I0129524

# Identity in Question
## The Study of Tibetan Refugees in the Indian Himalayas

**Swati Akshay Sachdeva**
Sikkim University, India

and

**Yumnam Surjyajeevan**
Sikkim Manipal University, India

**Series in Sociology**

**VERNON PRESS**

Copyright © 2021 Vernon Press, an imprint of Vernon Art and Science Inc, on behalf of the author.

All rights reserved. No part of this publication may be reproduced, stored in a retrieval system, or transmitted in any form or by any means, electronic, mechanical, photocopying, recording, or otherwise, without the prior permission of Vernon Art and Science Inc.

www.vernonpress.com

| | |
|---|---|
| *In the Americas:* | *In the rest of the world:* |
| Vernon Press | Vernon Press |
| 1000 N West Street, Suite 1200 | C/Sancti Espiritu 17, |
| Wilmington, Delaware, 19801 | Malaga, 29006 |
| United States | Spain |

Series in Sociology

Library of Congress Control Number: 2020940983

ISBN: 978-1-64889-231-8

Also available: 978-1-62273-912-7 [Hardback]; 978-1-64889-135-9 [PDF, E-Book]

Product and company names mentioned in this work are the trademarks of their respective owners. While every care has been taken in preparing this work, neither the authors nor Vernon Art and Science Inc. may be held responsible for any loss or damage caused or alleged to be caused directly or indirectly by the information contained in it.

Every effort has been made to trace all copyright holders, but if any have been inadvertently overlooked the publisher will be pleased to include any necessary credits in any subsequent reprint or edition.

Cover design by Vernon Press. Cover image: "Waiting for Dalai Lama", provided by the authors.

Dedicated to


Late Prof. Sameeera Maiti




"Don't Grieve.
Anything you lose comes round in another form."

-Rumi

# Table of Contents

# List of figures

# Preface

This book is based on the 2018 project report *Socio-Economic Conditions and the question of Identity among the Tibetan Refugees of the Indian Himalayas*, submitted to the ICSSR (Indian Council of Social Science Research), Government of India, which enquires the socio-economic conditions of the Tibetan refugees living in the Indian Himalayan regions, stretching from Dharamsala in Himachal Pradesh to Ravangla in Sikkim, and how the question of identity is being conceptualized, articulated and negotiated in their everyday life.

The initial conceptual backdrop of the study came through our interaction with the Tibetan refugees who are settled in Sikkim and Darjeeling, West Bengal. These are colleagues and friends with whom we sit and dine. (This is not to be confused with those Sikkimese citizens who are of Tibetan origin and lineage and are regarded as old settlers, such as Bhutias). Most of these colleagues and friends have accultured to the local cultural environment, in terms of speaking the language, food habits, fashions, and so on and forth, assimilating with the society where they are. Some have also established affinal relations successfully. Through our discussions with them, we have realized that the assimilation of the refugees and the question of their identity is an unexplored field with lots of scope for research, at least in this part of the country.

Following, back in 2016, we made a proposal for research to the ICSSR, which they accepted. Subsequently, in 2018, the project report with the combined effort of the research team based at Sikkim University was submitted. The observations, findings, and analysis of the report are those of the researchers based on their field analysis. The project's main objective was to explore the dynamism concerning both the socio-economic status and the question of the identity of the Tibetan refugees in general, and the youth and women in particular in the Indian Himalayan states of Himachal Pradesh, Sikkim, and West Bengal.

It is an independent, analytically- and empirically- grounded discussion of major sociological insights pertaining to the question of identity among the Tibetan refugees. The book is divided into seven chapters. The first chapter is an introduction to the background of the research question under study. Chapter two deals with the background of Tibetan Refugees in India; chapter three brings out the Tibetan refugees' socio-economic and demographic profile in India, using statistical tools. Chapter four provides a narrative account of Tibetans' lived experiences during their flight and the struggle in

India. Chapter five raises some questions related to the identity of the Tibetan refugees. Chapter six is on gender and identity issues among the Tibetan refugees. The final chapter brings out the major challenges and issues of the Tibetans and the way forward.

# Acknowledgement

The work is the result of the contributions made by numerous individuals and organizations, along with the collaborative efforts of the authors in shaping the final work in the form of this book. We would like to begin documenting those efforts by thanking the Indian Council of Social Science Research (ICSSR), Government of India, who sponsored the study. Without the financial assistance given by them, the work would have been almost impossible: collecting the colossal information on the Tibetan refugees who are spread across the length and breadth of India requires a tremendous amount of resources. We are honored for the privilege that the ICSSR has extended us by supporting the study. The original work, when it was proposed to ICSSR, was entitled *Socio-Economic Conditions and Question of Identity among the Tibetan Refugees of the Indian Himalayas,* and the report with the same title has also been submitted. The study explores the socio-economic background and the dynamic relationship between the formalization and negotiation of identity among the Tibetan refugees settled in the Himalayan regions of India, particularly among youths and women.

We will be forever indebted to (Late) Prof. Sameera Maiti, Department of Anthropology, Sikkim University. Prof. Maiti was a gentle yet vociferous and determined academician—an anthropologist par excellence, who always had a knack for research. Without her constant guidance and feedback, this work would have never set its first foot into academia, contributing to the discourses surrounding refugee issues, particularly the Tibetan refugees. It is heart-breaking to realize that she is no longer with us. We thank her for the guidance she has shown us, in both academic and emotional fronts, illustrated through her anecdotal worldview. We will miss you.

We are also grateful to Prof. T.B. Subba, an eminent anthropologist of international repute and former Vice-Chancellor of Sikkim University, for sparing his valuable time and sharing some of his experiences on the subject matter along with his continued inspirational intellectual advice, guidance, and thoughts. Going through his works and the discussion which we had with him has helped us in conceptualizing and charting the framework of the study.

Further, it would be an injustice to the study not to mention the name of Ms. Shristi Kala Chhetri, Research Assistant. It was her sheer professionalism, enthusiastic approach, and dedication towards the study that made it happen. Literature work on the historical background of Tibet and its people, the framing of questionnaires, and a major collection of the field data were her important contribution to the research work. We also are thankful to all the respondents and all other members who were directly or indirectly involved in the study for their most valuable feedback during the group discussions and survey. Without their kind help and support, this work would have been not possible. We are ever thankful and indebted to all our contributors for their help.

We are also grateful to the managers in charge of the Tibetan refugee centers for their guidance and support. The enthusiastic responses which we have received from the respondents further motivated us to complete the work successfully. Our special thanks go to Mr. Tenzing Wangda (Darjeeling), Mr. Lopsang, Mr. Tashi, Mr. Tenzing Pawo, Mr. Tenzing Nagwang, Mr. Sonam Dandul, Mr. Tenzing Zampa, Mr. Tenzing Norzin, Mr. Tenzing Jorden, Mr. Tenzin Nordhen (Ravangla), and Tsering Doma (sponsorship coordinator Ravangla). Sincere thanks to Tashi Rapten, Ugen Choden, Pema Tseten, and Tshering Wang (Ravangla), who aided and assisted in the focus group discussion, also sharing their personal narratives and experiences, which brought smiles and tears. Mr. Yalamber Subba and all the apala/pala and amala who have guided us during the fieldwork, given insights, shared their experiences, and showed love, support, and appreciation.

The consultations, discussions, and the great amount of homework held during the preparation of the manuscript with the generous support and help from family, friends, and colleagues will always remain in our heart with appreciation and respect.

We would like to acknowledge and express our gratitude to all the colleagues and faculty members of the Department of Sociology, Sikkim University. Dr. Sandhya Thapa (Associate Professor, Head), Dr. K. Indira, Mr. Shankar N. Bagh, Mrs. Sona Rai, and Mr. Binod Bhattarai (Assistant Professors) for their moral support and encouragement.

We also want to thank and appreciate the contribution of the anonymous reviewer, whose valuable feedback and comments have really helped in improving and (re)shaping the work.

Finally, we want to express our gratitude to the entire team of Vernon Press for giving us an opportunity to publish our work with them. We also want to thank Argiris Legatos, Editorial Manager, Victoria Echegaray, Assistant Editor, and Javier Rodriguez, Marketing Coordinator for helping and guiding us in every step in the process of preparation and publication of the manuscript.

Dr. Swati A. Sachdeva

Yumnam Surjyajeevan

Chapter 1

# Refugees and Identity: Problems and Challenges

## Introduction

Since the time humanity reached out from the plains of Africa to the continents of the world, humans have been migrating, making the history of migration as old as the history of human civilization itself. Till a few centuries ago, people nomadically ventured around in search of food, water, and habitable climatic conditions as borders were practically open. Migration at a later phase was mostly fueled by the need for trade and commerce, and expansion of territories—both in an economic and geographical sense, which paved the way for colonialization as well as the consolidation of nations, along with various other factors driven by socio-political undercurrents of the time. Nation-building also became an important state-sponsored project, which is a conscious strategy initiated by a state (Kolstø, 2000). The emergence of the modern nation-state was carried out through the 'process of collective identity formation... *to legitimiz[e]*...public power within a given territory' (Bogdandy *et al.*, 2005, p. 586; emphasis added). With the consolidation of the nation-state, restrictions were placed on the free movement of people, confining them within given geopolitically-defined boundaries along with particularities about citizenship and the creation of insider-outsider dichotomies. Migration, therefore, became a closely monitored and delimited phenomenon vis-à-vis international cross-border migration.

The existing global geopolitical scenario, which embodies the insider-outsider dichotomies, ethnic conflicts, civil wars, genocidal prosecution directed against particular ethnic group or community, has coercively compelled people to leave their homeland and seek asylum in some other country, such as the case of Rohingya and Syrian in recent times. These groups of people who leave their own country and sought shelter/asylum in a host country temporarily or on a permanent basis for political reasons are termed 'refugees'. However, defining a refugee is conceptually challenging when locating the reasons in historical contextuality, suggesting the adoption of a diachronic view rather than synchronic observation. There is a difference between the Protestants who fled 17th century France due to religious persecution and the Syrians who took flight from incessant bombings during the Syrian civil war. Further, in the Indian context, Bose has argued that 'Hindu migrants from Bangladesh are called refugees, while Muslim migrants are called "infiltrators" and illegal migrants' (2004, p. 4698). Owing to such a myriad of causes and reasons, The United Nations High Commissioner for Refugees (UNHCR) in its 1951 Convention and 1967 Protocol adopted the definition of 'refugee' as (UNHCR, n.d.; emphasis added):

> *Any person…*owing to wellfounded fear of being persecuted for reasons of race, religion, nationality, membership of a particular social group or political opinion, is outside the country of his nationality and is unable or, owing to such fear, is unwilling to avail himself of the protection of that country; or who, not having a nationality and being outside the country of his former habitual residence as a result of such events, is unable or, owing to such fear, is unwilling to return to it.

Such individuals are protected, and assured entitlements are provided in the host country. The entitlement for rights is bounded by the duties contained in the 1951 Convention and its 1967 Protocol, and it is 'the only global legal instruments explicitly covering the most important aspects of a refugee's life', besides, there are also other 'conventions and declarations that are of particular relevance in specific regions' (UNHCR 2011, pp. 2-5). In India, however, the legal status concerning refugees lack specific legislation. This led to the adoption of ad-hoc legal measures and approaches to look after refugee influx by the government, since India is neither party to the 1951 Convention on Refugees nor its 1967 Protocol. Therefore, refugee status in India is 'not governed by any codified model of conduct but rather it is based on political and administrative decisions' as per the administrative requirements and policy of the local government (HRLN, 2007, p. 2). The lack of uniform legislation led to a varying degree of unequal treatment of refugees 'resulting in a full range of benefits for some like legal residence and the ability to be legally employed, whilst others are criminalized and denied access to basic social resources' (Ibid., p. 2). The differential treatments of the refugees in India are also partly because of the adoption of the Foreigners Act 1946 and the Citizenship Act 1955, which govern the legal status of refugees in India. These Acts do not differentiate between individuals of foreign origin who fled their country from persecution with those who are visiting for any other purpose. In the absence of valid documents, the refugees are liable to 'deportation and detention'. Nonetheless, Tibetans who arrived in India in the late 1950s and early 1960s were accorded refugee status by the Indian government despite India being neither party to the 1951 UN Convention Relating to the Status of Refugees nor the 1967 Protocol (HRLN, 2007).

### Refugee Situation in India

Historically tracing, India has been providing asylum to refugees since the medieval period, as documented in historical records. For instance, Haneda (1997) pointed out that during the Mughal period, many Iranians who were suspected of being rebels or accused of being Sunnites or simply who had lost royal favor took political asylum in India and never returned. In contemporary history, the country also witnessed a massive influx of refugees during the 1947 India-Pakistan partition. Menon and Bhasin (1993, p. WS-3) wrote:

> Within a week of independence about 11 lakh Hindus and Sikhs had crossed over from west to east Punjab, and in the week following, another 25 lakhs had collected in the refugee camps in west Punjab. By November 6, 1947 nearly 29,000 refugees had been flown in both directions; about 673 refugee trains were run between August 27 and November 6, transporting 23 lakh refugees inside India and across the border-of these 13,62,000 were non-Muslims, and 9,39,000 were Muslims. Huge foot convoys, each 30,000-40,000 strong were organized by the Military Evacuation Organization and Liaison Agency to move the bulk of the rural population, especially those who still had their cattle and bullock-carts with them. The estimate is that in 42 days (September 18 to October 29) 24 non-Muslim foot columns, 8,49,000 strong, had crossed into India. By the time the migrations were finally over, about eight million people had crossed the newly-created boundaries of Punjab and Bengal, carrying with them memories of a kind of violence that the three communities had visited upon each other that was unmatched in scale, brutality, and intensity.

A similar refugee situation was felt during the Bangladesh liberation war, where many Bangladeshi refugees could settle in various parts of Bengal, Bihar, and North Eastern States (NES)[1] of India. Some of them, who had illegally entered the country, were termed 'infiltrators' or 'illegal migrants' (Banjan, 2009; Sarkar, 2010). Similarly, Bose's (2004) studies presented an insightful discussion about the arrival of less than 10,000 Afghan refugees in India during the 1980s and 1990s, who were mostly Sikhs and Hindus. Dasgupta's work, which discusses the repatriation of Sri Lankan refugees, highlighted their arrival in various phases: 'during the first phase (1983-89) 134,053 persons arrived from Sri Lanka. The second phase (1989-91) led to an influx of 122,078

---

[1] North Eastern States of India constitute of eight states, namely, Arunachal Pradesh, Assam, Manipur, Meghalaya, Mizoram, Nagaland, Tripura, and Sikkim.

persons. The number of refugees dropped significantly during the third phase (1996-2001), when 21,940 refugees arrived' (2003, p. 2365).

Likewise, since the beginning of the Tibetan crisis and the subsequent flight of the 14th Dalai Lama in 1959, India has been sheltering the Tibetan refugees. The U.S. Department of State reported that approximately 110,000 Tibetans refugees had settled in India by the end of 2001 (USDS, 2002). However, the figure has dwindled according to the Central Tibetan Administration (CTA) report, as there were only 94,203 Tibetan refugees living in India till April 2009 (Hindustan Times, 2010). According to USCR (U.S. Committee for Refugees), the difference in the number of Tibetan refugees in India in various reports is primarily due to the fluctuation of 'the arrival of more than 1,000 refugees from Tibet each year and the return of unknown numbers to Tibet' (USCR, 2002, as cited in USBCIS, 2003). This could also primarily be due to the historical contextuality of the unsettled Tibetan affairs, as unlike other refugees—who have settled and to an extent naturalized as Indian citizens—Tibetan refugees, on the other hand, desire to return to their homeland, to preserve their distinctive socio-cultural identity, and to reinstitute the government in Tibet someday. For such reasons, they have even formed their government-in-exile to look after the local and global affairs of their people. Owing to their unique situation, with the initiation of the then-Prime Minister of India, Pt. Jawaharlal Nehru, the state governments of Karnataka, Orissa, Himachal Pradesh, and Uttar Pradesh willingly came forward to extend a helping hand to Tibetan refugees. By 1984-85, the Government of India had assisted in the resettlement of about 37,399 refugees and was still engaged in the resettlement of about 3,300 refugees in the states of Jammu and Kashmir, Himachal Pradesh, West Bengal, Uttar Pradesh and Sikkim (GOI, 1984-85, p. 123). Further, the Government of India has also granted special status allowing them to stay in India until they find an amicable settlement with the Chinese Government (Subba,1990).

## Literature Review

The field of refugee studies has grown dramatically over the past few decades, with the intensification of forced migration taking place globally. Studies on refugees and related fields of studies such as exiles, homelessness and diaspora identities are indeed a fascinating area of research dealing with pathways, which seek to answer the ever-pressing issues of belonging and security. In relation to Tibetans, the cultural invasion and forceful occupation of its territories by China and the presented threat to their culture and civilization led to Tibetan exodus at a massive scale, fleeing their homes and homeland and taking shelter and asylum in unknown terrain and countries. The aftermath saw many countries opening their borders for the Tibetans who seek refuge, particularly its neighboring countries. In India, the then-Prime Minister, Pandit Jawaharlal Nehru, gave asylum to the Tibetans and welcomed His Holiness Dalai Lama, the spiritual leader. Thus, the rehabilitation and settlement process started. However, staying in an alien socio-cultural environment also presented a host of challenges. In the process of their settlement, though the rehabilitation is considered successful, they experienced numerous difficulties and hardships, along with going through the process of assimilation, acculturation, integration and transformation, and at times discrimination in the country of their refuge. This, to an extent, has propelled the phenomenal growth in scholarly work across all disciplines, particularly in the fields of sociology, anthropology, political science, and other allied social sciences disciplines.

Though there has been a deluge of publications on Tibetan Buddhism (Ray, 2001; Lama, 2001; Snellgrove, 2002) by Western scholars, spiritual leaders, and monks, all these mostly deal with the Bon religion, the rise and progress of Buddhism in Tibet, the practice of Lamaism, religious rituals, and practices. Sharma and Sharma's (1997) book describes Tibet from a religious perspective and concludes that Tibet is a land dedicated to religion. They also suggest that the Tibetan value system, which forms the basis of their social structure revolves, around religion or the practice of Tibetan Buddhism, their way of life. Like religion, Tibetan medicine is also a much-researched field, including the studies on the ancient system of medicine based on Buddhist philosophy and psychology such as those of Clarck (1995), Donden and Hopkins (1997), Janes (2002), and many others.

For the purpose of our study, we began with the work of Dalai Lama. His two works, *Freedom in Exile* (1991) and *My Land and My People* (1962), are worth discussing, as they certainly convey powerful first-hand experiences with autoethnographic details, giving authentic insights on the genesis and nature of Tibetan migration history. It also reflects the initial hardship faced by the Tibetan refugees in India and the Dalai Lama's negotiation with the then Prime Minister Jawaharlal Nehru for their rehabilitation in India. Next in the line of discussion, Dawa Norbu's *Red Star over Tibet* (1987) and *Tibet: The Road Ahead* (1997), which begin with a similar historical backdrop, but also illustratively bring into light the various events of Chinese occupation of Tibet, which have been discussed without any prejudice. There is a discussion on the process of the destruction of Tibetan Buddhism and the sinicization of Tibetans by the Chinese (Cultural Revolution and Cultural Destruction) and a chapter solely dedicated to the X[th] Panchen Lama. An effort has been made to disperse the dismal misconception people have regarding the Panchen Lama, whereby he has been regarded as the tragic hero of the Tibetan cause.

Discussion on the nature and genesis of Tibetan history and its people are found in different publications, both Indian as well as foreign. Francke (1994), in his book *History, Folklore and Culture of Tibet*, includes the history of Tibet, a brief picture of folklore, and cultural practices of the people, which also includes religious performances, marriage ceremonies, etc. and the social imprints that these cultural aspects have on society at large. Coleman's book *A Handbook of Tibetan Culture* (1993) is a comprehensive sourcebook of Tibetan organizations at the international level, and it also provides the biographical accounts of famous cultural personalities of contemporary Tibet. It contains a glossary of key Tibetan Buddhist and Sanskrit terms for the benefit of those interested in the study of Tibetan culture. Grunfeld's (1987) book *the Making of Modern Tibet* analyses almost all aspects of Tibetan society, the emergence of Tibet as an independent country, the institution of the Dalai Lama as a religious and administrative head, and the kind of relationship it had with Mongols. The Chinese occupation and the revolt of the 1950s, which led to a complete volte-face, have curiously been pointed out. The book *Tibet: The Country and its Inhabitants* by Grenard (1974) focuses on the life of the Tibetan people, their habitation, clothing, food, hygiene, and medicine. The author also highlights the accounts of population, their economic activities, occupation, climate, and geography. Publications such as *Cultural Heritage of Tibet* by Macdonald (1978), Michael's *Rule by Incarnation* (1982) and Tucci's *Tibet: Land of Snow* (1967), all generally discuss the traditional governmental system of Tibet under the institution of the Dalai Lama, regarding social structure, the class system and land relations. Various economic activities such as agriculture, animal husbandry, trade etc. have also been discussed. In his book, *The Revolt in Tibet*, Moraes (1960) broadly deals with the various events of Sino-Tibetan relations, the sudden occupation of Tibet by China and the flight of the Dalai Lama and his followers, and the negotiation with the then Indian Prime Minister. The impact of the Communist aggression in Asia, with special reference to India, has also been assessed.

Patterson (1960) also explores Sino-Tibetan relations and its occupation by China with equal importance. Richardson's *Tibet and its History* (1962) can be regarded as an elaborate analysis of almost all social aspects of Tibetan society as well as the history of the institution of the Dalai Lama. Conflicting relations between Tibet and China have also been highlighted. It concludes with a rough framework of the discussion on Tibetan people as exiles in the Indian Territory. Shakabpa's (1973) work exclusively deals with the political history of Tibet. It brings forth other aspects of Tibetan society, such as the origin and meaning of the name Tibet, its topography, vegetation, crops, transport, communication, and so on. Van Walt Van Praag's work, *The Status of Tibet: History, Rights and Prospects in International Law* (1988) mainly focuses on the independent status of Tibet and critically discusses the People's Republic of China's claim of Tibet as its motherland, which, according to him, is baseless.

Furthermore, treaties signed between Tibet and other European countries during the 19th and 20th centuries are discussed in the book. Statistics on the increasing population of Tibetans in Tibet and the peaceful co-existence of the Tibetan people of Han and other nationalities point to the fact that every community has been contributing harmoniously to the economic and cultural development of Tibet, thus forging a profound friendship with one another. Dawa Norbu (1979), in his article 'The 1959 Tibetan Rebellion' effectively deals with the independent status of Tibet. The victimhood of Tibet under the conflicting British, Chinese, and Russian imperialist interests in Central Asia have been well depicted. Besides, various other important points related to the cause of the 1959 Tibetan Rebellion—with emphasis on the imposing efforts by the Chinese government to change the Tibetan value system, which are founded on the principles of Tibetan Buddhism—are also discussed. Kasur's (2005) study refers to the debate by the U.S. Congress Sub-Committee on US-China relations on the question of whether to renew the MFN status (Most Favored Nation), which was a privilege granted to China in 1990. Although the administration approved granting the MNF status for the second time, however, there were appeals to revoke the status as China had been carrying out atrocities over the Tibetans with gross violation of Human Rights along with the imperialist occupation of Tibet. The author shows his desires and seeks support from the US Government and International Communities to come forward for a comprehensive solution to the Tibetan crisis.

Scholars, monastic clergy, and ordinary citizens escaping from Tibet have continued to describe the economic and political disenfranchisement, the pervasive suppression of cultural and spiritual life, and the extreme brutality by Chinese authorities in Tibet (Gyatso, Shakya and Palden, 1997; International Campaign for Tibet, 2005; Shakya, 1999). Cassinelli and Ekvall's (1969), Bhattacharjea's (1994), Ardley's (2003), Boyd's (2004), and Frechette (2007) and McConnel's (2009) works have extensively focused on how democracy is being conceptualized and operationalized among Tibetans, the unique evolution of and the rationale behind Tibetan democracy-in-exile, and the limitations faced by operating in exile.

This discloses that spacious researchers are directed towards the history of Tibet, the Chinese occupation, and Tibetans' revolt and flight. The beginning of the 21st century marked the exploration on the aftermath of the Tibetan Diaspora in different parts of the world; some of these important studies are by Korom (1997), Anand (2000), Bernstorff and Welck (2004), Yeh (2007), Basu (2008), and Hess (2009), and such studies are continuing. Surprisingly, not too many scholars seem to have sought Tibetan refugees in exile. Girija Saklani's

(1984) work presented extensive research on Tibetan refugees living in Dharamsala, Delhi, and Dehradun, and pointed out that they have 'successfully emerged from a self-sufficient barter economy into a competitive economy, and have adjusted to the new situation which is a tribute to the Tibetan community in exile' owing to their hard work, the active participation of women in economic activities, and being a born and instinctive traders (1984, pp. 216-219).

Subba's (1990) work gives an ethnographic account of the Tibetan refugee settlements in India and describes how Indian and foreign aid to the refugees have helped in their rehabilitation in India. The traditional economic system of the refugees when they were in Tibet, and the kind of economic activities they were engaged in in their country of refuge, have also been described. Their successful social adaptation in their host country has been attributed to the high degree of racial, cultural, religious, and other similarities between them and other Himalayan people like the Lepchas, Bhutias and the Nepalese. The scholar further pointed out that such similarities do not necessarily guarantee a situation free of ethnic tensions and conflicts. A chapter on the comparison of adaptation of Tibetan refugees in different parts of India, Bhutan, and Nepal has been included, with a brief discussion about the changes affecting the refugees and future consequences. Palakshappa (1978) has described the resettlement of Tibetan refugees in refugee camps in Karnataka set up by the Government of India based on field observation. The book mainly deals with the interaction between the refugees and the host communities. Both the negative and the positive aspects of the interaction have been efficiently discussed. Patel's (1980) book *Tibetans of Orissa* again discusses the changes in anthropological features of Tibetans in exile.

Datta and Chakraborty (2001) deal with various aspects of Tibetan Refugee migration from Tibet to India. The main area of study focuses on the Tibetans' compulsion to leave their homeland and their settlement in India, where Tibetans find a homely atmosphere to enjoy their basic human rights. In this context, they have regarded persecution as the main reason for Tibetan flight to India. Their successful social and economic adaptation in India points to the fact that they feel more at home in India than in Tibet, where half of their race is still living. The article also takes into account the vast changes which are affecting the refugees regarding their own status (regarding Tibet and the world at large), and who do not hesitate to acquire Indian citizenship—which is actually discouraged by the Tibetan Government in exile at Dharamsala, as this would hinder their effort to maintain and preserve their cultural heritage so that one day they can go back to their beloved motherland (Mishra, 2014).

Karthak (1991) mainly covers various problems the refugees encounter in the alien lands as well as the impact the alien societies may have on them. The main idea of their study revolves around the fact that changes in climate or geography lead to changes in the culture or living pattern of a human being. Norbu (2001) analyses the sociology of the refugee problems in general, focusing on theoretical concerns as well as empirical findings. His study deals with the political content of terror and flight, livelihood strategies and the impact of assistance programs, and interaction between refugees and the host population. The question of return and reintegration has also been raised. This paper gives special attention to the successful rehabilitation of Tibetan Refugees and explains its reasons. Why the Tibetan refugee community can be considered as a model refugee community both in India and the world at large has been clarified. Ray (2001), while writing about the refugees, their rights, and problems (specifically in the eastern and northeastern states of India), gives a brief demographic distribution of Tibetan refugees in India from the time they migrated in the 1950s, pointing out that they have the extraordinary ability to preserve their unique culture and identity, owing to the teachings of H.H. the Dalai Lama in relation to values like brotherhood, compassionate thought, honesty and decency for the attainment of world peace. While Thondup and Sinclair's (1999) work deals with school education of the Tibetans, another paper by Thondup (2000) sheds light on the influence of Indian cinema over Tibetan youths in India.

International level research on Tibetan diaspora is extensive and growing. Tibetan diaspora can be analyzed as both a condition and a process. Tibetan diasporic identities are contested, complex, and embedded in not one but multiple narratives of struggle. The Tibetan communities throughout the diaspora keep in close contact with one another in a variety of ways and on several different levels: personal, religious, and political (McLelland, 1986; Dargyay, 1988; McLagen, 1996). McLagen's (1996) study of Tibet activism is one of the few works on Tibetans in the United States, which discusses transnational connections in Canada. Tibetan research includes an official evaluation of the success of the resettlement scheme (Smith, 1975), and there are studies on the Tibetan communities in Lindsay, Ontario (McLelland, 1986; Dargay, 1988). These studies provide vital insight into diasporic identities and lived refugee experiences. More particular studies of the Tibetan diaspora appear to have focused on the resettlement of refugees in India; for example, Nowak's (1984).

An attempt to map the entire process of adaptation in India and Nepal was made by the German geographer Methfessel (1995). Otherwise, the focus on settlements has been limited to a few occasional papers like Goldstein's (1978) study of Tibetan refugees in Bylakuppe and other demographic surveys. One also encounters a sociological inquiry in the context of Sikkim Darjeeling Hills in Tanka Bahadur Subba's book entitled *Flight and Adaptation* (1990). Routray

(2007) describes that the exertion of the Tibetans to protect their cultural and religious identity has so far faced minimal opposition from their Indian hosts.

There are studies assessing the experiences of Tibetan refugees highlighting human rights abuses, hardships, and mental trauma (Mercer, Ager and Ruwanpura, 2005; Mills *et al.*, 2005). These studies highlight post-traumatic stress disorder, anxiety, and depression among Tibetan refugees. Many refugees suffered both serious psychological hardships and serious physical injuries. There have been studies that have examined the traumatic experiences and psychological reactions of adult Tibetan refugees residing in India (see Crescenzi *et al.*, 2002; Holtz, 1998; Keller *et al.*, 2006; Terheggen, Stroebe and Kleber, 2001, Sachs *et al.*, 2008).

In relation to gender, studies on Tibetan women are scantier; only a few pieces of literature were found during the literature survey. *Tibetan Women: Then and Now* (1990) by Indra Majupuria is a comparative study of the status and role of Tibetan women in the past and in the contemporary social situation. Datta (2002) deals with the changes that have taken place in the Tibetan refugee women's world by comparing their way of life in Tibet before the Chinese occupation, during the Chinese occupation, and after that in exile. The writer has concluded that though there was no sharp distinction between the sexes in Tibet, there was absolutely no scope for women in education and political participation in Tibet. In exile, they are getting educated equally on par with their male counterparts. They have become politically very conscious and have become important to the mainstream nationalist struggle of the Tibetan Nation as a whole.

Tibetan refugees, as a subject of research, represent a much wider substantive area of sociological inquiry. Even though Tibetan refugees in India have been the subject of much research, only a few studies deal with the Tibetans settled in the states of Sikkim, West Bengal (Darjeeling), and Uttarakhand. However, Dharamsala is over-represented in the study of Tibetan refugees in India. Most of these studies, as we see, deal with Tibetan civilization, diaspora, religion, medicines, and mythology. There is very little literature that focuses on the lived experiences of the people with the changes taking place in their culture and how they are struggling to preserve their culture and identity. The present study thus aims to explore this gap in research and literature. Further, scholarship on the question of Tibetans will be elaborately discussed on the theoretical framework in the subsequent sub-theme.

The lacuna is ostensibly visible; therefore, this book attempts to fill the void and subsequently aims to bridge the chasm by well-informed knowledge to a far more feasible extent, which might produce a tangible impact towards the chasm pointed above.

## Rationale of the Study

CTA or the government-in-exile was established for self-governance and to maintain solidarity among the Tibetan refugees with the determination to keep their distinctive socio-cultural identity intact and the hope of returning to their homeland. However, such political will and determination of the CTA are not without challenges, as there are issues concerning the question of socio-cultural assimilation and integration of the Tibetan refugees with the host society, which itself confronts the sanctity of maintaining the unique Tibetan identity. The study observed this phenomenon to be true predominantly among youths and those who are accultured to Indian society.

Identity, in a broader sense, refers to peoples' conception of 'who they are, of what sort of people they are, and how they relate to others' (Hogg and Abrams, 1988, p. 2). Suggesting that investigating what Tibetan identity is and/or what it signifies and represents for the Tibetan refugees requires inquiring, understanding, and analyzing the very question of Tibetan identity at various levels of conceptualization among different categories of refugees. These categories, which the study has conceptually segregated, are, firstly, those who came to India from Tibet seeking asylum (first generation); secondly, those who are born in India to refugee parents (later generation); thirdly, those who are settled within confined large cluster-settlement areas such as that of McLeod Ganj (Dharamsala) and Dalhousie with a distinctive socio-cultural and religious difference and lesser interaction with the surrounding community; fourthly, those who are settled in Ravangla, Darjeeling, and Sonada, which show shared communal relation as a result of their cultural, religious, racial and, to an extent, linguistic affinity. Finally, gender also has been considered as a category for the study. These segregations were taken into consideration owing to a prior observation made during the pilot survey, which shows a characteristic divergence in the conceptualization of Tibetan identity between these categories.

The study, therefore, seeks to explore the question of identity among the prescribed conceptual categories of Tibetan refugees in India. It aims to understand whether the conceptualization of Tibetan identity among the first and the 'later' generation of refugees differs. Studies have shown that there are socio-cultural differences among the first generation and subsequent generation of refugees. For instance, Bloch and Hirsch pointed out that native or heritage 'languages are found to be implicit in the construction, contestation and expression of identities among "second generation" refugees' (2016, p. 16). However, in relation to Polish immigrants in Australia, Forrest and Kusek's (2016) studies have observed that the retention of native language has significantly fallen among the second generation (children of immigrants), whereas it had virtually disappeared among the third generation (grandchildren of immigrants), at the same time educational and occupational attainment of these later generations were comparatively better than that of the host society. At the same time, there are also arguments that the later generation of refugees even bore the experiences of their parents and are often not seen as belonging to the country in which they are born and brought up and are commonly perceived as foreigners and even sometimes discriminated on such grounds (Chimienti *et al.*, 2019). Owing to such myriad discourses on the first and the later generation of immigrants and refugees, it becomes obligatory on the part of these studies to see whether the conceptualization of the Tibetan identity has generational differences and, at the same time—does it also entail differences based on the spatial organization of the settlements vis-à-vis cultural location and social positioning?

As discussed, analyzing identity requires factoring in the concept of socio-cultural assimilation. Therefore, integration of the Tibetan refugees becomes a necessary element in the analysis of identity formation, crystallization, and the crisis of identity of the Tibetan refugees. The aspects of cultural assimilation were observed among the Tibetan youths, thus leading to question how the youth negotiate between the identity they are ascribed with, juxtaposed with the identity they are acculturing/accultured to. Here, the question of identity crisis among Tibetan youths is one of the most important dimensions that the study seeks to comprehend. In relation to the crisis of identity, the conflicting gender role identity of the Tibetan women refugees is yet another significant element that the study endeavors to comprehend. The question, therefore, is: how much of their cultural past has been retained and how much of it has been sacrificed? These dynamic and transformative aspects of Tibetan refugees have been left largely unexplored in the existing studies. Therefore, sociological interpretation, which is very important, is still lacking because of the absence of adequate sociological research. A literature review has suggested that the area of our present concern has, however, been left largely unexplored.

Given the above facts, this academic exercise is an attempt to discover the range of unexplored nuances of the everyday experiences of the refugees. We are able to do so by presenting a comprehensive glimpse of their life and the challenges and problems they encounter. It also aims to get an insight into their worldview of the Indian society, which they are born to yet reluctant to embrace as their own. We shall try to explore and relate these lived experiences with the changing dynamics of society, economy, culture, and global politics, especially in the context of the bordering region of Sikkim and Darjeeling Hill.

## Conceptual and Theoretical Framework

For the present study, we have used both conceptual models and theoretical frameworks to understand the nature and characteristics of the integration of the Tibetan refugees at various levels. We have investigated how the theoretically-informed conceptual model on integration is particularly from a micro-sociological perspective and how it translated as participating in various domains of social transactions. However, the theoretical perspective on integration has not been discussed elaborately, as our main emphasis lies in understanding the question of identity for which integration is a means to an end.

Since the study deals particularly with the question of the identity of Tibetan refugees, it is important to look at two levels. First, on the question of what constitutes the idea of Tibetanness. Second, to see how that has changed over the years, and if not, then why. For the latter, it is important to see how much they have adapted and integrated into the culture and practices of the host society. Using the conceptual model developed by Ager and Strang (2008) in their work *Understanding Integration: A Conceptual Framework*, we assessed the level of integration of the refugees at four domains of integration. The conceptual model is represented in the diagram given in Figure 1.1.

**Figure 1.1:** Conceptual framework defining core domains of integration

| | | | |
|---|---|---|---|
| **Markers and Means** | Employment | Housing | Education | Health |
| **Social Connection** | | Social Bridges | Social Bonds | Social Links |
| **Facilitators** | | Language and Cultural Knowledge | Safety and Stability | |
| **Foundation** | | Rights and Citizenship | | |

Source: Ager and Strang (2008)

Firstly, at the level of major public arenas, which try to analyze their access to employment, housing, education and health care system, which Ager and Strang refer to as 'Markers and Means' to reflect the achievement of integration and the potential means required to attain said integration. Secondly, 'Social

Connection', which considers how they are socially bonded with people and families of their own community as 'proximity to family ...enabled them to share cultural practices and maintain familiar patterns of relationships'. Such connection played a large part in them feeling 'settled'. At the same time, how they are socially linked with the neighboring or the communities in the host society. Thirdly, at the level of means for 'facilitators' aimed toward 'language and cultural knowledge', and 'safety and stability'. Linguistic and cultural competence of the larger society where the refugees are located is necessary and effective markers of integration. Language, when sociologically considered, is an important medium for cultural transmission within and outside the community, particularly with the society at large. This leads to yet another dimension of the research, that is, how much the Indian born Tibetan refugees are linguistically informed about their Tibetan culture and identity. Within this parameter, as highlighted above, both safety and stability are another aspect of integration as the refugees themselves felt 'at home' if the community or their place of settlement is peaceful. Ager and Strang emphasized on these two parameters of facilitators, as they found that these two domains were lacking in the analysis of integration in other studies. This aspect leads to further integration in terms of 'economic and social participation in the mainstream society' as found in the case of Vietnamese refugees in 1970s UK in Hale's study (2000, p. 276). Fourth and final, in relation to 'citizenship and rights', as Ager and Strang pointed out that 'much literature concerning refugee integration uses the concept of citizenship' (2008, p. 174). However, the question of citizenship and rights are intertwined together. As the sense of right comes along with citizenship equipped by the sense of identity emerging from the fact of belonging to a nation, in the case of Tibetan refugees in India, the question on citizenship and right is thus misleading to an extent. Nonetheless, our study examines what kind of rights and privileges are guaranteed to them in India.

Theoretically considering the question of integration, we have focused on the micro-sociological phenomena rather than macro-sociological perspective, as integration can only be successfully translated when the participation of people is visible in the micro-social trends and activities; for example, a Tibetan refugee participating in full zest in the festivals of Indian people like Holi, Baisakhi, Id, Onam can be translated as integration, as social transaction and interaction have taken place.

Closely related to integration, the theoretical perspective looking into the concept of identity holds that identity or self-conceptions emerge from the interpersonal relations and interaction with the other; in fact, the self is a collection of identities as mostly propounded by symbolic interactionists (James, 1890; Cooley, 1902; Mead, 1934). Historically, identity was introduced in social sciences in the 1960s in the United States (Gleason, 1983), which was popularized in the work of Erik Erikson in the 1950s. Erikson characterized identity as 'a process "located" in the core of the individual and yet also in the core of his communal culture, a process which establishes ... the identity of those two identities' (1968, p. 22). However, the conceptualization of identity is narrowly restricted to the psycho-analytical framework. Later, under the influence of postmodern and poststructuralist discourse on the maladies of multiculturalism, many social theorists, particularly from the field of political sociology, adapted the concept to explore the territory of cultural politics revolving around race, class, ethnicity, gender, sexuality and so on with a renewed perspective (Appiah and Gates, 1995). James D Fearon (1999) referred to identity more in terms of socially constructed expected behaviors, membership rules and alleged attributes of the individuals defining the personal identity of the individual. For Dirk Jacobs and Robert Maier (1998), identity is a product of historical processes providing proficiency for the individual's identity in terms of dependability and continuity. Social values, collective symbols and norms determining behavior define one's identity. George Schopflin (2001) argues that identities are anchored around morale values such as right/wrong, polluted/unpolluted and desirable/undesirable.

The arguments presented above on the conceptual delineation of identity strongly suggests what Mead (1934) pointed out in his celebrated work *Mind, Self and Society*: the identity of the self arises in the process of social experiences and activities which are constrained and defined by the social structure (Mead, 1934). These social activities/actions of the agent/agency through which one's identity is being socially constructed are defined in accordance with the performance of established expected social roles in society. An identity consists of the internalized meanings of the self in a social position or role. An identity is the internal component of role identity, while a role is the external component (McCall and Simmons, 1978; Burke, 1980). Roles do not stand in isolation but presuppose and relate to counter-roles; the same is true of identities (Lindesmith and Strauss, 1956; Burke and Reitzers, 1981). The meaning of an identity is conveyed by its commonalities with one class of persons similarly situated and by its differences from other classes - those situated in counter-positions (Stone, 1962, p. 94). For instance, the social identity specified to an individual such as 'doctor' will only have meaning in relation to patients and the roles he/she performs; in the absence of the latter, the former ceases to exist and vice versa.

Similarly, parent as an identity is through the role of a parent, which becomes meaningful in relation to the role of a child. Relating to the study, it is important to enquire what most of the Tibetan refugees in India perceive themselves as: a Tibetan with distinctive Tibetan identity or as an Indian-born Tibetan with and without Tibetan identity; what makes a Tibetan identity distinctive from other communities at large; whether the refugee tag instills a sense of non-belongingness in the host society; if there is any discriminatory outlook presented towards them from the host society, and so on. Goffman pointed out that:

> When an individual enters the presence of others, they commonly seek to acquire information about him or to bring into play information about him already possessed... Information about the individual helps to define the situation, enabling others to know in advance what he will expect of them and what they may expect of him. Informed in these ways, the others will know how best to act in order to call forth a desired response from him... Many crucial facts lie beyond the time and place of interaction or lie concealed within it. For example, the "true" or "real" attitudes, beliefs, and emotions of the individual can be ascertained only indirectly, through his avowals or through what appears to be involuntary expressive behavior... (Goffman, 1959, pp. 1-2).

Goffman's introductory remark in his chef-d'oeuvre *The Presentation of Self in Everyday Life* suggests social interaction to be contingent on the identification of social objects involved in the process; identity, thus, can be argued to be the reification of these social objects embodied in the individual. In this case, how the Tibetans relate themselves with the people in the host society, and through this process, they define themselves and others and vice-versa 'on the basis of race, ethnicity, religion, language, and culture' (Deng, 1995, p. 1). In contemporary discourse, identity is generally linked to three concepts, the 'personal' – distinguishing characteristic(s) in which an individual take 'special pride in or views as socially consequential but more-or-less unchangeable', 'social' – a label with distinguishing 'membership and (alleged) characteristic features or attributes' (Fearon, 1999, p. 2), and 'collective' – referring to 'a shared sense of "we-ness" or "one-ness" that derives from shared statues, attributes, or relations, which may be experienced directly or imagined, and which distinguishes those who comprise the collectivity from one or more perceived sets of others' (Polletta and Jasper, 2001, cited in Snow, Oselin and Corrigall-Brown, 2004, p. 391). Cutting across the three definitive conceptualizations, interactionists view identity as constantly shaping and reshaping itself in everyday social practices, which creates a sense of self among the individuals; thus, in Bauman's (1988) words, identity is forged and realized in the domain of what is social. In a nutshell, identity is a subjective disposition of ego in relation to his alter, yet such subjective disposition of ego is the objective consequences emerging out of collectively shared values, what Turner and Oakes (1986) contended as social collectivity becoming self.

Suggesting that despite identity being an individual's subjective conception it attains an intersubjective ontological status which objectifies the nature of its existence by constructing the objective identity. Theoretically speaking, there is a question of how the Tibetans seem to attain an ontologically objective identity while staying miles apart in pockets of secluded settlements all across India or is such identity projection is a super-imposition by the CTA to bring a consensus universalis to its cause, if not what variance exists. Also, from the domain of micro-sociological theoretical perspective, the strands of phenomenological thought, particularly the Husserlian Phenomenology, appeals to the subjective micro-level understanding of identity as it is lived through via embodied subjects. However, the terms 'micro-level' or 'subjective' do not necessarily imply subjects existing independently of objects or bereft of their 'external realities'. The subject as an embodied agent, therefore, actively espouses the given parameters of identity, countering and dislodging some attributes while retaining some elements. The study, therefore, characterizes subjects as interpretive, coping beings perpetually engaged in a dialectic interaction of meanings with one's community and the society at large.

## Objectives of the Study

To explore the dynamism concerning both the socioeconomic status and the question of the identity of the Tibetan Refugees in general—and also the youth and women—, the study seeks to address the various aspects by means of the following objectives laid down.

1. To access the socioeconomic profile of Tibetan refugees settled in various settlements and undertake a comparative analysis.

2. To study the level of integration and assimilation of the refugees within the community and with the host society/community.

3. To undertake a comparative analysis of the lived experiences of the Tibetan refugees, between those who came from Tibet and those who are born in India.

4. To present a gender assessment and analysis on identity formation and crystallization, as, traditionally, gender norms and roles are more restricted and prevalent among women in a patriarchal society.

5. To examine the varied generation view, if any, towards refugee status and self-identity.

## Scope and Methodology

The scope of the study is limited only to five Tibetan settlements and centers in McLeod Ganj and Dalhousie in Himachal Pradesh, Ravangla in Sikkim, and Darjeeling and Sonada in West Bengal, which are highlighted in Figure 1.2 to

1.6. Although, conceptually, there is a difference between settlement and center, as Sudeep Basu (n.d.) in his paper *Organising for Exile! "Self-Help" among Tibetan Refugees in an Indian Town* has pointed out that 'settlements' primarily focused on 'rehabilitation strategy' for permanent agricultural settlement; whereas, 'centers', which has emerged spontaneously with the idea that no refugee could ever be rehabilitated in the fullest sense of the word without "Self-Help" focused more on making them self-reliant and economic independence. However, in our visit to these refugee settlements and centers, we could not observe the distinctive differences between the two, as in the case of Ravangla, both an agricultural settlement as well as self-reliant aspects— such as grocery shops, carpet and handicraft making and so on—were observed. At the same time, the subject matter of the present study is not dependent on differentiating the two conceptual categories; therefore, we will be using both the settlement and center simultaneously, as some are identified as settlements while others as centers.

Considering the nature and motif of the research problem in question, the study adopted 'mixed methods research' primarily for its advantage in a comprehensive understanding of social phenomena by synthesizing the merits of both qualitative and quantitative methods. The mixed research design generally employs three techniques for conducting interviews: structured, semi-structured and unstructured or informal (Morse and Field, 1995). Though we have used structured interviews for collecting socioeconomic and demographic details, we gave more emphasis on using a semi-structured and informal form of interview, primarily to control the nature and extent of vagueness in the response of the interviewees. Chambers (1994) pointed out that semi-structured interviews entail having a mental or written checklist but being open-minded and following upon the unexpected.

Accordingly, primary data were collected using interview scheduled, informal discussion, and both participant and non-participant observation based on the demand of the situation to bring out the ethnographic reality from the lived experiences of the refugees, as subjective experiential accounts of phenomena can provide rich descriptions of the experiential essence of the world which the refugees are in. The fieldwork was carried out between 1st October 2016 and 30th May 2017. The respondents were asked a set of prepared questions in the structured and semi-structured interviews, but as highlighted, giving more importance to informal discussion, at times dragged the interview to other areas of discourse which are outside the scope of research. The interviewees were Tibetan men and women from all walks of life, of various professions and backgrounds; the questions required their analysis of their own identity. Apart from the interviews, both participant and non-participant observation methods were employed, but banking more to non-participatory observation, as it allows the investigator to keep a degree of detachment from the group despite adopting the perspective of the subjects under observation through membership to the group (Nachmias and Nachmias, 1999). Living amongst the community during the fieldwork period gave the opportunity to carry out transect walk and field mapping for verification of the responses provided by the respondents through personal observations, at the same time to interact with others (who are not part of the study), giving a clearer picture and assessment of the view of non-Tibetan community perspectives.

## *Sampling*

The population of the study was identified from the five settlement areas from three states of India, which are Dharamsala (McLeod Ganj) and Dalhousie in Himachal Pradesh, Ravangla in Sikkim, and Darjeeling and Sonada in West Bengal. From these five settlements, 200 samples were studied, which are distributed proportionately into 50 samples each from the first three locations. Whereas in the case of Darjeeling and Sonada, the samples were divided into 30 and 20, respectively. Although the initial plan of the study was to focus only on one settlement in Darjeeling, however, later conceptualization suggested bifurcating the total 50 samples into two in the ratio of 3:2. One of the prime reasons for the sample bifurcation was to see any variance in the data. However, the hypothetical assumption was proven wrong, primarily due to the proximity of the two settlements, which are also surrounded by a negligible socio-cultural divergence of the surrounding community. In fact, the distance between the two settlements is approximately 16 km.

The sampled respondents were proportionately stratified between the first-generation refugees, which the study has conceptually classified as the older generation, while those who were born in India have been classified as younger/later generation. Among these two conceptual categories, further sampling stratification was made between the male and female. Overall, the entire sampling process was carried out using both probability and non-probability form of the sampling method. For the division of the older and younger generation and gender proportionality, we have used probability. Once sample stratification was completed, we used snowball and convenience sampling for the field study.

## *Household Survey*

The first step of data collection started with the household survey. The interview schedule was employed in collecting quantitative primary data. For this, we prepared a household survey form, which was administered to individual households. The idea of using the household survey method was to collect the data on individual households, demographic structure, family size, occupational structure, income, and expenditure. Besides the household surveys, the interview schedule was used to collect data relating to identity, gender, political participation, decision making, sources of income and expenses, etc. The data for the present study was collected primarily from two sources: the household census and interview schedule. At least one adult member from each household was interviewed to collect relevant data. 30 cases were taken for an in-depth case study so that the findings from the data obtained through other methods could be corroborated and substantiated. The data collected through fieldwork—household census and interview schedule— were classified, tabulated, and presented in a sample statistical method, i.e., the tables and graphs.

The field sites of the selected Tibetan refugee settlements are listed below. The star sign on the map marks the location of the settlement camp.

1. McLeod Ganj, Dharamsala, Himachal Pradesh

**Figure 1.2:** Map of the refugee settlement at McLeod Ganj, Dharamsala, Himachal Pradesh

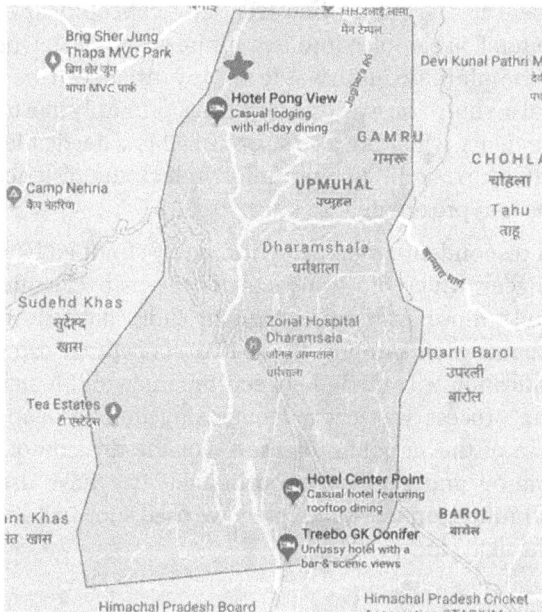

Source: Google Maps, viewed on 18/02/2018

## 2. Dalhousie, Himachal Pradesh

**Figure 1.3:** Map of the refugee settlement at Dalhousie, Himachal Pradesh

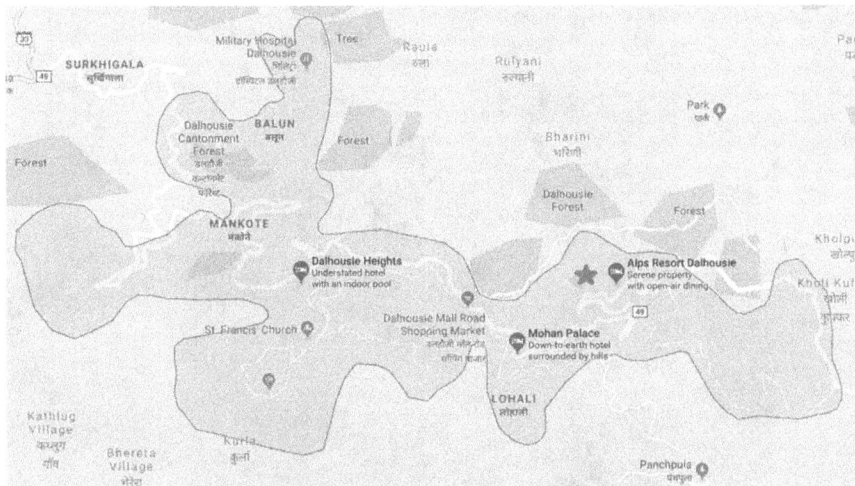

Source: Google Maps, viewed on 18/02/2018

## 3. Darjeeling, West Bengal

**Figure 1.4:** Map of the refugee settlement at Darjeeling, West Bengal

Source: Google Maps, viewed on 18/02/2018

## 4. Sonada, Darjeeling District, West Bengal

**Figure 1.5:** Map of the refugee settlement at Sonada, West Bengal

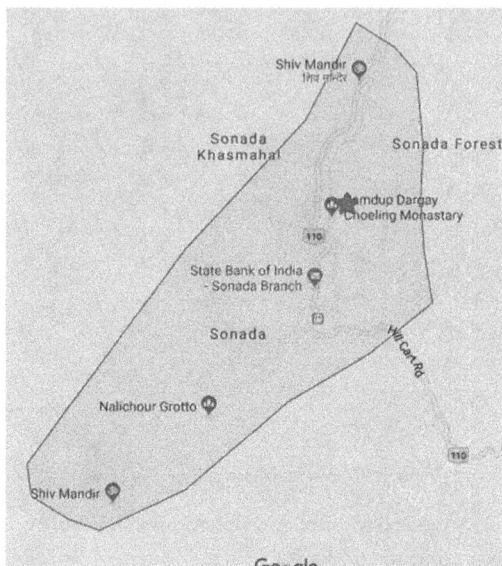

Source: Google Maps, viewed on 18/02/2018

## 5. Ravangla, South Sikkim, Sikkim

**Figure 1.6:** Map of the refugee settlement at Ravangla, Sikkim

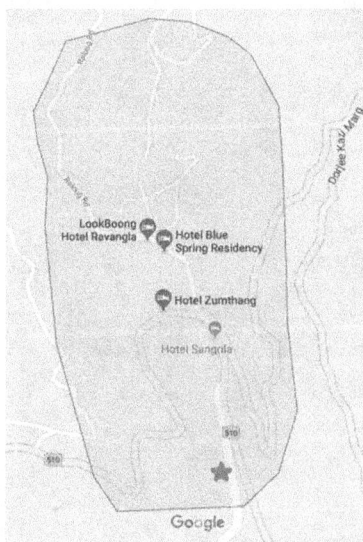

Source: Google Maps, viewed on 18/02/2018

Chapter 2

# Background of Tibetan Refugees in India

## Introduction

As per the CTA, there are 39 refugee settlement centers for the Tibetans, which are dispersed across the length and breadth of India. These settlements are broadly organized into three categories: agriculturally-based settlements (15 in number), 13 handicrafts-based, and 11 cluster communities. In these 39 settlements, there were about 94,203 Tibetan refugees living in India till 12 April 2009 (Hindustan Times, 2010). However, these figures do not always remain constant in all the mentioned settlements, as there is a persistent influx and efflux of the refugees from time to time, as already discussed in the first chapter. For instance, in 1976, in Arunachal Pradesh, the Tibetan refugee population was 6,247, which had increased to 35,000 by September 1985 (Subba, 1990). Similar instances were also found in other settlements located in Kalimpong, Darjeeling and Sikkim, which together stand at 8,854 in 1976, and by 1978 it was estimated to be more than 10,000. In Kalimpong alone, the numbers reported in 1976 and 1978 were 1,973 and 2,300, respectively (Subba, 1990). The national figure of Tibetan refugees in India, as per the data released by Dharamsala in 1976, stands at 68,784. A decade later, the Ministry of Home Affairs, Government of India, in its report for 1984-85, documented that only 66,130 Tibetan refugees had come to India since 1959. However, just a year later, the Rajya Sabha, the upper house of the Indian parliament, reported that 78,400 Tibetan refugees had been staying in the country as of 6th November 1986 (Subba, 1990). Further, the demographic survey of Tibet, 2009, reported that the Tibetan refugee population in India was surveyed to be 97,203. As highlighted, many of these 'early refugees eventually put down new roots in agricultural and handicrafts settlements established mainly in the 1960s and 1970s in southern India and other parts of the country' (USBCIS, 2003).

## Tibet: A Historical Backdrop

Providing a brief historical and cultural overview of Tibet is essential as it will assist in highlighting the necessary backdrop for better illumination of the study in pursuit. Tibet, popularly known as the 'Roof of the World' due to its great elevation, is also referred to as the 'Forbidden Land' because of its distinctive geographical terrain, which makes human habitation inhospitably difficult. Unreceptive attitudes by its leaders toward the entry of outsiders is also a cause for problems. Since this high desert area is barely habitable, its population is quite low (Kapstein, 2006).

The land of the snow-covered mountains, with rich cultural heritage and religious tradition dedicated to Buddhism, was once ruled by the successive incarnations of Chenrezig, also referred to as *Avalokitesvara* (one who looks with an unwavering eye). Tibet is generally divided into three regions: Eastern, Northern and Southern Tibet. The eastern part is mostly forested land areas, while the northern part—enveloping almost half of Tibet—is mostly open grassland, where nomads and their yak and sheep dwell. The southern region, consisting of central Tibet, is an agricultural region and all the largest cities and towns, including Lhasa, Shigatse, Gyantse and Tsetang, are in this area. There are several peoples of Tibetan origin, who follow the same spiritual tradition and speak Tibetan—and who are seen as Nepalese citizens these days—, like those residing in Upper Mustang or the Tamangs, who associate their name with a type of Tibetan cavalry, called *tamak* (Kapstein, 2006). The native religion of Tibet was *Bon* before the introduction of Buddhism. Lord Fonpa Sherab Miwo was its founder, and its followers were called Bonpas. In the Western countries, *Bon* religion was sometimes referred to as Shamanism, which was perhaps derived from the name of its founder Sherab Miwo. Worshipping of natural objects was the most important feature of this religion.

Historically, the 7th century A.D. is considered as the rise of the Tibetan Empire and the period when the Tibetan language and Tibetan Buddhist tradition were introduced and established (Kapstein, 2006). Ninety percent of the Tibetan population was made up of peasants, nomads, monks, and nuns. The remaining ten percent of the population consisted of nobles, civil servants, soldiers, traders, craft workers, and merchants. The peasants, who were mostly serfs living on large secular or monastic estates, were by far the largest group, making up the majority of average Tibetans (Goldstein, 1989). The next biggest group were the nomads who were scattered across the Plateau. Tibetan society was strongly differentiated. Social ranking in Tibet was an important aspect of both the legal system and the daily lives of Tibetans. The clearest evidence of the importance of social ranking, as discussed in Rebecca Redwood French's (1995) work *The Golden Yoke*, was the concept of the *tong* payment, which is basically 'monetary compensation for the act of murder' listed in the law codes (French, 1995, p. 303). Although there was no unified class system, Lhasa was the central authority, while more remote areas had clan-based governance. The majority of the poorer section of society were involved in cultivating the land and herding cattle, like yaks, which was the only source of food for survival in some provinces. Some social groups, like butchers or corpse disposers, were treated as outcasts (Snellgrove and Richardson, 1986). Snellgrove and Richardson further highlighted that monasteries and nunneries not only serve as spiritual and religious centers, but were centers for spiritual learning and education, and cultural dissemination, making monastic life pivotal in the society. Spiritual traditions were also maintained by lay practitioners and nomadic monks/yogis; the cultural heritage of Tibet flourished inside the monasteries, and committing one of the children to religion as a monk was beneficial for families.

King Songtsen Gampo erected the first Buddhist Temples, the *Kyichu-Lhakhang* in Paro and the *Jampe-Lhakhang* in Bumthang[2] (Snellgrove and Richardson, 1986). Following, in the 8th century, the 'Precious Master' Guru Padmasambhava, the founder of Tibetan Buddhism, was invited to come to Tibet by King Trisong Detsen to subdue the unbeatable indigenous forces and established the unbroken lineage of teaching in monasteries among the lay practitioners. The political life of Tibet of that period provided excellent conditions for the flourishment of spiritual tradition (Giles and Dorjee, 2005). The real establishment of Buddhism came into effect during the reign of the greatest King of Tibet, Chogyal Songtsen Gampo. In the later part of the 14th century, Tsongkhapa founded a sect called 'Gelugpa'. In the history of Tibetan Buddhism, the Gelugpa sect deals with supreme power. From the first part of the 17th century, under the leadership of the 5th Dalai Lama, the Gelugpa sect became politically and administratively supreme. They were known as 'Yellow Hat,' and the others were commonly grouped under 'Red Hats'. The Dalai Lama was regarded as their political and spiritual leader, as well as the head of the administration. Thus, Lamaism became the central character of Tibetan Buddhism (Grunfeld, 1987).

## Origin of Tibetan Crisis

During the 17th century, the Qing Dynasty marked the beginning of mutual relations between Tibet and China, particularly between the Tibetan spiritual leaders and the Chinese rulers. There was a tradition for seeking and turning to Tibetan monks for spiritual guidance, and this spiritual allegiance and respect resulted in granting the 5th Dalai Lama with the title of 'The Great Master' in 1653 (Erffa, 1996). Till 1949, Sino-Tibetan relations were considered peaceful; China recognized the theocratic rule of independent Tibet by the Dalai Lama. However, this changed when on 1st October 1949, Mao Tse Tung proclaimed Tibet as an autonomous region within the People's Republic of China (PRC),

---

[2] The erection of the monuments marked the victory of Buddhism over pre-Buddhist deities. Songtsen Gampo wanted to tame a huge demon whose body covered all of Tibet and its neighbouring areas, which posed a particularly big problem to the spreading of Buddhism. The king thus decided to erect a temple on each of the demon's joints so that she would no longer be able to move.

following which they attacked and occupied the Eastern part of Tibet. The new Chinese Communist regime set about expanding and consolidating its power; it quietly swallowed up the disputed outlying territories of its Western neighbor, i.e., Tibet. On 7th October 1950, which also marked the anniversary of the communists coming to power in China, the People's Liberation Army (PLA) invaded the heartlands of Tibet, starting their so-called 'liberation' and in the following year, the Chinese troops entered Tibet. The 'democratic reforms' in which the invading army was engaging faced resistance in some regions, while others met with cooperation (Vahali, 2009). The 15-year-old 14th Dalai Lama was granted full powers to rule, and upon his negotiation with the Chinese leaders, China pledged to abstain from any compulsion in altering the existing political system (Erffa, 1996).

On 23rd May 1951, during negotiations in Beijing, Tibetans, under duress, were offered a choice either to go for a 'peaceful liberation' by the Chinese or annihilation by its military force. Under such circumstances, the Tibetans were compelled to choose 'liberation', resulting in the signing of the Seventeen Point Agreement for the peaceful liberation of Tibet between the government representatives of PRC (referred to in the document as Central People's Government) and Tibet. The introductory of the document is read as (SPPPLT, 1951):

> The Tibetan nationality is one of the nationalities with a long history within the boundaries of China and, like many other nationalities, it has done its glorious duty during the creation and development of the great motherland. But over the last hundred years and more, imperialist forces penetrated China, and in consequence, also penetrated the Tibetan region and carried out all kinds of deceptions and provocations. Like previous reactionary Governments, the KMT [p.Kuomintang] reactionary government continued to carry out a policy of oppression and sowing dissent within the nationalities, causing division and disunity among the Tibetan people. The Local Government of Tibet did not oppose imperialist deception and provocations, but adopted an unpatriotic attitude towards the great motherland. Under such conditions, the 'Tibetan nationality and people were plunged into the depths of enslavement and suffering'.

The first clause of the agreement states that the Tibetan people shall return and be united with its motherland, i.e., PRC, and as one big family shall drive out aggressive imperialist forces from Tibet. This was simply not acceptable to Tibetans who claimed that Tibet had never been a part of China, and in fact, Tibet, as they claimed, had ancient claims to large parts of China. Moreover, the Tibetan people were ethnically and racially distinct, their language as well as script were different. Clause two directs the Tibetan local government to actively assist the PLA to enter Tibet and consolidate the national defense. Clause eight mentioned the reorganization and induction of Tibetan troops into PLA, thus becoming a part of PRC's national defense. Clause fourteen declared the immediate seizure of all external affairs relations by the Tibetan authority and to be handed over to PRC. Though in other clauses, assurance was given to Tibet of its religious freedom and protection of the Dalai Lama, the changing political climate clearly shows that the 'Land of Snows' has come under the clutches of the 'Dragon'.

During the period of the Peaceful Liberation Policy, extending from 1951-1959, the Chinese used the Tibetan people intelligently for their military preparation in Tibet, and no effort was made to indoctrinate them. As Tibetans were deeply rooted in Tibet and in anything that was Tibetan in nature, the majority were quite unreceptive to new ideas, especially of Communism, which was directly antagonistic to their way of life. There were few Tibetans who responded to the Chinese call. In the words of Norbu (1997), China had two courses; they could have taken Tibet by military force and imposed a military dictatorship without any difficulty. But this was considered non-communist in spirit and was also against World Opinion. She chose the second course on the pretext of 'Peaceful Liberation' by granting special autonomous status to Tibet. If China were to rule Tibet successfully, the intellectual backbone of the society had to be lulled, wooed, and deceived. In this way, the possibility of a revolt would be minimized, and the illiterate masses would follow the aristocrats, whom the Chinese had converted into the 'vanguard of revolution' (Norbu, 1997). Following this, the Dalai Lama realized that his life was under threat, subsequently leading to his flight to India from Tibet, overcoming the hardships and dangers of the mountain passages (Vahali, 2009).

## Beginning of Tibetan Refugee Era: India

PRC's invasion of Tibet on 7th October 1950 caused indescribable atrocities in the name of the Cultural Revolution. The cultural revolution carried out by the invading army was considered by many Tibetans as a direct assault on Tibetan culture, Tibetan Buddhism and a deliberate attempt to destroy Tibetan identity. Unable to resist the atrocious aggression, thousands of Tibetans, along with their spiritual and temporal leader, the 14th Dalai Lama, took flight from Tibet. On 31st March 1959, the Dalai Lama fought his way through the harsh snow-clad mountains and reached Chutangmu near Tawang, Arunachal Pradesh. A few weeks later, the then-Prime Minister of India, Pt. Jawaharlal Nehru, welcomed him in Mussoorie and formally offered him asylum in India. The Dalai Lama and his entourage were initially given temporary accommodation in Missouri-Birla house, a residence of one of India's leading industrial families, which was requisitioned for their use by the Government. From here, they were shifted to Dharamsala for permanent accommodation. Dharamsala became the seat of power from where the present Dalai Lama functions not only over the refugees settled in Indian territory but all refugees settled anywhere in the world. Initially, the proposal of the Tibetan Government in exile to settle all Tibetan refugees in the Northern part of India was not accepted; however, the Government of India was very liberal in allowing the refugees to relocate to different parts of India. In the following year, i.e., in 1960, the Tibetan *Kashag*[3] was formed, which later was renamed as 'The Government of the Great Snow Land'; presently, it is referred to as Central Tibetan Administration (CTA) or the Tibetan Government-in-Exile.

During the time, over 85,000 Tibetans followed their leader, seeking refuge in India (Vahali, 2009). Besides India, Bhutan and Nepal also became a major destination of these Tibetan refugees. Tibet used to trade with China, Mongolia, Nepal, Sikkim, Bhutan, and India since long past, and it had trade routes all around. The majority of the refugees entered India through Tse-Tang Tso-na Dzong to Tawang in Arunachal Pradesh. A large group of the refugees, particularly those settled in the Darjeeling Hills before 1959, took the route which starts at Phari, crossed the Chumbi Valley, entered Sikkim through Jelep-la pass and reached Kalimpong via North-eastern Sikkim, while many also used the Lhasa-Tawang-Assam route. As a result, today we find them scattered in various parts of the country, both in settlements provided by the government as well as privately settled refuges.

Although from the very beginning India regarded Tibet as a part of China and made it clear that it would not tolerate any anti-Chinese activities on Indian soil, India had its own interests and compulsion in the international scene. From 1959, Nehru, as Prime Minister of India, showed a keen personal interest in Tibetan refugee problems. It was as early as the 1960's when the Prime Minister started the process of rehabilitation of these refugees in the various states of India by providing them all possible assistance. In India, there were a number of settlement camps established at the request of His Holiness to the Indian Prime Minister, Jawaharlal Nehru. The main motto to establish such settlement camps was to preserve Tibetan identity and culture as His Holiness believed that if they are scattered, they might forget their roots. The state governments of Karnataka, Orissa, Himachal Pradesh, and Uttar Pradesh willingly came forward to extend a helping hand to Tibetan refugees as a response to the Prime Minister's initiative. By 1984-85, the Government of India had assisted in the resettlement of about 37,399 refugees and was still engaged in the resettlement of about 3,300 refugees in the states of Jammu and Kashmir,

---

[3] Traditionally Kashag refers to governing council of Tibet.

Himachal Pradesh, West Bengal, Uttar Pradesh and Sikkim (GOI, 1984-85, p. 123). Subba (1990) pointed that the Government of India (GOI) granted the Tibetans special status allowing them to stay in India if they wish to or till an amicable solution is brought into with the Chinese Government. Further, the GOI also made a formal request to the Government of Bhutan to cooperate with the Tibetan refugees, which the latter willingly responded. Many of the Tibetan refugees also took refuge in Nepal besides other foreign countries.

## Establishment of CTA

Tibetan refugees, as stated above, are unlike other refugees in Indian soil as they are in the hope of returning to Tibet and reinstitute their rightful rule over the land. For which, with the help of the Indian government, the Tibetan people have formed their government-in-exile known as Central Tibetan Administration (CTA), with the hopes of 'free democratic administration' of the Tibetan refugees and 'not designed to take power in Tibet' and 'would be dissolved as soon as freedom is restored in Tibet' (CTA, n.d.). The CTA, like all democratic institutions, operates through the three democratic pillars of the judiciary, legislature, and executive bodies. It also has apex bodies, such as an election commission to ensure the election of representatives democratically, a public service commission for fair appointment of CTA civil service staffs, and an auditor general established for the 'responsibility to audit the accounts of all the CTA Departments and its subsidiaries, … *including those* autonomous institutions that are fully or partly funded by CTA and self-funded autonomous institutions like co-operative societies, trading concerns, educational institutions, public health centers and hospitals and so forth that comes under the purview of CTA' (CTA n.d., emphasis added). The organizational structure of the CTA and functioning of the Tibetan Parliament in Exile (TPiE), keeping all the Tibetan refugees together and bringing solidarity among the people, particularly among those who are in India, reflects their determination in keeping their dreams and desire alive and the hope to return to their homeland.

## The Struggle in Progress

The Cultural Revolution (1966-76) or the Great Proletarian Cultural Revolution in China, with the indoctrination to bring true communist ideology and by purging the remnants of capitalist and traditional elements in society, caused a traumatic experience to the deeply religious Tibetans. It was considered by many Tibetans as a direct assault on Tibetan Buddhism and, therefore, a deliberate attempt to destroy Tibetan identity. Under the guise of people's liberation and establishing the ideals of communism in the proclaimed Tibetan Autonomous Region, the Chinese communist forces infringed on the religious, cultural, and linguistic rights and freedoms of Tibetan people (Jha, 1992).

Agricultural reforms on the territory of Tibet resulted in millions of people in China and Tibet starving to death (Vahali, 2009). 'Symbols of the feudal past', such as religion, native language, and traditions, were destroyed, and people were forced to adopt the new socialist identity (Vahali, 2009). After the so-called 'cultural revolution', a vast majority of Buddhist artifacts, temples and monasteries were destroyed. According to Jha (1992), the number of religious sites destroyed during the cultural revolution was 6,000. The turmoil of the cultural revolution finished in 1976, leaving Tibet with eight functioning monasteries out of 2,700 before 1959, and 970 monks and nuns out of 114,000 (Erffa, 1996).

Chinese cultural revolution was seen by the Tibetans as the strategic elimination of all signs of independent Tibetan culture. Not only was the Tibetan culture damaged, but the region itself was turned into a veritable war zone. The Chinese Government treated the province as a large military base, stationing 3,00,000 troops, hundreds of nuclear weapons, and many torture camps. It has been claimed that at present, approximately 3,000 religious and political prisoners are held captive in Tibet, being tortured and forced into labor camps. Since 1959 roughly 1.2 million Tibetans have died as a direct result of the Chinese occupation. It is widely believed that the Chinese Government is using the province of Tibet as a nuclear waste dump. There is no freedom, and even the Dalai Lama's photographs are banned.

According to a UN report, the Chinese occupation of Tibet has been characterized by acts of murder, rape, arbitrary imprisonment, torture, cruelty, inhuman and degraded treatment of Tibetans on a large scale. According to a document captured by guerrillas fighting the Chinese army, 87,000 deaths were recorded in Lhasa between March 1959 and September 1960. China's sustained, brutal occupation has resulted in a mass exodus of Tibetans to India. Over the years, thousands of Tibetans have taken dangerous, heartbreaking journeys over the Himalayas to enter India (Norbu, 1987).

In April 1954, India signed a new treaty, known as the Panchsheel Treaty, with China, which is based on the 'Five Principles of Peaceful Coexistence'. The memorandum agreed upon the understanding that India and China would under no circumstances interfere with each other's internal affairs, and that India should accept Tibet as an integral part of China. Respecting the agreement, the then Indian Prime Minister, Jawaharlal Nehru, made it clear to the Dalai Lama—when the latter visited India on a religious trip on the invitation of the Indian Maha Bodhi Society to attend the Buddha Jayanti—India's inability to support Tibet. When the Dalai Lama expressed his desire to seek exile in India, he was suggested to go back to his country and to try and work out the Seventeen Point Agreement with the Chinese government. However, members of the Indian polity (one of whom was Jaya Prakash

Narayan) promised that on some appropriate occasion, he would raise his voice in support of Tibetan freedom. Though Prime Minister Nehru was criticized by many for his China Policy, it seemed that he wanted to protect India's friendly relations with China and was determined to adhere to the principles of the Panchsheel memorandum. Thus, the Government of India could not contemplate taking the issue up with the Chinese over the question of Tibetan rights (Lama, 1962). However, the Sino-Indian war of 1962 proved the contemplation of Nehru and the agreement to be futile. It has been argued that he dreamt of a free Asia, where every nation would coexist in harmony.

The Dalai Lama, with his entourage, finally escaped from Tibet in 1959. This time, the Indian Government welcomed and granted asylum to the Dalai Lama on humanitarian grounds. Nehru showed a keen interest in the Tibetan affairs and refugee issue. During the 1960s, he prioritized the Tibetan refugee issue in domestic political agenda to compensate for his earlier inability to help Tibet. On 4th April 1959, Nehru publicly announced that India's policy was governed by three factors: the preservation of the security and integrity of India, India's desire to maintain friendly relations with the PRC, and her deep sympathy for the people of Tibet. This put the country in a dilemma. Norbu (2001) pointed out that, although it was the last component of India's foreign policy, the fact that the Tibetan people found their way in that official policy meant that the question of Tibetan refugees was high on India's agenda.

The danger posed to the independence of Tibet did not pass quietly without capturing the attention of the international community. The Government of India, supported by the British Government, protested to the PRC and stated that the invasion was not in the interest of the people. On 7th November 1950, the Kashag and the Government appealed to the United Nations Organization to intercede. Although the Tibetan delegation that was sent to various nations like India, Nepal, Great Britain, and the United States had been turned down initially, almost all Governments of different countries who the Dalai Lama had approached and requested for help and assistance were very sympathetic and promised support. The Federation of Malaysia and the Republic of Ireland sponsored a draft resolution, which was debated by the UN General Assembly during October. It was passed in favor of the Tibetans. A Tibet Support Committee was set up in India by Jaya Prakash Narayan. The International Commission of Jurists, an independent organization dedicated to upholding justice around the world, published a report on the legal status of Tibet in its favor and conducted a full-scale inquiry. The Afro-Asian Committee, which met in Delhi, unanimously supported the Tibetan cause. In 1959 the Central Relief Committee (India) and the American Emergency Committee for Tibetan refugees were set up to help the refugees. These were followed by other similar dedicated agencies in other countries all over the world. The Swiss Government was co-operative from the start and willingly sponsored 200 children for adoption and promised to take every possible step to preserve them and their unique Tibetan culture and identity. It introduced a scheme for some students to study in Switzerland and provided for the settlement of 1,000 adult refugees. The International Commission of Jurists published a report in Geneva during August 1960, which again vindicated the Tibetan viewpoint. It reiterated that China had violated sixteen articles of the Universal Declaration of Human Rights and accused China of committing genocide in Tibet. Countries like Thailand, Philippines, Malta, Ireland, Malaysia, Nicaragua and El Salvador discussed the Tibetan cause at the United Nations once again in autumn 1965 on the draft resolution. The International Red Cross and others helped the Tibetan resettlement program in other ways (Lama, 1962).

## Migration and After

The comprehensive examination of the history of Tibetan migration discloses that migration, in fact, started first within their own country. This mainly had to do with the question of inner and outer Tibet and differentiated Chinese policy for the same. It has also been regarded as one of the principal causes and characteristics of the 1959 revolt that rekindled the whole process of Tibetan Migration. According to Dawa Norbu (2001), inner Tibet includes Amdo and Kham, and the Eastern part of Tibet, most of which were already incorporated into neighboring Chinese provinces before 1951. Outer Tibet included Central, Southern and Western Tibet and some parts of Kham, which were under the effective control of the Tibetan Government in Lhasa at the time of the Communist takeover. This part of Tibet is what the PRC calls the Tibetan Autonomous Region today. Kham and Amdo are excluded from the Chinese conception of Tibet. The provisions of the 17-point Agreement, 1951, applied only to inner Tibet. Therefore, the communist leaders, for all practical purposes, treated Kham and Amdo almost exactly like China in terms of general policy implementation such as ideological campaigning, land reforms etc. Such policies were designed to replace core Tibetan Buddhist values and key institutions with Chinese Marxist ones. Naturally, Tibetans, who were deeply religious people, resented and resisted this widely in inner Tibet. This led to the first wave of displacement and forced immigration from inner to outer Tibet in the mid-1950s and then by 1959 into South East Asia, India, Nepal, Bhutan, and other foreign lands (Norbu, 2001). Of the total Tibetan refugee population, India sheltered approximately 80 percent, with the second-highest concentration in Nepal. According to the 1951 census, the number of Tibetan refugees in India was 3,000. In 1961, after the Khampa rebellion and consequent mass exodus, the number increased to about 43,000. This number grew to 50,000 in 1971. Between 1961 and 1971, the number did not grow much because the Chinese authorities sealed all the escape routes to India. Among

80 percent of the refugees living in India, 25 percent have settled in Karnataka, and the rest are settled in the Himalayan range in West Bengal, Sikkim, Uttar Pradesh, and Himachal Pradesh and so on. There are reports that the Government of India and the Government of Nepal have arranged for tight security at the border, and the Chinese authorities are blocking all efforts of the Tibetans to return home. Despite these tight security arrangements, Tibetans continue to sneak into the Indian Territory, although not in significant numbers. The Dalai Lama has set up his 'Government in Exile' at Dharamsala in Himachal Pradesh in North India with full cooperation from India and Western countries (Ray, 2001). The Dalai Lama was granted political asylum by the Government of India on 30th March 1959. When in 1960 the Indian authorities and the Dalai Lama's representatives decided that the refugees should be rehabilitated in permanent settlements, Nehru, as Prime Minister, wrote to the various Chief Ministers of Indian States, asking for the settlement of Tibetan refugees. All the State Governments of Karnataka, Orissa, Himachal Pradesh, Madhya Pradesh, and Uttar Pradesh privately responded to Nehru's request. The Government of India even persuaded Bhutan and Sikkim for the same. However, the proposal by the Tibetan Government-in-Exile for settlement of all the Tibetan refugees in one place in Northern India was not accepted by the Indian Government. Nonetheless, the Government of India's attitude toward the self- administration of the Tibetans was both liberal and generous. Consequently, groups of three to four thousand were considered large enough to preserve their language and other institutions. The Government of India also granted considerable autonomy to the Dalai Lama about the administration of his people (Goldstein, 1978; Subba, 1990). As a result, today we find a wide spatial distribution of the refugees, which goes beyond the Indian border to Nepal and Bhutan, and we also find many privately settled refugees in the Himalayan areas like Darjeeling and Sikkim. It is regarded that it is quite difficult to get the exact fact and figures of refugees settled in various parts of India. This is because their population has spread far and wide due to the constant inflow of their fellow nationals from across the border and because they are always moving from one place to another within the Indian Territory. However, in 'Tibetans in Exile', which was brought out by the information office of the Dalai Lama in 1969, an attempt has been made to depict their major settlements, location, and population as far as possible (Subba,1990). According to this report, there are 14 settlements distributed over seven states, namely Andhra Pradesh, Himachal Pradesh, Madhya Pradesh, Karnataka, Orissa, Sikkim, and West Bengal. However, it was found that the population figures for all the settlements were not available then, and the available figures for eight settlements could not be treated as authentic. But by 1976, the figures for their population in various places and countries became well documented. Consequently, it was recorded that India has 83.3 percent of

the Tibetans in exile. The remaining 16.7 percent are distributed over more than six countries, of which Nepal alone has 5-10 percent of these refugees. In India, the highest percentage of Tibetan refugees is in Mysore (Karnataka), i.e., 20.7 percent, followed by Dehradun and Mussorie (13.8 percent) and Arunachal Pradesh (7.6 percent). In the entire Darjeeling Hills and Sikkim, which are to be taken together, the percentage comes to 10.7 percent, which is slightly more than that in Nepal (Subba, 1990).

However, despite nearly 60-65 years having passed, Tibetan refugees, on the other hand, have maintained a separate culture and identity that they refuse to give up. Still, there are certain changes that have been taking place in the traditional Tibetan culture, social structure, and lifestyle in general because of various influences—modernization, globalization, enculturation etc. The present book aims to get an insight into the Tibetan refugee's worldview and perspective of their position in a country that they themselves do not want to embrace as their own. The scope of the study is, therefore, in regard to their flight to India and the process of their settlement and naturalization in India. It is primarily an empirical study where the focus would be on an intensive study of some refugee settlements in Darjeeling hills, Sikkim, and Himachal Pradesh. The study aims at analytical documentation of the struggle for a safe and secure life that the early settlers went through in the process of their flight to India. Also, their adaptation and adjustment into the new social, economic, and changed cultural milieu, especially from the viewpoint of the second- and third-generation migrants. Going beyond the scope of the field situation, the study would relate the life of the refugees in the hills with the larger Tibetan refugee community spread all over India to understand the process of reproduction of their separate identity as a Tibetan refugee community. The study would ascertain the role of Dharmasala in binding the community and its campaign for a separate homeland in Tibet.

The forceful occupation of Tibet by China in 1959 and its aftermath led thousands of inhabitants to flee Tibet as refugees to different parts of the world. India was one of the obvious destinations of these Tibetan refugees and had the highest concentration of their population after Nepal. Though very liberal, the Government of India did not allow these refugees to settle down in one place; as a result, they are scattered in different parts of the country. Darjeeling, a hill station of West Bengal, Sikkim, and Himachal Pradesh are a few of them. Along with all aspects of migration—such as its historical process, the process of adaptation, and integration in the host society—this study proposes to look at the identity of refugees as volatile and subject to change. The question of identity is intimately related to the question of migration as the phenomenon of migration is the outcome of a socio-historical process.

A brief review of the available literature on Tibetan refugees in India has revealed certain information gaps. For instance, Tibet was an independent country illegally occupied by China, who started indescribable atrocities upon the Tibetans in their own country, leading to the extinction of civilization of their race through the Cultural Revolution. This resulted in the fleeing of thousands of Tibetans, mainly to India and other parts of the continent. India, under Prime Minister Jawaharlal Nehru, gave asylum to these Tibetan refugees along with their leader, His Holiness Dalai Lama, and their rehabilitation and settlement started. In the process, they experienced many difficulties and trauma. Though their rehabilitation has been regarded as most successful (among the refugee groups settled in India), they had to go through the process of assimilation, acculturation and integration, and transformation in their country of refuge. The question, therefore, is: how much their cultural past has been retained and how much of it has been sacrificed? These dynamic and transformative aspects of Tibetan refugees have been left largely unexplored in the existing studies. Therefore, a sociological interpretation of the subject is needed, which is still lacking because of the inadequate sociological research.

Chapter 3

# Profiling the Tibetan Refugees
# in Indian Himalayas

## Introduction

The present chapter focuses on delineating the socioeconomic and demographic profile of Tibetan refugees in the Indian Himalayas. Socioeconomic profiling of the respondents is an essential element in sociological studies to provide a background insight into the lives of the subjects under investigation. In fact, any study would be superficial without taking into consideration the socioeconomic realities of the people. Profiling is important because it helps in statistical generalization in bringing out inferential interpretation of the data. Bhat and Ali (1994) had categorized what constitutes social and demographic profiles, which are a) age structure, b) age at marriage, c) death rate, d) birth rate, e) growth rate, and f) educational standards. Whereas the economic profile or indicators constitutes a) occupational structure, b) income distribution pattern, c) sources of income, d) borrowings and investments, e) house structure, and f) magnitude of fixed/variable asset.

As introduced in the first chapter, the study is conducted in Himachal Pradesh (Dalhousie and Dharamsala), Sikkim (Ravangla), and West Bengal (Darjeeling and Sonada). The chapter wholly focused on the quantitative aspect based on 200 samples, which were collected from the aforesaid areas which the analysis is based on. The distribution of the samples over these areas is diagrammatically represented in Figure 3.1.

Before we begin the data presentation and analysis, a brief description of the Refugee Centers from where the fieldwork was conducted is essential to situate the background of the respondents.

**Figure 3.1:** Sample distribution

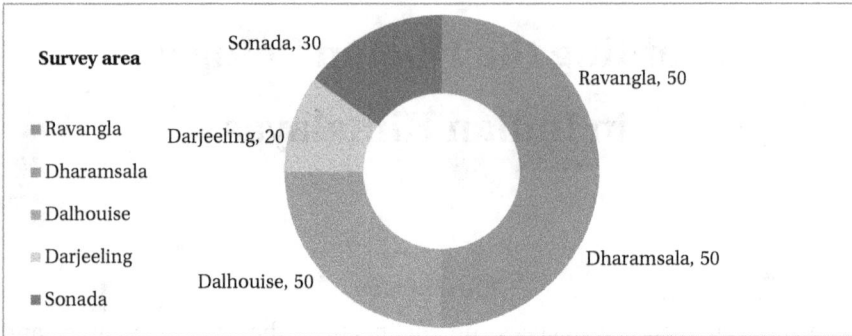

Source: Field Survey October 2016-August 2017

## Description of the Centers

When the Tibetan took refuge in India with His Holiness Dalai Lama, the Government of Indian generously extended its help in giving them political asylum as refugees in the country. The places which were arranged for their settlement in the country located across the length and breadth of the country. Two large transit camps, one at Missamari, Assam and the other at Buxa Duar, a former British prisoner-of-war camp situated near the Bhutanese border in West Bengal, were established to handle the influx of refugees. These 'camps represented an effort not only of the Indian government but also of the opposition parties...united to create a Central Relief Committee that was instrumental to obtaining food, medical supplies and international aid' (Avedon, 1984, p. 73). Within a few weeks of setting up these camps, they were flooded with more than 9,000 refugees, which was more than these camps were designed to accommodate. Therefore, efforts were made to engage the refugees in road building works in the cooler regions of North India to prevent disease due to heat and overcrowding. Several groups and batches of people in 1959 were sent for roadwork to Sikkim, Kalimpong and Darjeeling and some to Bhutan. Later, in early 1960, more people were sent for roadwork in the North Indian states of Himachal Pradesh, Arunachal Pradesh and Jammu and Kashmir (Basu, n.d.).

Basu's (n.d.) work has broadly classified the settlement areas of the Tibetan refugees into two aspects, firstly, permanent agricultural settlements with rehabilitation strategy as those in Southern India such as Bylakuppe Tibetan Settlement (BTS) in Mysore district, Karnataka, who is also known as 'Little Tibet of India'. Secondly, alongside the settlements, the Tibetan Refugee Self Help Centers (TRSHC), which has emerged spontaneously with the idea that no refugee could ever be rehabilitated in the fullest sense without the realization that 'vital element could only come from within the community from within one's selves' to empower oneself and the community by means of internalizing that one has only to help oneself—'Self-Help' (Basu, n.d.).

Keeping in mind the significance of these two dimensions of settlement areas, the five-field site is an amalgamation of both, which is further discussed.

### Phuntsokling Tibetan Settlement, Dalhousie

Phuntsokling Tibetan settlement is in the northern Indian town of Dalhousie in Himachal Pradesh. The settlement was established in 1959 when the first batch of 400 men and women, including monks, came from Missamari in Assam to settle in Dalhousie. Later, another two batches joined the settlement to form 1,500 Tibetan refugees; subsequently, many more took refuge, making it one of the biggest settlements in its initial years of the Tibetan rehabilitation program in India. Over the years, many Tibetans have moved to Southern India for resettlement. At present, there are about 450 Tibetan settlers, most of them earn their livelihood by hawking woolen hosiery goods in winter, engaging in making Tibetan handicrafts items, and readymade garment business in the local Tibetan market during the summer.

### Tibetan Refugee's Self-Help Centre, McLeod Ganj, Dharamsala

Mcleod Ganj Tibetan Settlement, Dharamsala, was established in 1959. Its history stretches long before the mentioned date as it was the headquarters of the Thirteenth Dalai Lama from 1910-1912 when China briefly occupied Tibet during the period and the leaders took temporary refuge in India.

### Tibetan Refugee Self-Help Centre, Darjeeling

TRSHC, Darjeeling, was established on 2nd October 1959. By 1961, the center was fully registered as a charitable organization and exempted from income tax on all gifts and donations received. The center, when it started, had only four members. However, today, the center is home to 300 refugees. The center focuses on giving hands-on training to artisans and craftsmen who want to learn the life skills to earn their livelihood through the production of handicraft items. The center also looks after the sick and needy people, working along with and taking care of the old and the orphaned.

The objective of the center revolves around rebuilding the future of the Tibetans, teaching children in overcoming the cultural differences and simultaneously (re)socializing them to maintain their unique culture, religion, and arts. In continuance of their decade's old tradition, the center extends their help to the less fortunate members of the Tibetan community following the ideals of the benevolent Buddha and his holiness the Dalai Lama.

### *Tashiling Tibetan Settlement, Sonada*

Tashiling Tibetan settlement was established in 1965 on a total area of 21.537 acres of land. The settlement is situated at Sonada, about 17km away from Darjeeling town. Initially, the population was 324. However, at the time of fieldwork, it had decreased to 256, as most of them had moved out from the center and had assimilated and settled alongside the local population as their earnings grew. The main source of their livelihood, in this settlement, is traditional apron weaving and petty business, etc. The center has one high-school (up to 10 standard), one crèche, one allopathic dispensary, and three monasteries.

### *Kunphenling Tibetan Settlement, Ravangla, Sikkim*

Kunphenling Tibetan settlement was established in 1978. The Government of India provided the necessary assistance to rehabilitate 1,000 Tibetan refugees in Ravangla, South Sikkim. A total of 600 acres of land was sanctioned for the settlement, of which 300 acres were initially given to the settlement. This settlement is situated at Ravangla, 66 km from Namchi, South Sikkim. Most of the families were provided a piece of agricultural land for their livelihood. Besides agricultural activities, the settlers also engaged in carpet weaving at the settlement carpet weaving center. The settlement also has a primary school, a dispensary, and a center for Tibetan traditional medicine commonly referred to as *Amji*. A Multipurpose Co-operative society registered under the Indian Co-operative Societies Act 1970 has also been established. The Society provides necessary services such as fair price shop, carpet center, workshop, restaurant and guesthouse, to meet the needs of the settlers. Currently, there are seven camps; two new camps were added in 2010-2011. A distinguishing feature of the settlement was, the houses were not concentrated in one location, but were spread out, and most of these houses were constructed by the inhabitants themselves with little aid. The settlement was also comprised of ex-army men and women who had served in the Indian army. The residents here converse more in Tibetan and Hindi.

### Socioeconomic and Demographic Profile

### *Age and Sex Composition*

As highlighted, a total of 200 samples were surveyed for the collection of demographic details of the refugees who are spread across in three states of India. The sex composition of the respondents is 49 percent and 51 percent for females and males, respectively (Figure: 3.3). In relation to age distribution, as shown in Figure 3.2, it is observed that only 1 percent each were represented in the age group of 10-20 and 80 and above years. The highest representation is found in the age group of 30-40 years, with 29.5 percent, followed by 24 percent in the age group of 40-50 years. The higher representation of these two-age groups is due to their settled nature in terms of jobs and residence. At the same time, respondents in this age bracket were also able to communicate easily in the local language, making them more sociable. It is also observed that the lesser representation of those who are septuagenarian and above are primarily due to their smaller demographic composition as well as their inability to communicate in local lingua franca. As pointed out, the highest population of respondents can be seen in the age group of 30-40 years; these respondents whom we interviewed were all born and educated in India. Therefore, for them, it is easier to navigate through the local social milieus being equipped with cultural sensibility.

**Figure 3.2:** Age composition (in range) of the respondents as per settlement areas

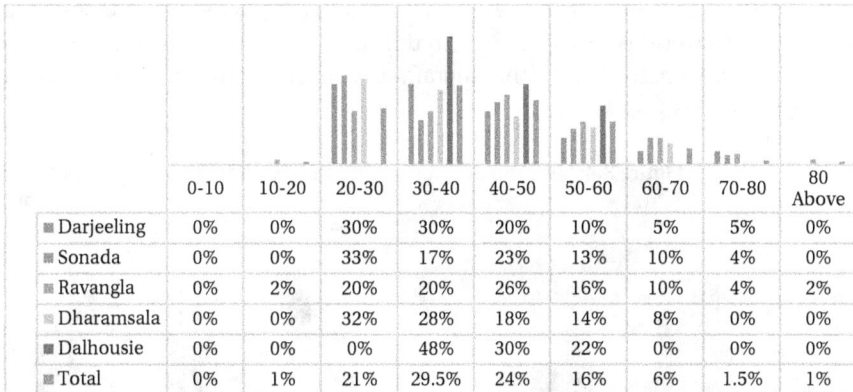

|  | 0-10 | 10-20 | 20-30 | 30-40 | 40-50 | 50-60 | 60-70 | 70-80 | 80 Above |
|---|---|---|---|---|---|---|---|---|---|
| Darjeeling | 0% | 0% | 30% | 30% | 20% | 10% | 5% | 5% | 0% |
| Sonada | 0% | 0% | 33% | 17% | 23% | 13% | 10% | 4% | 0% |
| Ravangla | 0% | 2% | 20% | 20% | 26% | 16% | 10% | 4% | 2% |
| Dharamsala | 0% | 0% | 32% | 28% | 18% | 14% | 8% | 0% | 0% |
| Dalhousie | 0% | 0% | 0% | 48% | 30% | 22% | 0% | 0% | 0% |
| Total | 0% | 1% | 21% | 29.5% | 24% | 16% | 6% | 1.5% | 1% |

Source: Field Survey October 2016-August 2017

**Figure 3.3:** Sex composition of the respondents

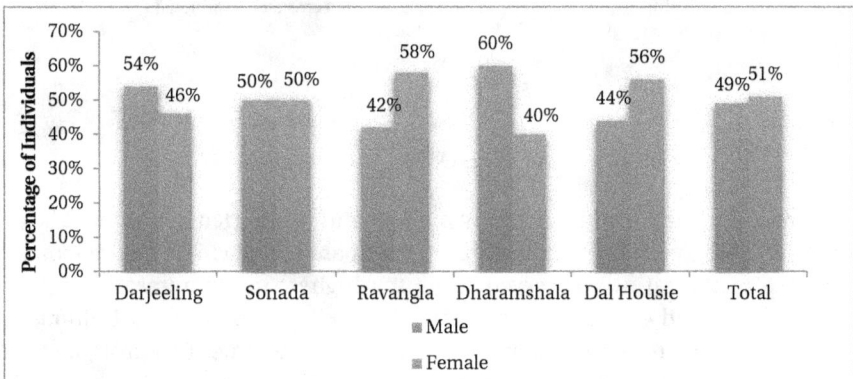

Source: Field Survey October 2016-August 2017

The study found that Darjeeling has 54 percent male and 46 percent female respondents; in Sonada, there is equal representation. Ravangla has the highest representation of females—with 58 percent—and 42 percent males, whereas Dharamsala has more male respondents (60 percent) as compared to female respondents (40 percent). Dalhousie has a male population of 44 percent and 56 percent female. During subsequent interviews, it was found that the higher representation of female respondents in Ravangla is due to the out-migration of the male population as most of them are working in the Indian army in various ranks. Further, a higher male population in Dharamsala where the study was carried out (i.e., TRSHC, Mcleod Ganj) also runs an old-age home, and a significant number of the residents were male with few female residents. The interview of the inmates was conducted to have a lucid picture of their struggle in the initial days of their flight and subsequent settlement in India, as well as to comprehend the changes that have taken place over the years. In relation to Dalhousie, the higher representation of the female respondents, which to an extent, is proportionate to the study population, is primarily due to their involvement in local handicrafts and participation in business and market activities.

**Figure 3.4:** Sex ratio of respondents' family members

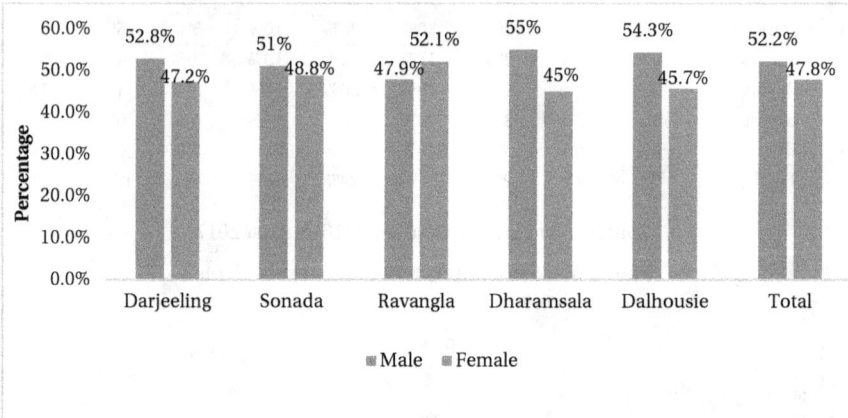

Source: Field Survey October 2016-August 2017

On average, the sex ratio of family members in respondents' households, as depicted in Figure 3.4, shows that 52.2 percent are male, while 47.8 are female. The gap in the ratio is observed to be the highest in Dharamsala, with 55 percent male and 45 percent female family members, followed by Dalhousie, where 54.3 percent are male, and 45.7 percent are female. The divergence is least observed in Sonada. However, the ratio presented a contradictory picture in relation to children, as 47.2 percent are male, while 52.8 percent are female

(Figure 3.5). A favorable sex ratio is observed in Dalhousie, where 48.7 percent are male, and 51.3 percent are female, while in Darjeeling the ratio is in favor of males, with 61.5 percent and 38.5 percent females. Nonetheless, in overall observation, the ratio stands in favor of the girl, which shows the non-discriminatory nature of Tibetan society towards a girl child in contradiction to Indian society. So far, there are no known reported cases of female infanticide within Tibetans in India.

**Figure 3.5:** Sex ratio of children in respondents' family

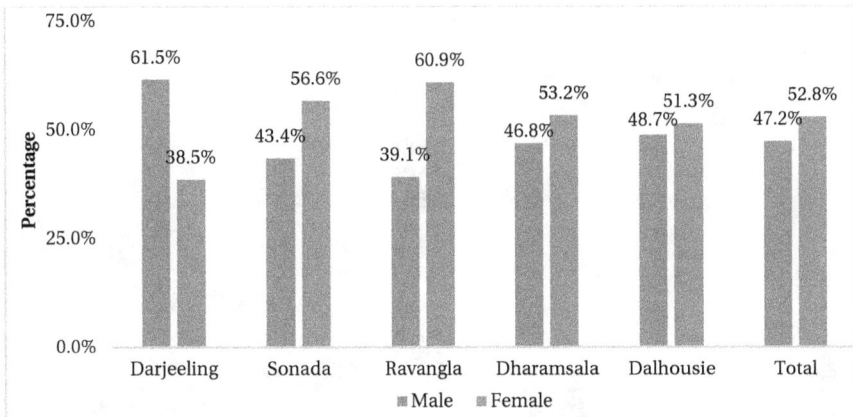

Source: Field Survey October 2016-August 2017

## Marital Status and Age at the time of Marriage

In relation to the marital status of the respondents, it was found that 61.5 percent are married, 35 percent are unmarried, 3 percent are widows/widowers, and 0.5 percent are divorcees. Few respondents who are divorcee were found during the field study in Darjeeling (5 percent) and Ravangla (1 percent); however, it also must be noted that the Tibetans themselves are governed by customary laws where divorce is attached with certain social shaming and stigmas which could be the reason for rare cases of separation. According to some respondents, marriage takes place between two people who are of the same age and based on this logic, some of the older generation could not find their match and remained unmarried; Dharamsala has more unmarried respondents (44 percent). Although initially, questions were put in relation to live-in-relationship, we have removed it from the statistical analysis since we did not find any cases, as given in Figure 3.6. When further enquired, few of the respondents have mentioned that live-in-relationship is uncommon among the Tibetans as such arrangements are not encouraged and supported by their elders.

**Figure 3.6:** Marital status of the respondents

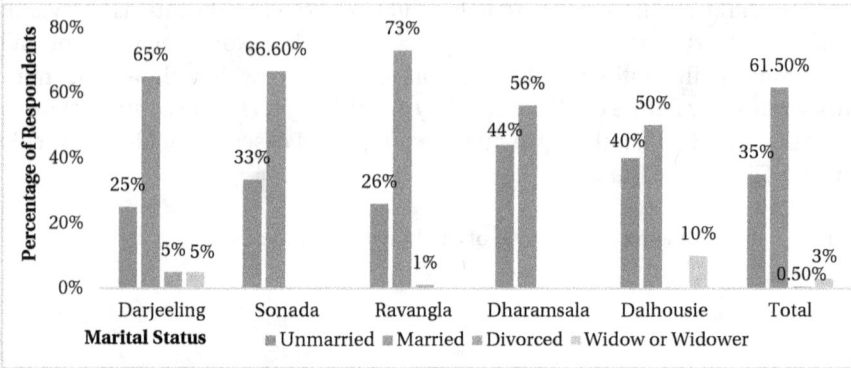

Source: Field Survey October 2016-August 2017

**Figure 3.7:** Average age of marriage of the married respondents

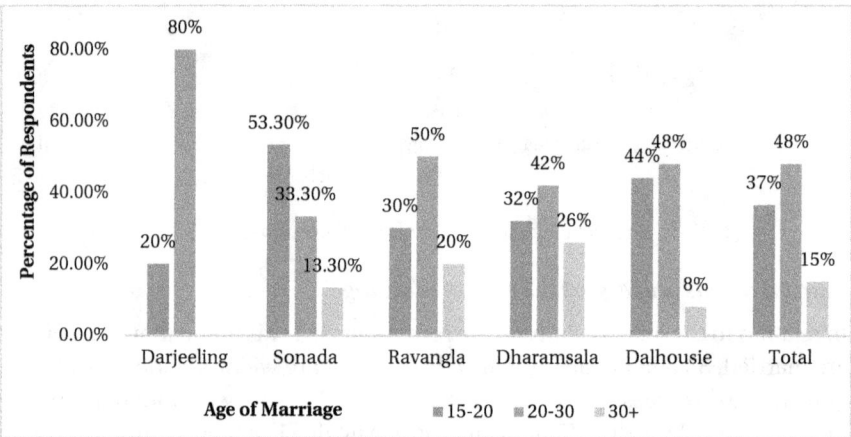

Source: Field Survey October 2016-August 2017

Marriage is an integral institution of any society; Figure 3.7 shows the average age of marriage of the married respondents, which is 65 percent or 130 (in absolute number) of the total respondents, as given in Figure 3.6. It is observed that 48 percent of the respondents married at the age between 20-30 years, while 37 percent between the age of 15-20 years and 15 percent were married above the age of 30. Similarly, as given in Figure 3.8, the average age of respondents' spouses at the time of marriage shows a comparable pattern: 49 percent of them married at the age of 20-30 years, while 35.5 percent at the age of 15-20, and 15.5 percent got married above the age of 30 years. It can be observed that in the given two data set, as given in Figures 3.7 and 3.8, not much difference can be seen between the two. This also proves the hypothetical statement made by some of the respondents in relation to the selection of spouses of the same age group. The data also reveals that more than one-third of the respondents have married below the age of 20-years-old; however, most of them belong to the older generation, and early marriage is common among their generation across the world.

**Figure 3.8:** Average age of respondents' spouse at the time of marriage

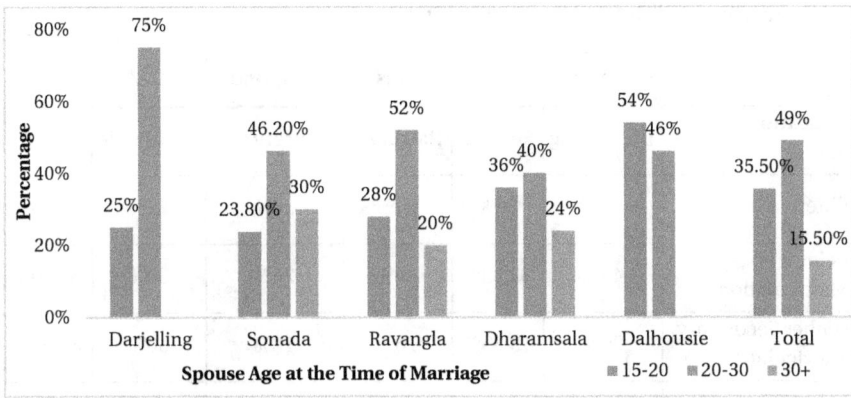

Source: Field Survey October 2016-August 2017

### *Educational Qualification*

Education is the index of human development, and it is also related to the socioeconomic empowerment of the people and the community. Educationally, as shown in Figure 3.9, 23.5 percent of the respondents are illiterate, 31 percent are below matriculation, 20 percent have successfully completed matriculation, and 16 percent have passed a senior secondary examination. Comparatively, a small percentage of the respondent has completed higher studies from which 7.5 percent are graduate, and only 2 percent have completed their post-graduate studies.

Statistical analysis of the educational qualifications shows that the maximum number of respondents had educational qualifications below matriculation (a total of 51 percent, including the illiterates). In contrast, 9.5 percent were graduates and above. Correlating with the age structure of the respondents, the level of educational attainment was found to be lower in the age group of 60 and above. The reasonable explanation which they have provided is that at the time of their arrival in India at a very young age (5-10 years old), the settlement centers did not have any formal and basic educational centers. At the same time, those from the older generation were mostly illiterate or below matriculate because when they arrived, they had already crossed the age for formal studies, and the education system in India was entirely different from that of Tibet. Another reason for the concentration of population in the below matriculate category is the fact that they believe that the education qualification up to class 8 was sufficient and the refugee belonging to not-so-economically-stable families had to give up education because earning a livelihood and supporting was more important, 10 percent of the respondents are postgraduates these are the respondent belonging from the younger generation whose families have understood the value of education and are pursuing their children to take up further studies.

**Figure 3.9:** Educational status of the respondents

| Educational Status | Darjeeling | Sonada | Ravangla | Dharamsala | Dalhousie | Total |
|---|---|---|---|---|---|---|
| Illiterate | 15% | 20% | 24% | 30% | 22% | 23.50% |
| Below Matriculation | 45% | 33.33% | 36% | 24% | 36% | 31.00% |
| Higher Secondary/ Matriculation | 20% | 13.33% | 16% | 18% | 30% | 20.00% |
| Senior Secondary | 15% | 16.66% | 18% | 14% | 16% | 16% |
| Graduate | 5% | 13.33% | 4% | 10% | 6% | 7.50% |
| Postgraduate | NIL | 3.33% | 2% | 4% | NIL | 2% |

Source: Field Survey October 2016-August 2017

In relation to the educational status of the family members of the respondents as given in Figure 3.10, it was found that 14.2 percent of female family members have education below matriculation and 8.8 percent are illiterate, 7.7 percent have education up to senior secondary, 6.9 percent have education up to matriculation, 6.5 percent are graduate, 3.5 percent are postgraduate, and 1.7 percent has a diploma. Unlike the female family members, male members of the family, i.e., 15.4 percent have education below matriculation that is more in comparison to the females, 8.8 percent of the male members have education up to higher secondary, which is more than the female members; 7.8 percent of the male members are graduates, which again is more than the female; 7.2 percent of the male members have education up to matriculation, which is more than the females; 6.8 percent of the male members are illiterate which is less than the female members; 2.5 percent of the male members are postgraduate, which is less than the females; and 1.5

percent of the male members are diploma holders. The only difference between the male and the female family members in terms of education is that more female members are illiterate, and there are more female members doing post-graduation and diploma.

**Figure 3.10:** Educational status of the family members

| Education | Sex | Darjeeling | Sonada | Ravangla | Dharamsala | Dalhousie | Total |
|---|---|---|---|---|---|---|---|
| Illiterate | Male | 7.10% | 7% | 6.80% | 7.40% | 6% | 6.80% |
| | Female | 7.10% | 14.10% | 10.50% | 8.50% | 4.50% | 8.80% |
| Below Matriculation | Male | 10% | 15.70% | 21.90% | 14% | 11.50% | 15.40% |
| | Female | 11.40% | 14.10% | 17.80% | 14% | 11.50% | 14.20% |
| Higher Secondary / Matriculation | Male | 11.40% | 8.60% | 6.80% | 2.50% | 10% | 7.20% |
| | Female | 5.70% | 8.60% | 5.40% | 6% | 9% | 6.90% |
| Senior Secondary | Male | 11.40% | 7% | 6.80% | 9% | 11% | 8.80% |
| | Female | 17.10% | 1.50% | 7.70% | 6% | 10% | 7.70% |
| Graduate | Male | 2.80% | 9.40% | 2.70% | 12% | 10% | 7.80% |
| | Female | 1.40% | 7% | 4.14% | 9% | 8% | 6.50% |
| Postgraduate | Male | 2.80% | 1.50% | 3.10% | 2.50% | 2.50% | 2.50% |
| | Female | 8.50% | 1.50% | 4.50% | 4% | 1.50% | 3.50% |
| Diploma | Male | 1.40% | NIL | NIL | 3% | 3% | 1.50% |
| | Female | 1.40% | 3.10% | 1.30% | 2% | 1% | 1.70% |

Source: Field Survey October 2016-August 2017

The analysis of the educational status of the children, as shown in Figure 3.11, shows that 16.9 percent of the female children and 15 percent male children have education below matriculation; likewise, 10.6 percent of female children and 7.5 percent of male children have completed matriculation, and 11.9 percent female children and 10.6 percent male children have completed higher secondary education. 7.5 percent female children are graduates in contrast to 8.1 percent of the male children; 3.1 percent female children and 4.4 percent male children are postgraduates; 1.8 percent female children and 1.2 percent male children are diploma holders, and 0.6 percent female members have other educational qualifications. It is seen that there is more representation of females in higher levels of education.

Education as a process provides the direction and guidance necessary for forming a social personality; good education drives occupational opportunities, which in turn provides the base for the relative social position of the people and mobility from one socioeconomic status to another.

**Figure 3.11:** Educational status of the children

| Education | Sex | Darjeeling | Sonada | Ravangla | Dharamsala | Dalhousie | Total |
|---|---|---|---|---|---|---|---|
| Illiterate | Male | NIL | NIL | NIL | NIL | NIL | NIL |
| | Female | NIL | NIL | NIL | NIL | NIL | NIL |
| Below Matriculation | Male | 23% | 13% | 17% | 6.2% | 16.2% | 15% |
| | Female | 15.3% | 13% | 19.5% | 12.5% | 21.6% | 16.9% |
| Higher Secondary / Matriculation | Male | 3.8% | 4.3% | 4.8% | 12.5% | 10.8% | 7.5% |
| | Female | 3.8% | 13% | 9.7% | 12.5% | 13.5% | 10.6% |
| Senior Secondary | Male | 11.5% | 4.3% | 9.7% | 15.6% | 10.8% | 10.6% |
| | Female | 3.8% | 13% | 17% | 15.6% | 8.1% | 11.9% |
| Graduate | Male | 15.3% | 17.3% | 4.8% | 6.2% | 2.7% | 8.1% |
| | Female | 7.6% | 13% | 7.3% | 9.3% | 2.7% | 7.5% |
| Postgraduate | Male | 7.6% | 4.3% | 2.4% | NIL | 8.1% | 4.4% |
| | Female | 7.6% | NIL | 4.8% | NIL | 2.7% | 3.1% |
| Diploma | Male | NIL | NIL | NIL | 6.2% | NIL | 1.2% |
| | Female | NIL | 4.3% | 2.4% | 3.1% | NIL | 1.8% |
| Others | Male | NIL | NIL | NIL | NIL | NIL | NIL |
| | Female | NIL | NIL | NIL | NIL | 2.7% | 0.6% |

Source: Field Survey October 2016-August 2017

### *Occupation and Income*

As per the study, the occupational status, as shown in Figure 3.12, reveals that 48 percent of the respondents are in the 'other' category, which includes professions such as army, teacher, nurse, governmental officials, etc., whereas 26 percent are involved in business activities, 7.5 percent were drivers, and the remaining 18.5 percent are homemakers. It was found that most of the Tibetan refugees were employed in the army or working as teachers and CTA officials. In most of the cases, the male family members were seen working in the army, and the other family members are doing business. Women in the family have also taken up a business, making them more independent and giving them equal rights in the decision-making process. In Ravangla, the majority of male respondents were in the army and women were seen working in the weaving section at the center or in small businesses, like tea stalls or seasonal businesses such as selling hosiery. In Dalhousie, most respondents were in business, and the rest were teachers; the older generation was seen in the weaving section. In Dharamsala, initially, they worked in the army, some were in the retail business, and some were employed as laborers. Now they were at the old age home spending their time doing their religious prayers.

**Figure 3.12:** Occupational distribution

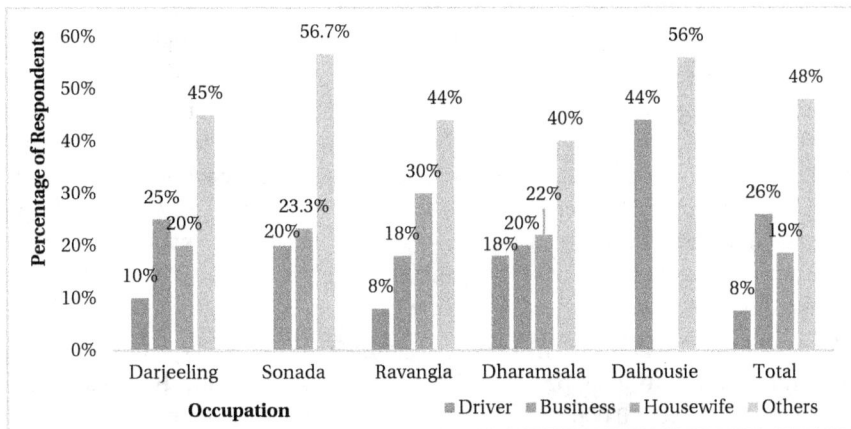

Source: Field Survey October 2016-August 2017

**Figure 3.13:** Average monthly income of the respondents and family

| Income in Rs. | Head | Darjeeling | Sonada | Ravangla | Dharamsala | Dalhousie | Total |
|---|---|---|---|---|---|---|---|
| Below Rs. 5,000 | Respondent | 40% | 16.6% | 18% | 24% | 18% | 21.5% |
| | Family | NIL | 6.6% | 12% | 14% | 10% | 10% |
| Rs. 5,000 to 10,000 | Respondent | 25% | 26.6% | 18% | 22% | 22% | 22% |
| | Family | 15% | 43.3% | 20% | 26% | 38% | 29% |
| Rs.10,000 to 20,000 | Respondent | 35% | 30% | 30% | 30% | 20% | 28% |
| | Family | 35% | 13.3% | 48% | 36% | 32% | 34.5% |
| Rs. 20,000 to 30,000 | Respondent | NIL | 13.3% | 20% | 8% | 20% | 14% |
| | Family | 25% | 13.3% | 10% | 16% | 8% | 13% |
| Rs. 30,000 to 40,000 | Respondent | NIL | 10% | 8% | 10% | 16% | 10% |
| | Family | 15% | 13.3% | 6% | 4% | 6% | 7.5% |
| Rs. 40,000 to 50,000 | Respondent | NIL | 3.3% | 6% | 6% | 4% | 4.5% |
| | Family | 10% | 10% | 4% | 4% | 6% | 6% |
| Above Rs. 50,000 | Respondent | NIL | NIL | NIL | NIL | NIL | NIL |
| | Family | NIL | NIL | NIL | NIL | NIL | NIL |

Source: Field Survey October 2016-August 2017

Figure 3.13 deals with the average monthly income of the respondents and of the family. The study found that 28 percent of the respondents earn between Rs. 10,000-20,000 per month, a high concentration of this income group is found among the respondents in Darjeeling, and the least was observed in Dalhousie (20 percent). It is followed by the income group of Rs. 5,000-10,000 constituting 22 percent, where 26.6 percent (which is the highest) is located among the respondents in the Sonada settlement center while the lowest is found in Ravangla (18 percent). The lowest percentage, i.e., 4.5 percent, is witnessed in the income group of Rs. 40,000-50,000, where respondents from Dharamsala and Ravangla with 6 percent each are highest in the category, while no respondents were found in Darjeeling.

A similar observation is discernible in the overall family income of the respondents, where 34.5 percent of the respondent's family belongs to the income group of Rs. 10,000-20,000, with a higher percentage being concentrated in Dharamsala with 36 percent, which is followed by Darjeeling (35 percent), and least in Sonada with 13.3 percent. Next to the highest income group is Rs. 5,000-10,000, with 29 percent, where Sonada has recorded the most with 43.3 percent and the least being in Darjeeling with 15 percent.

We can see from the above data that the families' monthly income increases as compared to the respondents. There are smaller numbers of families whose income is below Rs. 5,000 as compared to respondents' monthly income. The opposite remains true in the higher income group of Rs. 40,000-50,000, as the percentage of respondents is 4.5 percent while that of the family is 6 percent. An in-depth interview has revealed that those in the higher income group are also the ones who have higher educational qualifications. Further, the higher concentration of respondents and family in the income group of Rs. 10,000-20,000 is also primarily related to the types of occupations these refugees are engaged in such as weaving, retail shops, marketing seasonal clothes and other low paying professions. Contradictory to the general perceptions of the native communities, as highlighted in the work of Penny-Dimri (1994), the majority of the Tibetan refugees do not have a luxurious lifestyle backed by the high income, be it through engagement in various professions or through charities.

### *Household Infrastructure and Expenditures*

The symbolic manifestation of social change is discernible in the changing pattern of social action and behaviors in our daily interactions with others. These social actions and behaviors are, to an extent, determined by the adoption of tools and technology that ease the performance of our routinized task. The adoption of new technology has impacted the social relationship and the way we interact with others. Therefore, surveying the usages of various household infrastructure and gadgets among the refugees will let us analyze and assess the pattern of transformation; at the same time, it also is an indicator of the socioeconomic status and lifestyle.

In hilly areas, there are many villages that are isolated from any nearby motorable roads and highways. At the same time, due to frequent landslides, the already connected villages are often cut off for a good amount of time. In such cases, it is common among the local population to use an alternative cooking source, such as firewood or cow dung cake. However, in relation to Tibetan refugees, the clearly shows that every surveyed household usage cooking gas for their daily cooking task (refer Figure 3.14). It was also found that only 10 percent of the household has an induction cooktop in addition to the cooking gas; it was observed that many of them did not know about induction cooktops, and among those who knew about it tend to view it as a luxurious household gadget. 99 percent of the respondents' families have television, which is one of the main sources of entertainment for all generations. 86 percent have a refrigerator, while 36.5 percent had a radio; it has been seen that modern entertainment equipment such as television has taken over the radio. In the low-income group, the washing machine is considered a luxury rather than a necessity; 50.5 percent of respondent's families have washing machines. However, since half of the studied population has washing machines, it means that it has become a necessary household item rather than a luxury item. 20.5 percent of the population had fans; the percentage is low because most of the hill stations do not require a fan. 16.5 percent of the total population has four-wheelers; some are for private and some for public transportation use. 32 percent of the population have two-wheelers, 6 percent have bicycles. 92 percent of the total population had furniture; the rest do not since they were residing at an old age home. 58.5 percent has a water purifying system installed at home.

As shown in Figure 3.15, the various expenditures of the respondents. It was found that the maximum amount of expenditure is on household food items (32.5 percent), while only 4 percent is spent on eating out at restaurants and hotels. Followed by expenditure on education with 32 percent, this shows how the Tibetan refugees give more importance to education for their children. The third highest expenditure is on clothes (18.5 percent), which is followed by Transportation (8 percent), with the least on recreational activities (2 percent).

The respondent feels that there is more expenditure in food (household) as they take more protein and meat in their diet, they feel that there is more expenditure on education since they believe education is vital and necessary for making their children's future bright and opt for sending their children to the best educational institutions.

**Figure 3.14:** Respondent's ownership of basic household infrastructure

| Household Item Possessed | Darjeeling | Sonada | Ravangla | Dharamsala | Dalhousie | Total |
|---|---|---|---|---|---|---|
| Television | 100% | 96.6% | 98% | 100% | 100% | 99% |
| Refrigerator | 95% | 73.3% | 90% | 88% | 84% | 86% |
| Radio | 10% | 13.3% | 60% | 44% | 30% | 36.5% |
| Washing Machine | 5% | 10% | 72% | 72% | 50% | 50.5% |
| Fan | NIL | NIL | NIL | 72% | 10% | 20.5% |
| Cooking gas connection | 100% | 100% | 100% | 100% | 100% | 100% |
| Induction | NIL | 6.6% | 2% | 24% | 10% | 10% |
| Four-Wheeler | 10% | 16.6% | 12% | 30% | 10% | 16.5% |
| Two-Wheeler | 10% | 13.3% | 14% | 52% | 50% | 32% |
| Bicycle | NIL | 10% | NIL | 8% | 10% | 6% |
| Furniture | 95% | 100% | 100% | 100% | 70% | 92% |
| Water Purification System | 95% | 83.3% | 28% | 58% | 60% | 58.5% |

Source: Field Survey October 2016-August 2017

**Figure 3.15:** Particulars of respondent's average monthly expenditure

| Expenditure | Darjeeling | Sonada | Ravangla | Dharamsala | Dalhousie | Total |
|---|---|---|---|---|---|---|
| Clothes | 20% | 23.3% | 4% | 24% | 20% | 18.5% |
| Transportation | 5% | 3.6% | 8% | NIL | 20% | 8% |
| Education | 30% | 26.6% | 20% | 40% | 40% | 32% |
| Recreation Activities | 5% | 3.3% | 4% | NIL | NIL | 2% |
| Religious Practices or Customs | 10% | NIL | 4% | 4% | NIL | 3% |
| Food (Household) | 20% | 36.6% | 60% | 20% | 20% | 32.5% |
| Food (Restaurants/ Hotels) | 10% | 6.6% | NIL | 12% | NIL | 4% |

Source: Field Survey October 2016-August 2017

### *Access to Basic Amenities and Other Social Welfare Schemes*

Access to basic amenities and other social welfare measures of the government is an important dimension of the social inclusion of the refugees. Here, we have taken into consideration access to water, communication, and rations. It was found that 85.5 percent of the respondents get their water from the connection source provided by the government, while 14.5 percent had to arrange it themselves, Figure 3.16. Among those who had to arrange themselves for private connection was reported highest among those who are in Dalhousie (30 percent), followed by Darjeeling (25 percent).

Regarding access to communication devices, such as landline connection – telephone, and mobile devices, it was found that 98 percent of the respondents are using one of the means or both form of communication, while 2 percent of the respondents differ to use any (Figure 3.17). The highest number of respondents who do not use any of the mentioned communication devices are reported highest in Dalhousie (10 percent). Respondents from Darjeeling, Ravangla and Dharamsala reported using only mobile phones, while those in Sonada reported using mobile phones as the main means of communication, and at the same time, 3.3 percent of these respondents have an additional landline connection.

Certain welfare schemes are extended to the Tibetan refugees by GOI. Ministry of Home Affairs, GOI, in a press released notes reads:[4]

It has been observed that there is no uniformity in extension of benefits of central schemes to the Tibetan refugees. Government of India categorically wishes to clarify to the state governments that the Tibetan refugees living inside the settlements and outside are as entitled to all the development schemes of the government of India as any Indian citizen... Tibetans living in India can now avail the benefits of the MGNREGS, Rajiv Awas Yojana, NHRM and the public distribution system. Tibetans can also avail loans from the nationalized banks.

Regarding which, we assessed which social welfare card they have in their possession along with the refugee card. The study found only three types of cards in their possession, which are BPL (Below Poverty Line), APL (Above Poverty Line), and Refugee card. As shown in Figure 3.18, APL cardholders account for 19 percent, while 5 percent are BPL cardholders, and 82.5 percent of the refugees have refugee cards. However, in Dharamsala, Dalhousie and Ravangla, we found only refugee cardholders, with the least percentage in the latter (64 percent). One of the striking features of the finding is that not all Tibetan refugees have a refugee card in their possession. Those who hold BPL cards are entitled to ration under the PDS (Public Distribution System) in India.

---

[4] Tibetan refugees to be given benefits of welfare schemes. Hindustan Times, Jun 02, 2014 https://www.hindustantimes.com/chandigarh/tibetan-refugees-to-be-given-benefits-of-welfare-schemes/story-2AqbgUwlFM2S8VsGfEzShL.html

**Figure 3.16:** Basic amenities: Water supply

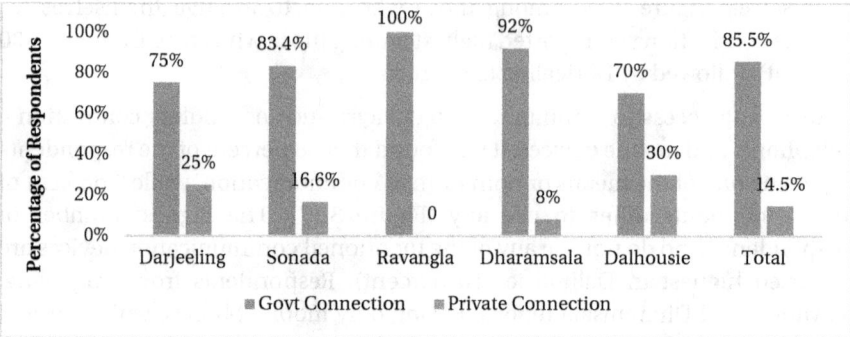

Source: Field Survey October 2016-August 2017

**Figure 3.17:** Basic amenities: Communication device

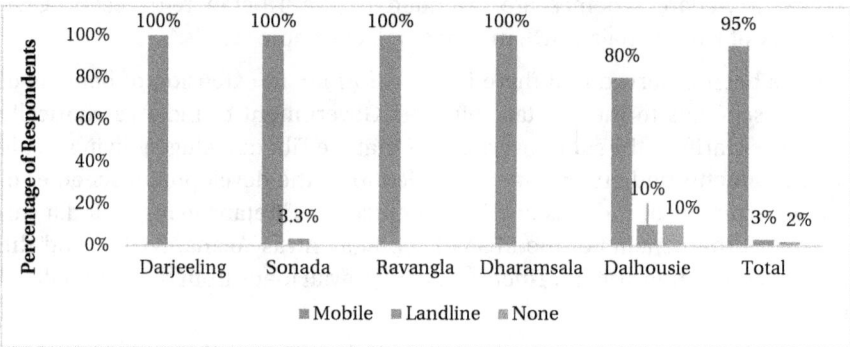

Source: Field Survey October 2016-August 2017

**Figure 3.18:** Types of welfare card

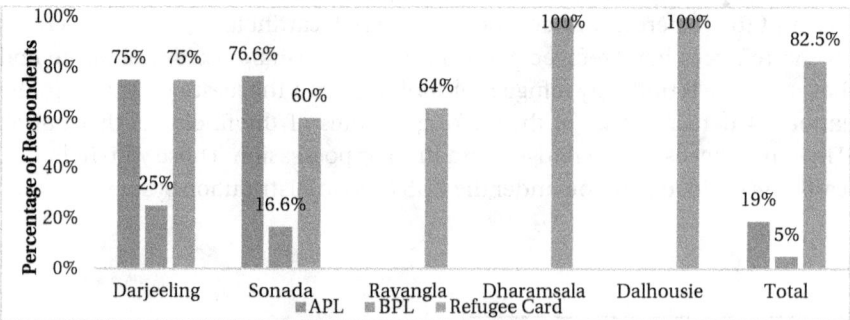

Source: Field Survey October 2016-August 2017

### Health Care and Sanitation

Health is one of the essential elements of human life. Traditionally, the Tibetan community has its own form of medicines, commonly referred to as *Amji*, with its own methods of curing illness. However, their flight to India has, to an extent, changed the practice of Amji, and they have adopted the modern allopathic medical system along with the Indian Ayurvedic based treatments. According to the study, 50 percent of the respondents were found to be using the allopathic treatment, while 32.5 percent still follow the traditional Tibetan system, 13 percent believe in homeopathy, and only 4.5 percent are inclined towards ayurvedic; see Figure 3.19. The change in the medical system is due to the settlement of the Tibetan refugees in India; most of the population resorts to allopathy for any kind of illness, though the traditional Tibetan system is followed side by side, more importance is given to allopathy in terms of severe illness.

Figure 3.20 shows that many of the respondents, 92 percent, reported that they did not know about the health system of Tibet. Most of them pointed out that their lack of knowledge is because when they left Tibet, they were too young to remember, and at the same time, more than 70 percent of the respondents were born in India. However, those who can recollect and are able to encounter the prevailing condition in Tibet claimed that the health care system in Tibet is not good as compared to the Indian health care system (8 percent). The primary reason being, as per their argument, in Tibet people still follow the old traditional Tibetan system to cure all illnesses, which is often not enough to combat new diseases. Another reason which they have pointed out is that after the occupation of Tibet by China, the Chinese government has not provided necessary medical amenities.

Vaccination of children is one of the essential aspects of the medical system of India; the survey conducted takes into account the number of children and enquired whether they have been given necessary vaccinations. Every single respondent and their family members have reported of cent percent vaccination of their children. Another facet that the study has found out is that all the refugee camps have health centers where the refugees are given special care and are provided with awareness programs from time to time.

Proper sanitation is considered as one of the essential factors in terms of hygiene; it generally refers to the provision of facilities and services for the safe disposal of human urine and feces. Inadequate sanitation is a major cause of disease worldwide. Improving sanitation has a significant beneficial health impact for the individuals, their households and across the community.

**Figure 3.19:** Health system

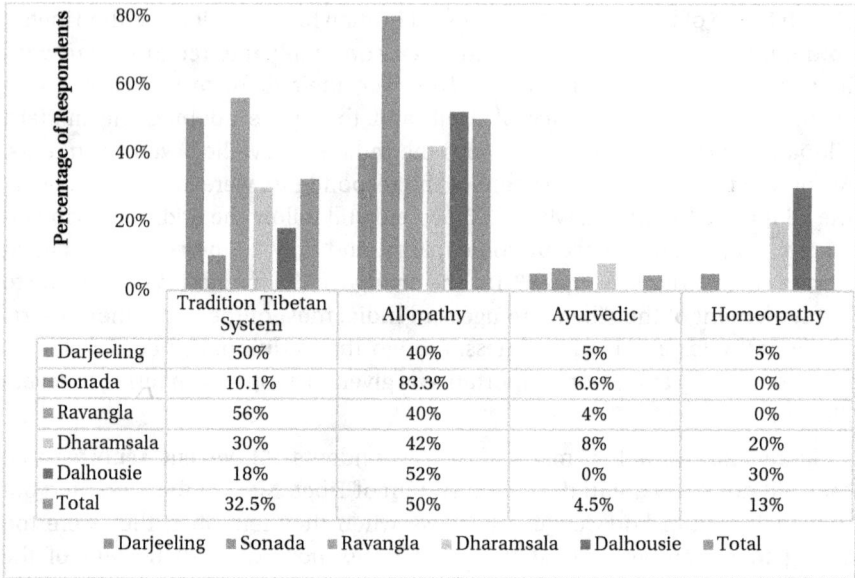

| | Tradition Tibetan System | Allopathy | Ayurvedic | Homeopathy |
|---|---|---|---|---|
| ▪ Darjeeling | 50% | 40% | 5% | 5% |
| ▪ Sonada | 10.1% | 83.3% | 6.6% | 0% |
| ▪ Ravangla | 56% | 40% | 4% | 0% |
| ▪ Dharamsala | 30% | 42% | 8% | 20% |
| ▪ Dalhousie | 18% | 52% | 0% | 30% |
| ▪ Total | 32.5% | 50% | 4.5% | 13% |

▪ Darjeeling   ▪ Sonada   ▪ Ravangla   ▪ Dharamsala   ▪ Dalhousie   ▪ Total

Source: Field Survey October 2016-August 2017

**Figure 3.20:** Medical health system of Tibet

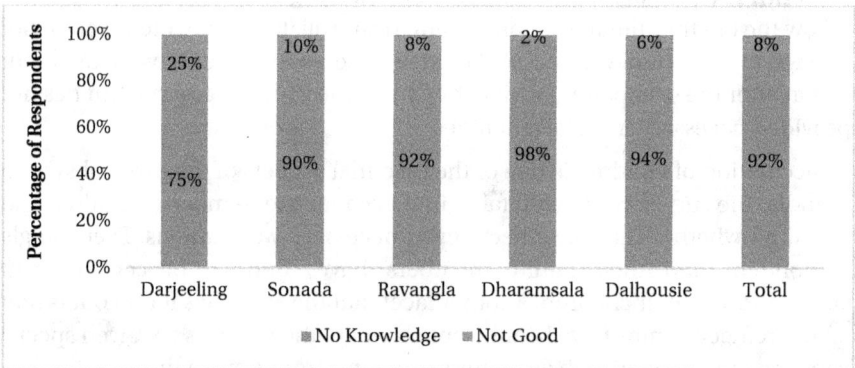

▪ No Knowledge   ▪ Not Good

Source: Field Survey October 2016-August 2017

During the survey, it was found that only 27 percent of the respondents have easy accessibility to sanitation facilities, whereas 73 percent of the respondents face difficulties in accessing the clean and hygienic sanitation facilities, as given in Figure 3.21. Inaccessibility of proper sanitation facility was reported highest in Ravangla (86 percent), followed by Sonada (80 percent) and Darjeeling (75 percent).

**Figure 3.21:** Accessibility of sanitation facilities

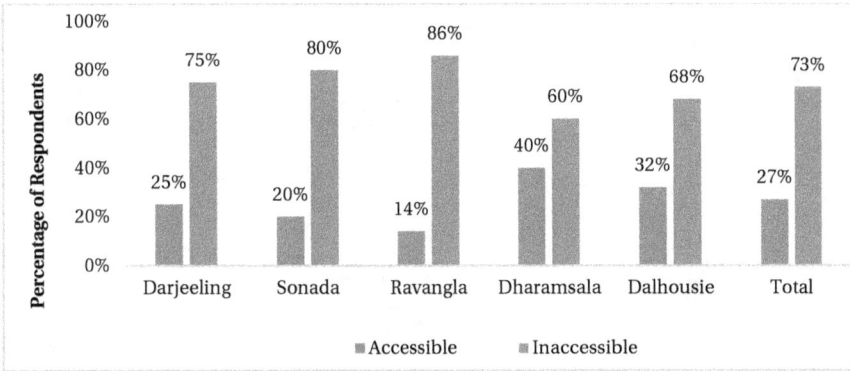

Source: Field Survey October 2016-August 2017

**Figure 3.22:** Types of accessible sanitation facility

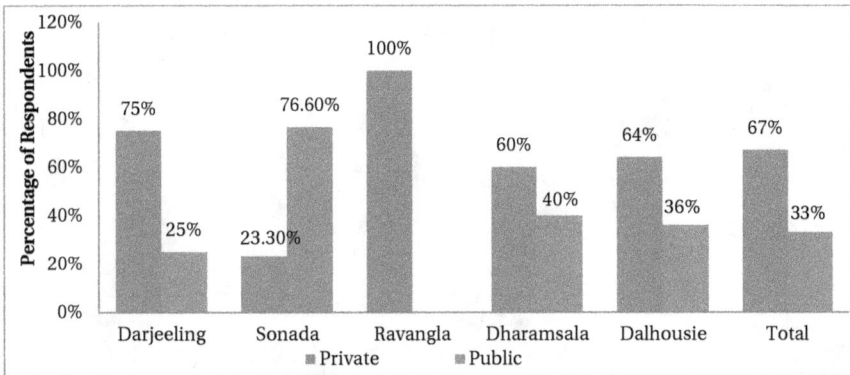

Source: Field Survey October 2016-August 2017

Among those who were able to access the sanitation facilities, respondents in Dharamsala center reported the highest with 40 percent (Figure 3.21), of which 60 percent are of private ownership while 40 percent are of public use (Figure 3.22). In Ravangla, only 14 percent of the respondents reported being able to access clean and hygiene facilities, as these facilities are privately owned, as shown in Figure 3.22.

One of the issues which many of the respondents have raised is the lack of proper sanitation facilities in these settlement areas. Further, many female respondents have also complained about the absence of separate toilets and bathrooms for men and women in most public utilities. This has created inconvenience for both the sexes.

Chapter 4

# Documenting the Experiences
# of Tibetan Refugee

## Introduction

The present chapter posits a descriptive and insightful account of the lived experience of the Tibetan refugees. Works of literature documenting Tibetan diaspora have received increasing scholarly attention, particularly after 2000 (Routray, 2007; Hess, 2009; Basu, 2018). Bentz (2012), in her article *Being a Tibetan Refugee in India,* discusses how Tibetans managed to establish a strong exile community, and how they succeeded in preserving a distinct Tibetan identity in a context of increasingly numerous interactions with Indian society. The study also focuses on analyzing the challenges of the Tibetans vis-à-vis the tensions between being/remaining a refugee and acknowledging the diasporic status. In another ethnographic work by Diehl (2002), the author deliberates on how the Tibetan community struggles with the contradictory notion of cultural homogenization, hybridity, ethnic identity and assimilation. In this work, there are rich narratives that focus on cultural preservation and what it means to be truly 'Tibetan', and how the notions of Tibetanness are imagined and debated, especially when old and new cultures meet. There are several other studies that discuss or focus on Tibetan migration (Dolma *et al.*, 2006; Choedup, 2015; Frilund, 2018). Choedup (2015), in his work, analyzed the lived experiences of three generations of Tibetans in exile; the study concludes how a group of people, despite being stateless, continue to engage and negotiate with the host nation for their individual and collective identities. Basu (2018) studied the exodus of Tibetan refugees in diasporic lands focusing on how places and Identities are redefined and transformed by refugees negotiating their belonging in an alien country over time. He tries to comprehend how the Tibetans have negotiated their identity as refugees while coming to terms with their existence as a 'permanently exiled' diasporic group. The author further argues that with diminishing prospects of return, Tibetan refugees find it difficult to create a sense of solidarity in this far away land. Rather, 'refugee diaspora' identities are seen as historically and culturally constituted and are born out of the constant and shifting movement and homecoming practices of refugee groups in varied local settings (Basu, 2018, p. 212).

To date, there has been little published academic literature documenting the lived experiences of the Tibetan refugees. This chapter attempts to proffer an analysis of the changes they witness in their society, economy and culture as a result of adjustment with the local population. In a similar vein, their journeys of escape from Tibet and their notion of Home and Homeland is also examined in this chapter.

In an attempt to document their lived experiences, we conducted interviews between February–March 2017. We administered semi-structured interviews to 30 refugees at the different centers identified for the study, in Himachal Pradesh (Dalhousie and Dharamsala), Sikkim (Ravangla), and West Bengal (Darjeeling and Sonada). The questions were pretested, and all interviews were conducted individually and privately. We had a Tibetan translator in Dharamsala and Dalhousie. However, in Darjeeling Himalayas, Nepali being the lingua franca of the region and our proficiency with the language, conducting interviews was easier. We also hired a Tibetan translator in Sikkim, but the majority of the respondents could comprehend and converse in Hindi and Nepali; hence the services of the translator were not availed extensively. In-depth semi-structured interviews were conducted and audiotaped, field notes were taken, and data was shown to participants to ensure accuracy.

Thematic analysis is one of the most common forms of identifying, analyzing, and interpreting patterns of meaning (or 'themes') within qualitative research (Braun and Clarke, 2006). The study relies on Inductive Thematic Analysis (ITA) developed by Braun and Clarke, wherein they define the approach as underscoring the empirical data first, which is not shaped or influenced by any theoretical considerations. The method employs a phenomenological approach to data analysis since it offers an opportunity to facilitate and describe the lived experience and perceptions of research participants of the community in exile. The phenomenology of Edmund Husserl articulates lived experiences or *'erlebnis'* by utilizing the methods of reduction or epoch and eidetic variation to deduce the very essence of a given phenomenon (Moran and Cohen, 2012). Invoking Husserl's pithy phrase, *'back to the things themselves'* wherein the 'things' refers to the phenomenon as they appear in one's consciousness, Husserl was invested in inquiring about the internal structures of consciousness which he believed harbored indubitable essences of a given phenomenon. However, the present book employs a descriptive methodological tool of subjective lived experiences of Tibetan refugees in conjunction with the thematic analysis to extract commonalities of themes and patterns as and when they emerge post the completion of holistic reading and coding. The study benefits from *Husserlian* Phenomenology because he conceives of lived experiences as an act of intentionality of consciousness directed to the phenomenon.

Similarly, the research utilizes the human science approach of lived experiences as envisaged by Husserl but does not deploy the methodological reductions of *epoch* and *eidetic* variations to ascertain the immutable structures of consciousness. The study, therefore, attempts to build a thematic narrative predicated on the subjective/interpretive experiences of the Tibetan refugees depicting their personal meanings, episodes, and encounters. In his phenomenological enterprise, Husserl lays emphasis on the 'things themselves' or how things manifest in one's consciousness without meditating much on the subjective meaning-making capabilities of individuals (Smith and Smith, 1995). Considering the limitations imposed by Husserl's theoretical framework, the study benefits by selectively utilizing *Husserlian* phenomenology sans the rigor of the methodological suspension for the discovery of essential and unchanging essences.

Thirty cases were picked for an in-depth case study and narrative analysis, after completion of preliminary fieldwork.

Following each interview, the researchers identified themes through holistic reading and rereading of transcripts. Themes derived from the interviews were grouped in the following categories:

1. Dangerous journeys of escape

2. Being Tibetan in a different home

3. Integration with Indian culture

4. Preserving Tibetan identity

5. Future aspirations

These thematic analyses are based on the observations which can be broadly classified as experiences of those who are born in Tibet and experiences of those born in India.

## Dangerous Journeys of Escape

Most of the Tibetan refugees have experienced multiple devastating occurrences of violence, terror, and destruction during their journey of escape. Psychological studies conducted on Tibetan refugees have largely focused on understanding various pathological symptoms resulting from traumatic exposures (Mills *et al.*, 2005; Servan-Schreiber, Lin and Birmaher, 1998). Elsass and Phuntsok's (2009) work elaborately mentioned the traumatic experiences, witnessed violence and terror in their escape journeys and discussed the coping mechanism with the intervention of counselors. The study revealed that Tibetan torture survivors used their political engagement and Tibetan Buddhism as an important coping mechanism. Similarly, Dolma *et al.* (2006) documented a group of Tibetan refugees who made their journey of escape to

Nepal. This study informs findings of similar nature, that refugees experience mental hardships, physical torture and often abuse of their basic human rights.

Corroborating the above assertion, the present study is also supported by poignant descriptions and accounts of similar nature. For instance, the narrative of a 76-years-old married man, who was living with his wife and a married son in Ravangla (Sikkim), recounts that he was only twelve years old when he fled from Lhasa with his family in 1960. He had two younger siblings—a brother and a sister—and an elder sister. His father was a monk and a doctor of Tibetan medicine. His mother was a homemaker and a very religious person. He narrated, 'When I went to school, I would hear from friends that they (referring to Chinese army) are coming, and they will not spare anyone.... if you are old, they will kill you, and if you are young, they will induct you in the Chinese army'. According to him, during those times, the religious and political climate in Tibet was hostile, but his parents always kept him and his siblings motivated by narrating stories of joy, courage, and happiness. In order to remain concealed at night, they were not allowed to light any lamp. Recalling the experience of that fateful cold night, he mentioned there was a thumping on the main door, and his father quickly hid them in the basement of the house. It was the Chinese soldiers who had come to take his father, as some Chinese soldiers needed medical attention. 'My father left with the soldiers and never came back. The next morning my mother packed whatever little belongings we had, and we started our long journey in the wildernesses'.

He shared the rumination, how his little feet would often give way, despite that he had to keep following his mother and elder sister who had been carrying his two younger siblings on their back. His general perception about people was that they were not nice as each one of them wanted some favors, be it money or other little things which they had been carrying. They had been traveling for almost 17 to 18 days, and about 23 or more people had joined them. At night they would often hide behind big rocks hurdling together to brave against the relentless cold. One night his little brother had gone to the toilet and was attacked by the wolf and taken away '...I saw my mother cry and scream as she saw them eating and tearing his flesh away'. He mentioned after this incident, his mother did not speak; she was mourning the death of her son and never overcame her grief. Just when there was a ray of hope, they were attacked by Chinese guards. They said they would let the men and children go if they left the women behind. 'Almost all the middle-aged and older women came forward and told the rest of us to run.... which we all did. My sister ran with us, and my mother was left behind. On the Indian border also, the Indian guards asked my sister to give her earrings, if we wanted to enter'. The narrative highlights the pain and anguish experienced by the people when they were fleeing from Tibet. There was a sense of uncertainty among the community member, but a strong desire to live and not give up; this optimism, according to many, probably came from their belief in Buddhist Philosophy.

Collyer (2007), in his work *In-between places: Trans-Saharan transit migrants in Morocco and the fragmented journey to Europe*, highlights the meaning of the journey as the most important analytical category in understanding the migration of his sub-Saharan interviewees who belonged to 'yet to be recognized refugees', 'previously recognized refugees' or 'those with other protection needs'. Since many of the Tibetan refugees had already crossed over to India, they were already in the 'recognized' category by the Indian government. The journey across the Himalayas and escape to neighboring countries, as reported by many respondents, is long and arduous, with frequent reports of hypothermia, snow blindness, and frostbite. The story of a 79-years-old man, living with his family in Dalhousie, highlights the health hazards the refugees experience in their journeys. The respondent, along with his parents, crossed the border in 1959 as an entourage of the group that followed His Holiness. At that time, the situation in Tibet had become very hostile; his father informed them that '…. Even if we live here, we are going to die, let us give life a chance and try to live'. Recollecting the hardships they faced while crossing the Himalayas. He mentioned, 'we chose the lowest range of the Himalayas, which is the Nathula pass, as you cannot cross the pass during June or July so I assume it must have been the months of September, October or November'. He mentioned that the weather was very harsh, and they had to prepare themselves for the worst. 'We had no glasses to protect our eyes and no warm clothes to protect us from the cold. We used homemade remedies to protect us from frostbites … we mixed the residue from the smoke with butter to protect our skin, and for the eyes we made yak wool fringe and yak woolen clothes to cover hands and feet and protect us from snow'. The journeys of exile were fraught with difficulties; it is a test of resilience, physical hardiness, and a check of psychological steadiness. Considering the interviewee's existential remark imbued with hope and optimism, striving for the continuity of life in the face of adversities, the subjective human experience and individual as a meaning-making and the interpretive agent becomes foregrounded as a point of analysis. Phenomenology emphatically speaks of the salience of intentionality wherein one directs one's consciousness towards objects extending in space or intangible phenomenon experienced within one's mind viz. fear, hope, belief, and the meanings associated with the same (Berger & Luckmann, 1966, p. 14). Going by this premise, humans, therefore, do not live through experiences by intending it in a state of vacuity. Similarly, when examining the lived experience of the interviewee's narrative, the respondent reminisces about his episode of exodus as an instance of survival, surmounting enormous hardships and suffering to bring to fruition his personal meanings of striving for a 'second chance to live' than resigning to one's fate.

The account of a 15-year-old when he escaped from Tibet also gives references to the same fact. Recollecting the struggles he and his friends braved while making the great escape from Tibet, He mentioned '...going by foot was posing a big problem as the Chinese had become alert and were keeping a vigil on the Tibetan's that were escaping and if the Chinese government found out, they were given severe punishments. They would be stripped and beaten; their precious belongings would be taken away. Some would be subjected to extreme torture and would have iron roads pushed down their private parts'. To escape this drudgery, he and his friends decided to take help from their friend, who was a taxi driver that ferried goods across the border. It took one day to reach the Nepal border from Lhasa. They hid amongst the goods; he mentioned that due to the heavy load, they nearly got crushed, and one of his friends fainted, but luckily, they managed to cross the security check. They entered Nepal, anticipating that their ordeal was over, but it continued. They escaped from the Chinese government, but they encountered dacoits and were on the verge of being robbed, but the Nepal police intervened. Having failed to mollify the Nepali police, why were they fleeing? They were handed back to the Chinese government. He narrated that his only goal was to meet his Holiness, '....I was ready to die for him, sacrifice my life for him. I got lost in the forest, almost drowned in a river and spent the entire night clinging on the rock, until I was rescued by local people'. These local people gave them a place to stay, food was served, but due to the trauma, they could barely eat '....They tried to make us comfortable and mentioned that we were in safe hands, the host made noodles for us with chicken, and this was the first time we ate chicken as we don't have chicken or egg at Tibet. In Tibet, it is believed that when you kill many animals for food, it is more sinful as you are taking many lives. On the contrary, killing one animal would feed many mouths, and at the same time, it is less sin'. He left his family with the desire to meet his holiness and feels blessed that he is close to his God.

A report published by UNHCR, *Addressing the causes of migratory and refugee movements: the role of the European Union* (2002) by Boswell informs about the macro theory approaches to migration, which chiefly expounds upon the larger structural push and pull factors as reasons for humans to relocate in other places. Nonetheless, such an overarching theory fails to explain or consider certain discrepancies with respect to human motivation that fuels their urgency to undertake migration. A case in point is the aforementioned young interviewee as his *raison d'être* for migration seems not to stem from socioeconomic/political or other structural concerns but his insistence on being near his spiritual/religious leader. One's interaction, socialization, subsequent renderings of meanings and one's acquired knowledge collectively constitute one's natural attitude when embedded within socio-cultural milieus. The symbolic and spiritual sense of refuge/haven the interviewee experiences with the presence of his holiness is indicative of the importance of micro-level interactions humans forge with society and its institutions. The dynamics of such interactions, the salience of the individual agency and the dominance of meaning in the lives of humans can be collectively attributed as factors producing multitudinous personal narratives, each infused with possibilities of experiences of personal loss, trauma and triumph and the individual's navigation of meanings when encountering phenomenon of migration and displacement.

In another ontological narrative, a woman mentions being separated from her parents in her flight from Tibet. Her family had taken shelter in the house of an influential Tibetan family, and they felt this would be advantageous for them and aid their escape. However, someone disclosed the secret and the house was raided. In the commotion, her mother hid her behind the cupboard and told her that she would come back for her. 'I waited for a very long time and slept...I woke up because something was biting on my feet; it was a rat.... I screamed and came out of hiding.... There was no one'. She described with sadness that she stayed in the house for two days, and later, the owner of the house came to get her. *He did not tell me anything, but I just followed him.* She joined a group that was trying to cross the border since she was alone; others helped her (65 years, Ravangala).

Similar experiences have been shared in another ethnographic study by Frilund (2019), *Tibetan Refugee Journeys: Representations of Escape and Transit*, where she explores Tibetan journeys to India via Nepal at least partly on foot. The findings reveal that risky journeys have a remarkable meaning for those who make the journey individually or collectively. Corroborating this study, in another journey narrative, a widower, living with his two daughters at the camp in Ravangla (Sikkim), shared the story of his escape from Tibet. He was four years old when he, his uncles, father, brother, and cousins made their first attempt to escape from Tibet because of Chinese atrocities. In their first attempt to escape, they were caught, sent back and badly tortured. In the second attempt, his uncle took a gun to protect them. When they were crossing the Chinese border they were again followed '....they indiscriminately fired at us and my father was hit on the leg...but my uncle was a hero, he fired back and killed the Chinese on the horse, after which the others ran away. The journey was very tough since my father was hit, he was losing a lot of blood, and then we met some lamas who were also escaping, and they rubbed some plants on my father's wound, which stopped the bleeding'. This incident left an indelible mark on his psyche; he decided he would join the army when he grows up. He eventually did join the army, but he laughed and said, '... I thought I would fight the Chinese, but I am fighting the Pakistanis'.

The respondents mentioned that the rigid unaccommodating nature of the Chinese, especially towards religion and culture, was one of the main factors that drove the Tibetans to exile. The journey from Tibet into India was a treacherous one fraught with physical and psychological hardships. Refugees experienced severe hardships such as robbery, torture, beatings with rifle butts, threats of being shot, and sexual assaults. The refugees took buses to the border areas and walked across the mountain range. They had severe exhaustion during the journey like nausea, vomiting and frostbites. There were narrations of sacrifice by the parents to see their children cross the border. Many of them sacrificed their affluent life for survival and to be with His Holiness. However, respondents entering India from Sikkim did not mention any atrocities being committed to them. Those reaching Dharamsala mentioned parting with their precious stones and gold, which they had to give away as a bribe. All the respondents conveyed that these experiences changed their views about life. Despite these personal traumas and experiences, they wanted to navigate further in life, forgetting the past events and following the Dalai lama.

The respondents recall incredible experiences of courage, will and personal sacrifice to ensure the safe passage of their family and themselves surrendering their homes, comforts, and material securities. Owing to the unfavorable political climate, the Tibetan refugees became victims of forced displacement, coercing them to leave their homeland to flee with the Dalai lama. Considering their narratives of resilience and spirit, the lived experience brings to the fore subjective meanings accorded by the interviewees when reminiscing about their forced departure, violence and countering their adversary. The exigency to leave their place of origin, release memories of their past and willingness to encounter life-threatening experiences whilst escaping to maintain proximity with one's religious/spiritual leader demonstrates their personal internalized meanings and the subsequent coping mechanisms espoused to survive and sustain themselves. Mark Wrathall, in an introduction to Dreyfus's work, ' Skillful coping: Essays on the Phenomenology of everyday perception and action' (2014), mentions that Dreyfus acknowledges both the mental states and the impact of the external world upon the individual because the former cannot exist in a mode of solipsism and the external world cannot exert influence unless mediated by a mind. The interplay of both elicits responses, action, meaning, and behavior embodied and enacted by the individual. In a similar strain, the respondents embroiled in the dominance and hegemony of the Chinese tyranny are directly impinged by their experiences of political hostilities, social insecurities, deprivation of individual autonomy and discrimination becoming immediately susceptible to the odious repercussions of one's external realities. The series of successive experiences of torture and brutality, the intolerance and ostracization of the Tibetan community/culture, their intra-group companionship, the meaning, and salience accorded to the departure of his holiness collectively constitutes the dialectics of meaning mediated by the consciousness allowing for the individual to respond and act accordingly.

## Being Tibetan in a Different Home

In recent years there has been a myriad of writing on the meaning of home within social sciences, and the concept of home is being visited with academic interest. It is well acknowledged in the literature that 'home' is a 'multidimensional concept' (Mallett, 2004). The concept has been extensively discussed in the literatures of Somerville (1992), Mallett (2004), and Moore (2007). Home is a symbolic place, where space and time are controlled and structured functionally, economically, aesthetically, and morally and where domestic communitarian practices are realized (Rapport and Dawson, 1998; Douglas, 1991). The relationship between house and home has been acknowledged in relevant interdisciplinary literature (Chapman and Hockey, 1999; Wright, 1991; Saunders and Williams 1988). In recent times since millions of people are being displaced from their homes because of war, economic instability, or genocide, the meaning of the term home is becoming significant. The concept has been widely discussed in the literature of migration, diaspora, and cultural studies (Tarodi, 2011). Sarup (1995) states that 'home' is in a place, and places are socially constructed and not static. Here, 'place' is a crucial variable, as all relationships are embedded in a place, which gives 'placeable bonding', a fundamental human importance (Tarodi, 2011). Sarup (1995) suggests that the concept of home is tied to a sense of one's identity, which is that story which we tell ourselves and which others tell about us. Cooper's (1976) article conceives the home as an inalienable source of identity. The discussed literatures opine that home is a socially and culturally constructed place. However, in the context of displaced people, it invokes a sense of identity, conflating with the notion of 'homeland' and, therefore, is intertwined with citizenship and belonging. In the discussion on the Tibetan refugees' perceptions of home in the next section, the multiple understandings are brought to the fore.

Since the Tibetan government in exile, CTA, is based in India, it is pertinent to understand if India has become a home to the Tibetan refugees or is it still a shelter. Falcone and Wangchuk's (2008) work mentioned how the exiled Tibetan people tend to hold on to certain deep constructions of Tibetanness. Through the experiences of the Tibetan community in exile, this work asks the question: what is the 'homeland' for Tibetan exiles today?

This section of the book studies how different generations of Tibetan refugees after migration and their settlement in India craft their definition of home. Tibetans in exile tend to romanticize Tibet, and this is not uncommon even among second- and third-generation Tibetans in exile who have never been to Tibet. In this study too, the older generation remembers Tibet in its long-standing glory, when it was pristine and beautiful, the mountains were covered with snow, the air was clean and pure, the place was sacred and holy, and there was no pollution. They reminisce about their houses, clothes, occupation, and the relatives they had to leave behind. A similar recollection was also made by Tarodi (2011), who, in his work, explores the notion of home from the perspective of the Tibetans living in exile in India for the last five decades. According to one respondent, 'we lived in a small house and ate the meat of Yak. Life was not easy… but it was home' (75 years, Ravangla). He narrated that now '…. Tibet is not the same; it has become barren; all the beautiful houses and gompas are destroyed'. But he still yearns to go back some day and stay in his home and cherish old memories. For him, going back to Tibet is a reality that remains merely postponed. The nostalgia of home, the hope to return, and the feeling that their present dwelling is a temporary shelter made him feel that Sikkim is not his home.

C. Wright Mills, in his insightful work, 'The Sociological Imagination' (1959), categorically asserts the importance of acknowledging the interplay between an individual and his/her acquisition of lineage or history wherein alterations in the latter inexorably produces impressions on the former. Mills, therefore, underscores the inextricable nexus between 'biography' and 'history' wherein history also implies the larger macro social and structural transformations which for Mills engenders subsequent shifts produced in the lives of individuals. For Mills, therefore, the very processes that supposedly define the contours of individualism expressed via multiple sites of identity, one's fluxes in employment, income determination, one's class, gender, *et al.* cannot be understood without invoking one's social, cultural matrices and one's life history (Mills, 1959, pp. 3-5). Similarly, the idyllic image of the respondent for his homeland and the perception of Sikkim as a 'temporary shelter' speaks of his internalized mental dichotomy of 'us vs. them' in which 'us' for him symbolizes a native spatial site to call his own, and 'them' here refers to the 'othering' of a seemingly foreign land. His personal identity and belonging, therefore, are derivative of his memories of his erstwhile existence. For him, 'the temporary shelter' viz. Sikkim fulfills his pragmatic concerns to inhabit spaces of safety but does not necessarily associate his aspirations, hopes, identity and nationalism. Reverting to the premise proposed by Mills (1959) of the significance of the connexon between the individual and history and juxtaposing the narratives of the interviewee, it becomes understandably clear that one's social/cultural milieus and historical specificity render itself cardinal when attempting to apprehend one's conception of personal identity and imaginations of nationalism.

For another respondent (60 years, man, Dalhousie), who belonged to an affluent family and enjoyed all the luxuries in Tibet and misses them in India, India is not completely his home, because he feels that in India they are here because of 'kindness', and fears that at any time the state or the local people may decide to withdraw this kindness, and then he will have no choice but to leave. However, he felt that he should not be ungrateful to the Indian Government because they have helped him in times of crisis, which makes India his second home. He mentioned '...Tibet is my first home and I always want to go there, and I want to die there. But in case I am not able to go there, India is now my second home'. He was grateful that he was able to send his children to good schools. India has given him freedom, and he will stay here till Tibet is free. In the same strain, a 60-year-old man and caretaker of the old age home at Dharamsala mentions he did not marry because he did not have a place to keep his family; it is difficult for him to accept an alien environment as his homeland.

The key proponents of the existentialist school of thought, a divergence from pure phenomenology, posits that one's existence precedes meaning or essence. This implies meaning as a fluidic, forever shifting, and amorphous activity which individuals in their everyday lived experiences embrace, consider, or reject. Individuals, therefore, actively operate in a realm of what can be called as the 'dialectics of meanings' wherein they may produce a new synthesis of meanings or choose to disregard it altogether. In a similar strain, the above interviewees engage and fashion meanings when coping with their everyday experiences. The respondent from Dalhousie, for instance, articulates his idea of 'home' in gradations of natal connections and pragmatic concerns. The contours and meanings of what constitutes a 'home' for the denizens of diaspora, therefore, remains amenable to revision and recreation. The flight from home, the assimilation and adaptation of foreign cultures and the gradual acceptance of the place of refuge (India) as a haven and a home demonstrates the possibilities of hermeneutics as the interviewee continually revises, assimilates, and repudiates meanings. Lived experience as a conceptual and theoretical framework, therefore, allows for countering dominant narratives on the idea of a home and the conservative parameters/traditional attributes arbitrarily demarcating the meaningful limits of the same.

For most of the younger generation respondents who are born and brought up in India, they envision Tibet through the eyes of their parents. Tibet was a place of mountains, snow, yak, and monasteries, where many of their parent's relatives still live. As narrated by a young respondent, '... I have been born and brought up in Sikkim, I have heard a lot of stories from my grandfather about Tibet, but I like being here. I have friends, life is good, and I am thankful that I have home...' He further added that 'Since my parents, siblings and friends are here, this is home'. He felt that there was no religious or political freedom in Tibet, so there was no need to return. This narrative reflects the feeling and emotions of the respondent about his meaning of a home. He experiences mixed feelings about Tibet because the picture of Tibet is based on the narratives given by their elders or grandparents. For another young generation respondent pursuing her Ph.D., Sikkim is her home, and she has no desire to go back to Tibet. She mentioned that she would support a protest for Tibet but would stay back in India. 'I have everyone in Sikkim and lots of friends in Delhi; I do not feel like a refugee here… our generation does not take interest in identity issues, it is always the politicians who play these games'. She expressed that she was grateful to people in Sikkim for accepting them and allowing them to do business… she mentioned even more than Sikkim, she enjoyed being in Delhi '…. All my friends love me, I can speak Delhi type Hindi…my friends find me very stylish, and I love the attention that I get from them'. She also mentioned that her grandparents have very fond memories of Tibet, and as a child, they narrated to her a lot of stories '…they also question whether my studies will help them in going back to Tibet…I feel sorry for them, because their heart is in Tibet. My parents are also very happy here. We feel safe'. For her, freedom is essential for a human being, and India has given them this; now, after so many years, no one is even interested to know who they are? If given a choice, she would prefer to live in India as it is her home now.

Most of the respondents belonging to the older generations reconstructed Tibet as being pure, both in religious and environmental terms. The old generation reminisced about their houses, the food and yak. They mentioned that life was not easy, but it was 'home'. However, most of them felt that Tibet is no longer the same. The houses have been destroyed and dilapidated, the monasteries are in ruins, and this was a very emotional issue for them because they attach great value to religion in their life. They wanted to return and were worried that they are now aging and that they will never be able to go back. For other generations, though Tibet is 'home', the experience they hear from people who have recently traveled to India makes them believe that the social, religious, and political climate in Tibet is unconducive, making survival difficult. On the other hand, for the younger Tibetans, Tibet is an unfamiliar place. But the territorial space they refer to as their home country is a place where they have 'nothing'; there are no connections except narrations from memories of previous generations. For them, Tibet is the first home, the land from where their parents have come from, but at the same time, India is a second home, too, the 'home' where they were born and their children have been raised. The respondents who have grown and have lived in India, their food and lifestyle now resonate with the Indians. They enjoy a measure of freedom, especially religious and cultural freedom in India.

The inter-generational variances, in terms of meanings assigned to the idea of 'home', warrants the premise that meanings are in a state of continual 'becoming' or 'being'. The prior meanings of their 'first home' are seemingly transitions from harboring idealistic aspirations to return to their homeland towards acknowledging the futility of the whole enterprise. It would necessitate recalling Phenomenologist Heidegger's remark that beings are 'thrown into the world'. In context to the first, second and other successive generations of Tibetan refugees, the world is indicative of the specificities of spatial, temporal, historical and cultural milieus which for Heidegger 'beings' are proverbially thrown at. This state of thrown(ness) implies that all beings are not ahistorical and continually interact, experience, and hold meanings that are relevant to their existence. The young and old generations alike because of their thrown(ness) at particular junctures of history, social/political upheavals and displacement along with their experiences of a 'second home' (of peace and stability) contrasting the imagery of their ravaged sovereign (Tibet) produces myriad (polarized) responses from the interviewees varying from romanticizing their 'first home' professing their unwavering commitment to return towards expressing alienation with regard to Tibetan culture and the territorial site they refer to as their 'first home'. The narratives of the cumulative generations of Tibetan refugees and their personal meanings associated with the idea of home reveals the provisional nature of subjective interpretations vulnerable to time, space, history and social interactions/intersubjectivity.

## Integration with Indian Culture

'Meanings of integration vary from country to country, change over time, and depend on the interests, values and perspectives of the people concerned' (Robinson, 1998). The conceptual model of Integration by Pennix is based on four dimensions, i.e., cultural, social, economic, and political integration. Cultural dimension aims at an understanding of the language, ethics and norms of the host society, social integration means inclusion into education and welfare systems, economic refers to economic enterprise and outreach and political is equated with participation in politics with the right to vote, which would later acquire through naturalization (Pennix, 2009). Most writings testify that Tibetans in exile have assimilated and adjusted with the host country and their new situation due to continuous support and assurance from Dalai Lama's leadership (Goldstein-Kyaga, 1993; Palakshappa, 1978). Saklani (1978) fieldwork and research among Tibetan refugees living in Dharamsala, Delhi, and Dehradun also have a positive connotation. She mentions Tibetans have 'successfully emerged from a self-sufficient barter economy into a competitive one'.

Since 1959, the focus of the Government in exile is the preservation of linguistic, religious, and cultural identity through documentation and education. They are skeptical about two aspects firstly about the erosion of Tibetan culture in Tibet under Chinese rule and secondly disappearance of their indigenous culture when in constant socialization with the host societies. This is reflected by the emphasis on the use of language, dress, marriage ceremonies or food preparation. In his work *Tibetan Refugees in India: Integration Opportunities Through Development of Social, Cultural and Spiritual Traditions* focusing on the newly arriving Tibetan refugees in India, Adams (2005) asserts that new refugees are often without skills or qualifications, a disadvantage that may seclude them from both the community in exile and the larger Indian host community. However, by highlighting the wealth of cultural heritage, they may regain their lost social capital and sense of belonging. In an interview with One World South Asia, Thubten Samphel, secretary of the Tibetan Government-in-Exile's Department of Information and International Relations, asserts that the Indian government has been very generous with the Tibetan refugees, and according to them, enjoy most of the rights of Indian citizens. He shed light on the grim and pathetic conditions of Tibetans in China and discussed the 'Middle-Way Approach,' which is a proposal for an autonomous, rather than sovereign Tibet.

Nevertheless, despite their constant effort in preserving their cultural identity, the Tibetan refugees are challenged with the herculean task of integrating with the host societies (Bureau Reporter, 2003). As rightly mentioned by Crescenzi *et al.* (2002) in their work, Tibetans are said 'to be rightly proud of their traditional collective coping mechanisms ... these are mostly cognitive and spiritual: reciting mantras, visualizing His Holiness, and focusing on Karma, patience, compassion, impermanence, and the suffering of others. Without access to the collective coping mechanisms, the refugee appears to be left isolated – especially since the display of emotions is socially discouraged'.

The living narrative of a 66-year-old man from Dharamsala highlights how, in order to integrate with the host country, they are developing diverse linguistic skills '....I learnt Nepali and Hindi when I was in Dehradun, I accompanied my mother whenever she went for business, and since in the market place there were many Nepali- and Hindi- speaking people, I learnt both the languages'. He added, '....it has really helped me assimilate with the people in India, they also feel happy when they hear me talking in their native tongue, I generally do not hear people talk about us and calling us refugees'. He mentioned that language is a medium by which an individual, even from a different land, will be able to make a 'home' for himself in an alien land; it aids and accelerates the process of assimilation and integration.

In his work, *Survival of a Culture: Tibetan Refugees in India*, Michael (1985) writes that the Tibetan economic order and Tibetan Buddhism is open to economic enterprise, and this proved to be beneficial when the Tibetans had to survive in the new host land. Economic participation is a precondition for integration with the host country. Bentz (2012) paper discussed how the Tibetan refugees are employed in agricultural activities (e.g., Bylakuppe, Karnataka), traditional Tibetan carpet weaving (e.g., Tibetan Refugee Self-Help Handicraft Centre, Darjeeling, West Bengal), businesses (e.g., Majnu-Ka-Tila, New Delhi), small businesses, restaurants, taxi driving, and cattle rearing (e.g., Gangtok, Sikkim). Scholars who have worked on the Tibetan refugee settlements agreed that the economic success in India is exceptional. The following narrative explores how their enterprising nature and economic outreach have, to some extent, aided and assisted them in the process of integration. A 40-year-old respondent from Darjeeling talked about the perils his parents encountered while escaping from Tibet. He recollected when his parents came to Darjeeling; they were not welcomed by the local population. They felt very secluded and, at one point in time, wanted to go back to Dharamsala. Gradually, they started conversing in the local language, and they felt the attitude of the people change towards them. He mentioned that his mother would prepare some *momos* and sell them in the market, and this would be relished by the people. He narrated that 'despite our best efforts, the people do not accept us completely, they feel we are sharing their resources, Tibetans who stay at the centers face fewer problems than those outside; initially the attitude of the people was not nice'. He also mentioned that his children do not face any discrimination, they have all Nepali friends, and they are invited for the birthday party of their friends; they can barely speak their own language, which, according to him, is a loss of their Tibetan culture. He added that sometimes the problem of assimilation can be from both sides '...I have Tibetan friends who do not want to mingle with the local population, they view them with suspicion, and on the other hand, sometimes the local inhabitants do not accept us. I hear many of my Tibetan friends say that they should only marry a Tibetan girl'.

Assimilation and integration with the host country is a two-way process, which requires adjustment and acceptance from both the ends, the host country as well as the migrating population. The major credit for the survival of the Tibetans in the host societies belongs to the charismatic leadership of His Holiness Dalai Lama. He has been instrumental in uniting the Tibetans in exile, responsible for reconstituting their social and political organizations and strengthening their faith and political will. He has been efficacious in enthralling the leaders of the host country who have exhibited an exceptional understanding of the spiritual and social values of the exiled cultural group and have welcomed them. Tibetan society is blessed for maintaining a balance between the two macrocosms of tradition and modernity.

Nowak (1984) mentions that the Tibetan administration in Dharamsala feels that the Tibetan culture in their homeland will disappear under the Chinese regime, and there is also a likely hood of the indigenous Tibetan culture disappearing in the host societies. Hence, they are focused on the preservation of linguistic, religious, and artistic knowledge through both documentation and education. 'A more conservative notion of preservation has informed innumerable official policy decisions by the Tibetan government-in-exile as well as individual choices regarding every aspect of daily life, including language use, habits of dress, marriage ceremonies, and food preparation' (Basu, 2018)

Women have always been regarded as the harbingers of culture and traditions. Even among the Tibetans, women carry the onerous task of preserving the cultural identity but, at the same time keeping in mind the element of integrating with the host nation. The first sight of a respondent 30-year-old woman (Ravangla, Sikkim) was very interesting because she was wearing a Tibetan *baku* with a *pangden* (marriage symbol among the Bhutia community*)* and was also wearing the green *pothey* thread (marriage symbol for Nepali community). She mentioned that she was married to a Nepali, who was a doctor by profession. She recollected that when she visited Gangtok hospital for her treatment, she met her husband and fell in love with him. She narrated that she lived with her parents in the Ravangla center and was born in Sikkim. She felt 'people in Sikkim are very nice and loving; they generally do not discriminate, the adjustment was not very tough for my parents. In Sikkim, if you work hard, you can make money; they will not trouble you regarding that. However, they will reserve the Government jobs for the Sikkimese people'.

When she married, her parents were very annoyed, and her husband's parents were also not happy, but her husband was very supportive, and now things are favorable for her. She mentioned that my parents chastise me that '…. your children do not know Tibetan, and I just laugh it off. I have no memories of Tibet, I grew here, met my husband here, got my happiness here, this society has accepted me, and that is enough'. She further added that her marriage has entitled her children to all the benefits that Sikkimese subjects are entitled to. Hence they will receive all the benefits from the state regarding education and occupation. For this respondent, she has asserted her Tibetan identity by adorning the Tibetan dress, but at the same time, by symbolically wearing the green beads, she has announced her integration with the host society.

For another respondent (55 years, woman, Ravangla), marriage with a non-Tibetan was an answer to her prayers. She narrated that at the age of 20, she escaped from Tibet to Lachen, North Sikkim. She used to work as a laborer in a construction site. It was there that she met her husband, who was of Nepali ethnicity. He was a lorry driver and carried raw materials for the construction site. However, she never had the courage to tell her parents about their relationship. She recollected that during those days, her encounter with the Bollywood blockbuster movie *Dil* (Heart), which picturized the girl eloping with the boy of a different community, gave her both assurance and clarity in regaining her courage to elope with him. Initially, both her husband's family as well as her family did not accept their relationship '...but soon I won their heart'. She mentioned, '... I was initially stressed, because I had married outside the community, but following my example, many girls and boys eloped and married outside the Tibetan community'. She added that her in-laws were very happy with her, and she has given her children the finest attributes of both the communities. Social and cultural integration with the asylum country has stood her in good stead. Nevertheless, successful socio-cultural integration requires a common sympathetic understanding from both sides.

The assumptions made in the writings of Kabuya (2008) and Nezer (2013) reveal that socio-cultural aspects influence the chances to establish social relations with indigenous communities. Tibetan refugees, on the one hand, try to hold on to their cultural identity, but constantly make efforts to integrate with the local populace. Consistent effort creates long-lasting relations, as shared by a respondent '... at that time, the people in Sikkim were not very friendly with us, they addressed us as '*Chin bhote*' (Chinese Bhutia). We were very scared and just bore that insult quietly'. He mentioned that, with the passage of time, noticing their hard work, the local population started accepting them, but they were paid very meagerly for the work. He enjoys being in Sikkim '...there is no problem here, so why complain'. Even in the face of extraordinary pressure to assimilate with the host populations, Tibetans living in exile in India have been extremely successful in charting out a life-in-exile for themselves. The respondents mentioned that they were able to manage boundary regulation without changing their own emotional attitude to the locals; they felt that a flexible attitude is much better than fixed borders and prejudices.

Drawing on Amartya Sen's work, *Identity and Violence: The Illusion of Destiny* (2006), wherein he lays emphasis on the possibilities of individuals holding multitudinous identities, each varying in importance which is contingent upon the context, the Tibetan refugees to espouse a similar strategy of shifting the emphasis of identities in a given context. The displaced refugees, when living amidst the Indians, attempt to embody the cultural and regional traits peculiar to the territory or settlements they reside in. The act of cultural malleability and the ability to adapt and assimilate into the customs of the host country by the refugees represents their willingness to shed rigidities of religious and nationalistic identities. Sen, therefore, brings to the fore salience of shifting contexts and the relative autonomy of individuals to embody identities in terms of their importance and relevance. The acceptance of the refugees by the local economy, entitlements of citizenship and other pragmatic benefits provided the necessary impetus for the refugees to reconcile with their hybrid nationalistic identities of being Tibetan refugees settled in India.

### Preserving Tibetan Identity

Tajfel defined social identity as 'the individual's knowledge that he belongs to certain social groups together with some emotional and value significance to him of the group membership' (1972, p. 292) or 'a self-definition in terms of social category membership' (Turner, 1999, p. 10). Multiple factors may constitute Tibetan cultural identity; Tibetans strongly identify with their Buddhist spirituality and attach the greatest emotional significance to it (Venturino, 1997). Like all other ethnic groups, Tibetans share a language identity (Giles, 1978). However, there is a dearth of Western scholarly journal articles devoted to the efforts of Tibetan diasporas to preserve their culture and identity, and they continue to struggle in preserving their language, religion, and culture. The largest publication on Tibetan identity was largely European because in Lopez (1998), Dodin and Räther (2001), and Schell (2007) Tibet was studied via religious manuscripts, 'Western and Tibetan accounts have together played an important role in the development of an ideal Tibet and by transference, of an ideal Tibetan refugee' (Diehl, 2002, p. 20).

In their work, Houston and Wright (2003) mention that 'they are communities that live religion'. They cite Warner (1998), who notes 'religion for most Tibetans is not just a weekly gathering or the recitation of a particular text. One reason quoted by many researchers is that Tibetans have been able to preserve their own culture due to the leadership of the Dalai Lama's recognize. Holiness commands a pivotal and powerful position in Tibetan communities worldwide. 'Through his global profile, and a transnational nationalist political structure, he creates images of Tibet, and thus builds the idea of community'. The structure and functioning of the Tibetan government in exile and the Tibetan national flag also undeniably indicate the importance of Buddhism in Tibetan society. Even the Tibetan government in exile is referred to as *Choesid nyisden gyi zhung* or 'spiritual and political government', similarly the national flag (*Bod kyi gyal dar*) symbolizes the spiritual and political identity of Tibet. Tibetan school children sing the Tibetan national anthem on regular school days, thereby communicating their pride for their cultural identity (Giles and Dorjee, 2005).

According to a Respondent (65 years, woman, Dharamsala), being 'Tibetan' means compassion, sympathy for all human beings, love for religion and love for one's culture. It is the Tibetan language and religion that makes the Tibetans unique from the rest of humanity. To preserve the Tibetan identity, language and religion need to be protected from contamination. According to her 'In our Tibetan society, everyone is treated equally, I heard of the caste system the first time when I came to India, how does being born in a caste makes one lower and higher. In the Tibetan culture, everyone is respected, and we are all equal'. The Tibetan identity can, therefore, be conserved by preserving the language and religion.

When a young respondent (26 years, woman, Dharamsala) was asked what it means to be Tibetan and what Tibetan identity is for her, she mentioned that essentialized categories of language, culture, religious affiliation and even race provide ready building blocks and templates for one's identity. 'For us Tibetans, Buddhism is our way of life, and the philosophy of Buddhism is compassion, love and surrender to the divine, and we all believe in that... Dharma is what differentiates us from others'. According to her, identity is not solid and stable, but rather an ever-developing phenomenon manifested and formed via negotiation in the process of social interactions. Although she believes life in exile reinterprets the meaning of some traditions, but it also establishes entirely new ones. She wants to preserve her language, her religion, but was confused about her traditional dress '...I do not know whether I should go to the monastery in a pair of jeans, or wear the traditional dress, I can't go because you're not supposed to go in jeans'. She mentioned that since she is born in India, she has non-Tibetan friends, and this is viewed as abandoning Tibetan identity.

According to a 70-year-old man, living in Ravangla (Sikkim) with his wife and two children, cultural identity remains consistent, 'Nothing has changed for us, we are Tibetans, and we will remain so, whether we stay in Sikkim or any other part of India. We have a responsibility, and that is to preserve our culture, and we are doing that'. One of the very important factors influencing one's cultural or national identity is the 'new identities of hybridity that are taking place' because of intermarriage. He mentioned that in Ravangla, many inter-marriages are taking place, and the Tibetan race is not pure anymore.

Language has become a symbol of Tibetan identity as a 'means to create a new national or ethnic identity' of Tibetans that is based on secular and political purposes (Fox, 2013, pp.38-39). To preserve the Tibetan identity, the language needs to be preserved, religion needs to be preserved, and the Tibetans should stay together. The size of the Tibetan community, the settlement structure, the vicinity of cultural and religious objects all have a positive effect on the preservation of culture and assimilation. The factors that hinder cultural preservation are western influence and materialism, which are slowly eroding human values. Therefore, the younger generation needs to be given more guidance.

According to the arguments of a 55-year-old man living in Darjeeling (West Bengal), 'Tibetans are unique because they have been able to preserve their religion, language and culture. He felt that identity needs to be preserved but it cannot be rigid… I was against my son marrying the Nepali girl, but she is very nice and really takes care of my son'.

From this narrative, it can be seen that along with maintaining the Tibetan identity, integration is also essential; otherwise, it creates hostility among the inhabitants of the host community. Since it is a question of survival and acceptance by the host country, many of them learned the local language, and they were gladly accepted by the local population. Modern education is the reason for transformation taking place in Tibetan society and in the mindset of the people. The educated younger generation of Tibetans felt that knowing and understanding the situation in Tibet, it is impossible for them to go back there, and they should instead use India as a gateway and passport to other countries so that they can have a better life. After living in India for so long, some of them were even born there, and they felt that life there is good, they have access to most things; the only thing they do not have is an Indian Citizenship.

This can be validated in the narrative of a young Tibetan boy from Darjeeling (West Bengal) pursuing his higher studies in the United States. According to him, Darjeeling has always been his home, the place where he spent the first sixteen years of his life. He did not grow up in a Tibetan society as his circle of friends and relationships outside his family were essentially non-Tibetan. In fact, linguistically, he was more comfortable with English than Tibetan while his interest in books and music stretched from Gabriel Garcia Marquez to the Beatles. Therefore, the first sixteen years of his life were without any strong identification to his own community or culture, with the stories of Tibet told by his grandparents being the only discernible link to his identity as a Tibetan.

According to him, The Tibetan Children's Village was the largest and oldest Tibetan School in exile, attracting students from all corners of the exile community as well as a sizeable number from Tibet itself. It was a closed community that was rich in its celebration of Tibetan culture and emphasis on its language, history, and heritage. 'Looking back now, I can positively say that it was during this period that I was (re) introduced to my Tibetan identity, as for the first time I was attending Tibetan prayer sessions, participating in cultural shows, and generally was surrounded by Tibetan classmates and teachers'. He further added that the connection language builds to one's community is a strong one, and during the two years he spent in Dharamsala, speaking and writing in Tibetan truly gave him a sense of organically relating to his Tibetan identity. He recalls that, after moving to Delhi for his graduation, he dabbled in a myriad of ventures, some good and others not so productive. Since he was the only Tibetan in a Hostel of almost three hundred students from all over India, yet he did make some very good friends that have remained close to him till the present moment. He narrated '… I was very fortunate to have never experienced the racial discrimination that many Tibetans (as well as people from the Northeast part of India) face from the local North Indian community in terms of our physical appearances and manners of speaking. Those around me were always very interested when I mentioned my Tibetan heritage, and I was able to share with them the history and culture of my country while listening to their own stories. Therefore, although almost paradoxical, I have been very proud of my identity as a Tibetan Refugee, which, although stems from the loss of my country, is one that has a rich history and connected to a larger Tibetan diaspora that has done very well over the past many decades in preserving its unique culture while also learning from the modern world, such as our experiment in democracy which is the Tibetan Government in exile'.

After spending a year in a monastic college in Dharamsala, and in order to focus on studying Tibetan and Buddhist Philosophy, he got the opportunity to converse with many Tibetan monks who had recently escaped into exile from Tibet. According to him, having been born in India, his imagination of Tibet was one built around the tales of his grandparents, about the herds of yaks and sheep they drove across the rocky plains and the idyllic nomadic lifestyle they led before they had to leave it all to come into India during the late 1960s. 'Therefore for a long stretch of time, I was never able to identify with the Tibet that was on display via the images and videos that came from the region, or the one that was running on the industrialization and 'modernization' brought upon the railroads and might of the Communist Party of China. The presence of two Tibet, the past which I grew up on and the present, which I did not know at all, has always been a source of tension every time I attempt to reconcile my Tibetan identity in a non-Tibetan environment. Talking to these monks who were from Tibet provided me with a very real-time sense of connection to Tibet, and since many of them were from nomadic families, it gave me a sense of continuity in hearing that the old ways still survived, albeit under great pressure from the Powers at Beijing'.

In India, he rarely explains to people about the political existence of Tibet since many had a basic understanding of the circumstances that led to the exile of Tibetans into India, 'In the US, every time I introduce myself as Tibetan, I must first answer the question "But aren't you Chinese?". The sense of being a refugee in a land where very few know your story is much stronger than in one where the history of the country is so intricately linked with your own, yet it also spurs on a sense of responsibility, one that was not so prevalent in India'. Therefore, now he is quite actively engaged with attempts to promote the Tibetan culture through organizing talks and cultural shows while attempting to work, with a few other Tibetan students and professionals in America, towards building a mentorship network for those Tibetan students who are unable to enter their desired professional fields due to lack of networking access.

Tibetan communities themselves are still compact regarding communication of language and knowledge about culture and customs. They are bent on maintaining their traditional Tibetan identity without giving up the hope of going back one day to their homeland. The intermediate generation, 20 to 40 years old, of working age, was mainly keen on the economic and educational opportunities, but Tibetan identity needs to be upheld and Tibetan culture, language and traditions need to be percolated down to children. In India, the Tibetan community remains very tightly knit because of the social environment. But even in the West, there is very little intermarriage, and the extended family is still the model when family reunification immigration laws make this possible.

Most of the respondents felt that whether they stayed in India or even in foreign countries, their identity was not compromised. There may be external changes, but internally Tibetans do not become or feel less Tibetan. They felt they were only transforming because they lived in a different society, and assimilation was needed for acceptance. Some respondents complained that they did experience less cooperation initially, but with the presence of his Holiness at Dharamsala, things were quite negotiable with the Indian Government. Initially, the local population did feel that they were going to usurp their resources, and they were jealous, but now, emotionally, the relations between the local population and Tibetans are cooperative, friendly, regardless of cultural, ethnic, and religious differences. Nevertheless, the size of the Tibetan community, the settlement structure, the vicinity of cultural and religious objects serve as positive factors and helps them to maintain their identity.

### Future Aspiration

With every passing year, the prospects of return are diminishing for the Tibetan community in exile. They are constantly grappling with the interplay and complex definition of home and homeland. The preoccupation of the exile community with the preservation of tradition has resulted in a degree of 'enclavement' (Klieger, 1989) or 'emplacement' (Diehl, 2002) from Indian society that has come with its own set of costs and benefits. Sudeep Basu (2018) examines how diasporas re-territorialize notions of belonging, home, culture, and community in a host society. Tibetans have always remained grateful to India, since India has given them space to exercise their identity to the fullest, as Falcone and Wangchuk (2008) in their work mentions that for many Tibetans, India is 'Home away from Home'. The relation between India and Tibet is based on a strong spiritual and cultural connection. Buddhism is a gift to Tibet from India, and it has significantly influenced Tibetan heritage, and linguistics has always played a very important role in this relationship. Similarly, the Tibetan diaspora in India has also instigated a cultural and religious revival of Buddhism (Dolma, 2016). However, despite this mutually symbiotic relationship, the Central Tibetan Administration has not conferred a legal or political recognition as a government by India.

Dolma (2016), in her research, mentions that the political and legal identity of Tibetan in India is very abstruse. India provides a registration certificate RC to individuals above 17 years, which needs to be renewed every year, this is a legal document which gives the Tibetan all the rights and privileges as the Indians, but they are not given the right to vote or work in government offices. Apart from this, they are given a travel document called an Identity Certificate (Yellow Book), which also acts as a passport, but does not allow travel abroad like the Indians. Acquiring Indian Citizenship is another difficult task. However, despite having an amicable relationship with the home country, there is always a yearning to return home. The meaning of home, as mentioned earlier in the study, varies from individual to individual. An 82-year-old respondent yearns to go back to Tibet. She narrated, '…. His Holiness has told us that we will get Tibet and he will take all of us…it is nice here, but this is not home. I am very old now, and I want to see my home'. She recounts Tibet as a beautiful place, covered with fields of barley and mustard. There were plants all over, yaks were more common, and they were very precious. She remembers her home and a big dog which she had.

On the one hand, where there is a sentiment and nostalgia towards Tibet, there are others who feel a sense of responsibility towards the Indian government. A 30-year-old teacher from Dharamsala says the Indian government has been generous to give asylum to the Tibetan refugees, but when the time comes to repay, many leave for foreign countries. He mentions that there are numerous cultural changes that are taking place in the Tibetan community since they are away from their homeland; he gave an example in relation to food items and changes that have occurred; he narrated '…Tibetan people believes in killing once; therefore they took beef or buffalo as their staple meat, they say that slaughtering a bigger animal once can feed many and only has to be killed once but in comparison to chicken and other meats one chicken or goat won't be sufficient to feed many therefore the slaughtering of many animals is involved but after coming to India and specifically residing in

Himachal Pradesh and with the ban of beef here they have to shift to chicken and mutton as their staple meat'.

He added, 'the food items have not changed much because the climatic condition of Himachal is somewhat similar to Tibet so the dishes which were prepared in Tibet can be prepared in India, but the basic ingredients are not found here, and so they have adapted to locally available food items; the basic example of that can be seen in the consumption of rice and chapatti'.

In terms of clothes, he preferred wearing western clothes as he found those comfortable and suitable to the climate, and he wore his traditional dresses during festivals or when his holiness came. He narrated, older generations are more particular about the traditional clothes, but the younger generation looks for comfort; the authentic cultural dress is also seen among those who have just come back from Tibet.

The respondent mentions that the Tibetan population can be easily outnumbered by the Chinese, so instead of having dreams to go back, he believed every Tibetan should stay back in India and repay the debt. He also believed that one should marry in one's community, speak the Tibetan language, follow the religion but at the same time adapt to another culture, and he believed that Indian culture is also very rich, and it is the land of Buddha. However, since they do not have a homeland of their own and if their culture too fades away, then their identity will be lost, so it is important to protect their identity and to get ready for any kind of struggle in the future; they must understand the power of unity and stay united and keep the culture and religion intact. The narrative highlights the aspect of dual loyalty, which means a diasporas commitment both to his homeland and the host country. The loyalty will depend upon the interplay of various factors.

Another respondent explained how she preserves her Tibetan identity, born to a Bhutia mother and a Tibetan father and hence both the cultures are reflected in her personality. She can speak both Sikkimese and Tibetan fluently. Like the youngsters her age, she also enjoys the latest western music and clothes, but at festivals, she always wears her traditional clothes. She is very grateful to the Indian Government for the shelter and refugee that they have given them '…I am very happy here, I was born here, and since my parents are here, this is my home. But I feel very sad for my grandparents; they always want to go back to Tibet'. She mentioned that till the time she was in Sikkim, she was not conscious of her identity; it was only after she went to Dharamsala that she realized how important one's identity is. As a result, she started writing blogs, generating interest, and creating awareness about the plight of the 'Tibetans in Exile'. She added that 'I do not say we are refugees, but we are in exile; it gives a sense of hope that someday Tibet will be free'.

A crucial role is played by His Holiness for the Tibetan; he has been able to inculcate Tibetanness in the minds of the Tibetans. Personal loyalty to the Dalai Lama plays a key role in creating unity among the community, 'He is our God'. He was unhappy that even after so many years of being there, they cannot vote and have no identification. He was very upset with the green book given to the Tibetan refugees because it conveys that they do not belong in India. He was very happy when the Aadhar Card became mandatory because the green book '…was just a proof of identification and not saying that they are citizens'. However, this is also a misreading of the Aadhaar card as a 'proof of Indian citizenship' according to the respondent. As Chaudhuriaand and König (2017, p. 127) pointed 'Aadhaar does not authenticate citizen identity, nonetheless, in its promise to build a 'national grid' of identity information infrastructure, it indicates a meta-structure of anew inclusion/exclusion paradigm of citizen formation in India that appears to reinvent early liberal values of civic republicanism based on property rights'.

In terms of future aspirations, the aspect mentioned by all Tibetans respondents was the preservation of their religion. They see religion as an attitude, a philosophy, a value system, and not as a formal tradition. The other important aspect to preserve is the Tibetan language. When language script is preserved, then other cultural parts will be preserved. However, the language, despite its crucial importance for the preservation of Tibetan culture, loses its priority as a means of communication since they must operate in an entirely different social environment. The third aspect of Tibetan culture to be preserved, according to the Tibetans, is the desire to return to Tibet. On a personal level, some respondents also see marriages with non-Tibetan as a threat to preserving one's culture but, on the other hand, also as a medium for assimilating with the local populace.

Evidently, the Tibetan refugees express a multitudinous range of stances with respect to their native identity, culture, and religion. A pervasive sense of dilemma and insecurity clearly sets the dominant tone in most of the narratives articulated above. The Tibetan refugees experience the predicament of maintaining the sanctity, integrity and contours of their indigenous culture and religious practices whilst concomitantly managing to interact freely in the process absorbing local practices, customs, partaking in the economy and marriage alliances between ethnic communities to remain culturally inconspicuous. Multiple stratagems like inculcation of the native language, indoctrination of the tenets of their spiritual leader, the Dalai Lama and the preference to marry within one's own community are some measures adopted by them to preserve and secure their indigenous cultural moorings. But because of their displaced reality (as a refugee) and their settlements in India, some stratagems to protect their culture are often forsaken to ameliorate the possibilities of cultural differences and alienation between them and their local/regional cultures. Overall, the Tibetan refugees experience what can be termed as a paradoxical equation with India with regard to identity and future aspirations for their community wherein they strive for social and political inclusion, thus acquiring citizenship rights and security for their denizens whilst simultaneously harboring aspirations of returning to their homeland. In a similar vein, Bauman, in his incisive analysis of modernity and globalization, describes the contemporary zeitgeist with the metaphorical liquid or 'liquid modernity' to expound upon the uncertainty and instability characteristics of the modern age. Bauman posits the possibilities of the collapse of seemingly stable and powerful macro-level state apparatuses and other allied institutions promising security (Bauman, 2012). Similarly, the conceptualization of such 'liquid fear' as promulgated by Bauman in modern societies resonates with the ever-looming dangers of identity, nationhood, citizenship experienced by the Tibetan refugees in India. The constant threat of losing their indigenous culture, their identity coupled with their struggle for seeking security, shelter and refuge and the gnawing uncertainty of reclaiming their lost pristine homeland produces the possibilities of constantly negotiating their identities and micromanaging strategies in their everyday encounters to maintain the semblance of balance between one's indigenous identity and the espousal of a hybrid cultural identity formed with the assimilation of local/regional practices of the host country.

Chapter 5

# The Objective Tibetan Identity:
# Formation and Crystallization

## Introduction

Identity has become part of both psychological and sociological lexicons. It has been conceptually derived from the Latin word *idem* (sameness and continuity). Studies of contemporary society reflect the necessity to address the historically and spatially contingent concept of 'identity'. It has been subjected to objectification and used by numerous social actors and groups as a tool for articulating and claiming their space (both personal and social) in the society at large. This aspect reflects on the political dimension of Tibetan identity, especially on understanding how various actors/agencies use identity as a tool for realizing their political endeavors, particularly in relation to their assertion against the Chinese incursion and occupation of Tibet. Therefore, problematizing identity in all domains of social life should be meticulously yet circumspectly handled considering its fragility and dynamic nature.

Giddens (1991) highlighted that late modernity is one of those particularly volatile moments where individuals and groups face crises and dilemmas of identity leading to 'identity politics and movements' and 'collective searches for identity'. Snow, Oselin and Corrigall-Brown (2004) pointed out this apparently underlying proliferation of identity problems and concerns in so-called late-modernity or postmodernity. These are numerous well-chronicled sociocultural challenges and changes: state breakdown, increased immigration and refugee flows, multiculturalism, technological advances such as the Internet, globalization, ethnic revitalization, and movements against socioeconomic and political exclusion. The confluence of such factors loosens in some instances and shatter in other. The cultural and structural moorings to which identities were once anchored gave rise to the construction, reconstitution, extension, negotiation, and challenges of various combinations and permutations of identities. Because of such factors and trends, identity-related issues are particularly relevant to social life as we move deeper into the new century.

Identity politics, thus, has become a multi-disciplinary study with strong roots in poststructuralism. The 70s and 80s saw increasing attention to those categories of people who had long been left out from the centralized predominant discourses; subsequently, there were concerns to give voice to those who had long been silenced. Intersections of race, sex, class, sexual orientation, ethnicity, and nationality were among the many identities that began to draw the attention of social scientists. This focus on cultural identities represented a marked shift from the economic and political based analysis that had dominated the sciences of the time. This assertion of the individual, and especially of those individuals who were outside of the social norm, caused great instability in the comfortable split between the personal and the public, the family and the nation, and the state and the civil worlds. Feminists were among the first to assert that 'the personal is political', giving rise to a notion of identity politics based on the unique social locations of a given individual. The claim to identity was a political assertion rather than a personal one because identity also brings with it membership to a community. In turn, membership demands equality with others in that group, and so those with identities that disrupt the status quo are a threat to the hegemony of the ruling class. Allowing members of a social minority equal claim to social goods would call for a reshaping—often a radical reshaping—of societal values, norms, and even sometimes laws. A culture of identity politics represents a multicultural approach calling for loyalty to various, and often multiple, categories of one's identity. This challenges the foundations of the modern nation-state, which has been supported by the existence of homogenous group identity. Who is to be included for membership has always been an important social question, but the dawn of the era of identity politics seems to usher in a new hope for those who have long been left out in the cold of the social world? Feminists, people of color, gays and lesbians, and ethnic minorities are among the many who have been eager to embrace such politics to gain a voice and end their historical silence. At the same time, theorists have recognized the limits of identity politics and the view of personhood and community that it endorses. Identity politics, it is argued, promotes the notion of stable, essential identities and, as such, privileges difference over the reconciliation of difference. To counter this trend, some theorists have proposed a 'relational' politics, which assumes that identity is always the product of relationship and, therefore, never an essential aspect of a person's identity. In contrast to an identity politics that seeks to assert individuality, relational politics aims to overcome the ever-present threat of interpersonal conflict by privileging the flux relationship and social 'conversation' over the stability and privilege of identity.

## Conceptualizing Identity

Identity can be thought of as the cover term for the name humans impute and avow while interacting with others and orienting themselves to their various social worlds. A central principle of interaction between humans, or with other social objects that constitute their world, is that interaction is minimally contingent on the identification of the objects involved. In other words, before we can act toward or interact with some object, it must be situated in time and place. To do so is to give the object a name in the sense of classifying it as a member of a category (e.g., a soldier, a woman, a man, a chef, a student, and so on). Such naming entails the imputation and/or avowal of identities. Not all identities are the same, however, as there are at least three types of identity that are featured in the relevant literature on identity in the social sciences: social identity, personal identity, and collective identity. These three concepts, however, are interconnected and overlap with each other. From a sociological standpoint, social identity is the foundational or anchoring concept it is grounded in and derives from social roles, such as police officer, physician, or mother, or broad social categories, such as gender, racial, ethnic, and national categories. This structural grounding is captured in the parallel concepts of 'role identities' and 'categorical identities'. Interactionally, social identities can be both imputed or avowed. They are imputed when the ego assigns to alter an identity based on presumed category membership (he/she is a Tibetan!) or the role alter is thought to be playing (he/she is a refugee!) or the role ego would like alter to be playing, which is referred to as alter-casting (you are a Tibetan refugee, aren't you?). In each of these cases, a social identity is ascribed to others, and interaction is likely to proceed in terms of this identity. Social identities can also be avowed or claimed, as when ego announces, 'I am a Tibetan' or 'I am a refugee' and so on. It is because of such category-based avowals that some social psychologists define social identity in terms of self-definitions or identifications associated with social category memberships, or as one's self-concept derived from one's knowledge of membership in a social group, as well as the emotional significance that this membership produces. But such self-definitions are perhaps more appropriately conceptualized as personal identities, which also include aspects of one's biography and life experiences that congeal into relatively distinctive personal attributes that function as pegs upon which social identities can be hung (Goffman, 1963). The importance of distinguishing between social and personal identities rests not only on the fact that the latter are self-designations, but is also suggested by the observation that individuals sometimes reject other-imputed social identities, especially when they imply social roles or categories that are demeaning and contradictory with an idealized self-concept (Snow, Oselin and Corrigall-Brown, 2004). Such observations suggest that personal identities may sometimes be grounded in social identities derived from role incumbency or category-based memberships but without necessarily being determined by those social identities. The term self-concept has been used to explain the negotiation or compromise that is reached between an individual's ideal conception of the self and the information they receive from the social world, with the resulting negotiation capturing the tension that often exists between an individual's social and personal identities. The difference between the social and personal identity is rather mere disciplinarian boundaries, as both are inseparably intertwined with each other signifying the dualistic characteristics of one's identity. As Erikson has pointed out that identity is both located in the core of the individual as well as in the core of her/his communal culture, and the discordance between the two is resolved through his conceptualization of ego identity – which functions to ensure sameness and continuity in one's identity, suggesting that one's identity is inherent of both personal and social identity.

Collective identity, on the other hand, overlaps with the kindred concepts of social and personal identities yet differs from them. It is loosely defined as a shared sense of 'we-ness' or 'one-ness' that derives from shared statues, attributes, or relations, which may be experienced directly or imagined, and which distinguishes those who comprise the collectivity from one or more perceived sets of others (Polletta and Jasper, 2001). Identifying with a collectivity is often based on an individual's social identity, such as identifying as an ethnic minority or a citizen of a country, but such category-based associations do not automatically give rise to collective identity. Instead, the development and expression of collective identity is often triggered by contests pitting one group against another, as in the case of the World Cup and the Olympics, by unanticipated events, such as the World Trade Centre terrorist attacks of September 11, 2001, or by threats to group or community integrity or viability, as in the case of much social movement activity. A significant part of the power of collective identity comes from the collective solidarity, efficacy, and agency it provides, which individuals are not as likely to experience via their personal or social identities.

How identity is conceptualized and analyzed is based largely on orienting perspectives of Essentialist, Dispositional, and Constructionist. Essentialists reduce the sources of identity to a single determinative attribute regarded as the individual's or collectivity's defining essence. Essentialist perspectives encompass both structural and primordial logic. Structuralists understand identity to be rooted in elements of the social structure, such as in roles, networks, and broader social categories, such as social class, ethnicity, and nationality. Alternatively, Primordialists understand identity as deriving essentially from presumed biological givens, such as sex and race. Neither of these essentialist variants ignores historical factors or social changes, but these factors are treated more as intervening variables that affect the relative salience and pervasiveness of the structural or biological roots of identity.

The dispositional perspective posits a connection between various personality traits or tendencies and behavioral prospects. This perspective is based on the idea that certain social psychological traits or states predispose individuals to adopt or claim some identities over other possibilities. According to the authoritarian personality thesis, for example, dogmatic and insecure individuals are highly susceptible to identification with extremist social movements. In general, there are at least two major dispositional hypotheses. One is the troubled or spoiled identity thesis, which holds that individuals with unsatisfactory or stigmatized identities are open to and likely to be searching for more satisfactory identities. The other dispositional thesis is that individuals look for and adopt identities that verify their existing identities or self-concepts. Standing in contrast to both the essentialist and dispositional perspectives is the constructionist perspective. It holds that there is considerable indeterminacy between identities and their theorized ascriptive, structural, and personality moorings. From this perspective, identities are regarded as the product of negotiation, interpretation, and presentation rather than biologically preordained, structurally given, or dispositionally determined (Cerulo, 1997).

Language and interactionally based discursive processes, such as framing, figure prominently in identity construction. Although the analytic utility and credibility of these perspectives vary among scholars, it is arguable that together they contribute to a fuller understanding of identity than is provided by just one of them. For example, while it is historically indisputable that ethnic and national identities are constructed (Cornell and Hartmann, 1998), they are not fabricated whole cloth apart from past and current cultural traditions and structural arrangements and the flow of political events and happenings, which together exercise constraint on the interpretive processes associated with identity construction.

## Questions on Tibetan Identity

In consideration of the historical circumstances in which the Tibetan refugee movement took place, the Tibetan refugees have a unique status in India. This status is reflected in the concessions from certain procedures governing other refugees, and certain rights enjoyed only by Tibetan refugees and some facilities provided by the Central Government. While the Ministry of Home Affairs is responsible for regulating foreigners in India, the Tibetan refugees also have the government-in-exile established in 1960 by the Dalai Lama, the spiritual and temporal leader of the Tibetan refugees. With headquarters in Dharamsala, India, and through its Central Tibetan Administration (CTA), it has a presence in all the Tibetan settlements. The Settlement Officer (SO) appointed by the CTA represents the government-in-exile and looks after the day-to-day affairs in the settlement.

So, to say, the conceptual operationalization of identity vis-à-vis Tibetan identity concerns with trying to understand how the Tibetans collectively yet objectively see the Tibetan identity, what determines the membership – like ethnicity, does belonging to the group automatically grant them the objective identity or is there any ritualized role(s) to be performed in order to become a member of the 'we group' Tibetan identity. Is conformity to the objective identity strictly followed, does deviation from it invites social sanctions? Based on this conceptualization, the study seeks to delineate the conformity and deviation to the objective identity and raise the various issues revolving around. As highlighted in the first chapter, the question of identity will delve with those who came to India seeking refugee asylum status from Tibet. Secondly, among those generations who are born to refugee parents in India since they have not struggled and lived through the experiences as their parents and did not directly descend from Tibet during the crisis period. Thirdly among those refugees who are confined in cluster settlements in large Tibetan refugee communities, such as those that are in McLeod Ganj and Dalhousie. Their settlements are located and surrounded by communities that are distinctively different from their own, in terms of cultural, religious, and racially. These factors posed a severe challenge in the process of their integration with the host society, making them maintain their distinctive identity. Fourth and finally, those refugees who are settled in the parts of India where the mentioned distinctive differences are less, such as those refugee settlements in Ravangla, Darjeeling and Sonada. Therefore, the level of differential integration among these settlements with the communities of the areas also determines the formation and crystallization of their identity. Contextualizing, the study seeks to explore the question of the identity of the Tibetan refugees in India by questioning and investigating whether the notion of identity among the Tibetan refugees are constant regardless of spatial organizational settlement and historical position in time or is differential and in flux.

Further, understanding of integration is also a necessary element as, to an extent, it is important for understanding identity formation, crystallization, and the crisis of identity of the Tibetan refugees. Exploring the question on identity of the Tibetan refugees, particularly among the youth, is pertinent, as on the one hand where the CTA and the Tibetan Parliament in Exile (TPiE) are in hopes of returning to Tibet, which to an extent imposes a restriction on the practice and maintenance of their distinctive cultural and traditional identity, and on the other hand due to their social linkages and bridges in their social interaction for the various purposes they are more attuned towards the host society. Aspects of cultural assimilation in their outlooks are observed among the Tibetan youth, thus leading to question how the youth negotiate between the identity they are ascribed with when in interaction with the identity they have accultured. Here, the question of identity crisis among Tibetan youths is one of the important dimensions that the study seeks to comprehend. In relation to the crisis of identity, the conflicting gender role identity of the Tibetan women refugees is yet another significant element that the study endeavors to comprehend.

## Relation between Integration and Identity

As highlighted above, integration is an important constituent part of identity formation, consolidation and crystallization. However, before we relate how integration constitutes identity formation, we need to discuss how assimilation plays a vital role in integration. Assimilation involves some level of integration. The term integration is often used in conjunction with the legal term desegregation, the process of ending legally sanctioned racial separation and discrimination. Desegregation often involves removing legal barriers to interaction and offering legal guarantees of protection and equal opportunity. Integration occurs when two or more groups interact in a previously segregated setting. That integration may be court-ordered, legally mandated, or the natural outcome of people crossing the 'color line' once legal barriers have been removed. When evaluating the extent of integration in society, it is important to ask the question: With whom do you live, learn, pray, celebrate, and mourn? If the answer to this question involves only people of a single race or ethnicity, then one must conclude that he or she lives a segregated life. An un-segregated life leads to pluralism where different groups coexist in harmony, have equal social standing, maintain their unique cultural ties, communities, and identities, and participate in the economic and political life of the larger society. These groups also possess an allegiance to the country in which they live and its way of life. In a pluralistic society, there is no one race or ethnic group considered as the standard to which other races should aspire. Rather, cultural differences are respected and valued. Operationalizing the concept of integration, the study evaluates how the Tibetan refugees are integrated within their own community and with the larger society. As introduced in the first chapter, we will be looking through the various aspects of integration using the model developed by Ager and Strang (2008). As discussed, it is an established fact that for the comprehension and formulation of identity, integration is a fundamental part of the process. This integration model is divided into four domains or levels of integration, which will be discussed in detail.

### *Markers and Means*

Firstly, at the level of major public arenas, which tries to analyze their access to employment, housing, education and health care system, which Ager and Strang refer to as 'Markers and Means' to reflect the achievement of integration and the potential means in attaining integration. First, however, certain facts about the Tibetan refugees need to be highlighted; for instance, Tibetans refugees who came to India between 1959 and 1962 were issued Registration Certificates (RCs) according to which they were given leased agricultural lands for their livelihood and resettlement; however, these lands cannot be bought or sold or enter into any form of transference by them. Roemer (2004) has also highlighted that those Tibetans who came in the mentioned period also enjoyed access to the formal Indian economic sectors, such as employment in the Indian government and entrance to Indian Universities. However, those who came after 1962 were not given any entitlement to the mentioned facilities. Apart from the refugees of the Partition and some Bangladeshi refugees who came before 1959, no other refugee group in India has been leased agricultural lands for establishing settlements anywhere in India. The Tibetans do not need a work permit in India and may be employed anywhere in the informal sector. Government employment (except for serving in the Indo-Tibetan Border Police Force and in CST schools up to standard IV) is, however, closed to them as they are not Indian citizens (Chimni, 2000; Vijaykumar, 1998). A very important facility provided by the Government of India to the Tibetans, which no other refugee group in India enjoys, is providing exclusive schools for Tibetan children, the Central School for Tibetans (CST) under the Central Tibetans School Administration. The expenditure of these schools is fully met by the Central Government. Tibetans, however, do not have access to higher education in India except for some scholarships provided by the Indian government. In the state educational institutions, a domicile certificate is required, which only the citizens are given (Chimni, 2000). Hence, Tibetans are forced to pay fees as foreigners and do not have access to higher education at par with Indians.

## Employment

Employment constitutes one dimension of the integration in relation to refugees, as it is the means through which a sense of being independent of the shackles of bondage is instilled among the refugees with 'economic independence'. Economic independence can be thought of as a major integrating factor of the refugees; as a result, it is also the most researched area of integration (Castles *et al.*, 2001). As discussed in Chapter three, Figure 3.12, 48 percent of the respondents were employed in various occupations such as teachers, army, nurses, officials, etc. whereas, 26 percent were involved in various kinds of business activities, and 7.5 percent were engaged as drivers. Briefly, 81.5 percent of the Tibetan refugees are economically integrated into Indian society. The remaining 18.5 percent constitute homemakers. However, these groups of women are not to be seen as economically unproductive; they engage in various kinds of seasonal micro-economical activities such as making candles, jewelry, incense sticks, weaving and selling seasonal clothes, etc. In the studied five field areas, Sonda (56.66 percent) and Dalhousie (56 percent) constitute the highest number of employed respondents, followed by Darjeeling (45 percent), Ravangla (44 percent), and Dharamsala (40 percent). The highest average income of these individuals ranges mostly between Rs. 10,000-20,000 (28 percent) with the highest concentration of these income category groups in Darjeeling (35 percent), followed by Dharamsala, Ravangla and Sonada with 30 percent each, with least recorded in Dalhousie (20 percent). However, in terms of family income, Ravangla (48 percent) has the highest concentration, which is shown in Figure 3.13.

It would not be wrong to argue, deriving from the statistical facts from our study, that the Tibetan refugees in India are economically very much integrated into society. A transit stay in Delhi on the field visit to Dharamsala and Dalhousie reflects how various clothes, bags, shoes, and numerous items sold in the *Majnu ka Tila* market, mostly owned and run by Tibetans, are preferred by Delhiites for its superior qualities in cheap prices. Such aspects were also visible in Dharamsala and Dalhousie.

## Housing

As already highlighted, those Tibetans refugees who came to India between 1959 and 1962 were issued Registration Certificates (RCs), as per which they were given leased agricultural lands for their livelihood and resettlement. In these lands, they have settled and carved a little Tibet out for themselves. In the Darjeeling and Ravangla areas, it was found that many Tibetan refugees are staying in rented places outside the settlement camps. Besides the settlement and housing issues, we also enquired into various household infrastructural facilities. Figure 3.14 shows that cent percent of the refugees have availed the facilities for cooking gas consumer connections; about 85.5 percent of the households were found to be connected to main water supply sources operated by the State, whereas the remaining 14.5 percent of the respondent's household had private water connection. Out of the places where the study was conducted, Ravangla had a cent percent water pipeline connected to the public water distribution system; however, the lowest was found in Dalhousie (70 percent). These households were issued various kinds of beneficiary cards to avail of the various subsidies given by the Indian government. In Dalhousie, Dharamsala, and Ravangla, the Tibetan refugees only have a Refugee card for availing various facilities. However, in the case of West Bengal, both in Darjeeling and Sonada, a high number of refugees have APL and BPL cards, as well as a Refugee card. In Darjeeling, the total percentage of APL cardholders was 75 percent, BPL 25 percent, and Refugee card 75 percent. In the case of

Sonada, APL cardholders were 76.6 percent, BPL was found to be 16.6 percent, whereas Refugee cardholders were 60 percent, as given in Figure 3.18.

## Education

Educationally, 31 percent of the respondents are educated below matriculation, 20 percent of the respondents had qualifications up to matriculation, 16 percent up to higher secondary, 9.5 percent had higher education. A significant number of respondents were illiterate (23.5 percent). The illiteracy rate of the respondents is highest in Dharamsala (30 percent), below matriculation is highest in Darjeeling (45 percent), and matriculation is highest in Dalhousie (30 percent). The higher rate of illiteracy and below matriculation of the respondents is due to a larger number of the respondents belonging to the older generation who were mostly illiterate or below matriculate because when they arrived in India, they had already crossed the age for formal studies and the education system in India was entirely different from that of Tibet (refer Figure 3.9).

In relation to the educational expenditure of households, it is highest in Dalhousie and Dharamsala (40 percent), followed by Darjeeling (30 percent), Sonada (26.7 percent), and Ravangla (20 percent), as shown in Figure 3.15.

## Health

In the third chapter, Figure 3.19 shows how most of the Tibetan refugees preferred the modern or allopathic form of health system, which was recorded highest among those staying in Dalhousie, i.e., 52 percent, Dharamsala 42 percent, and 40 percent each in Darjeeling and Ravangla. However, it is also important to note that besides the allopathic medicine, they also equally prefer traditional Tibetan healing practices popularly known as Amji. This was recorded to be the highest among those staying in Ravangla (56 percent), followed by Darjeeling (50 percent). In fact, Amji is the most preferred form of health system among the Tibetan refugees, particularly in Darjeeling and Ravangla. However, it was also observed that, besides their preferences, the children of the Refugees born in India were all vaccinated as per the medical system or health guidelines of India, suggesting that the Tibetan are integrated into the health system of India. However, whether any distinctive health facilities were given to them or not could not be ascertained.

### Social Connection

For the integration of the refugees, or whether they feel they are integrating with the larger social system, it is important to enquire about the mediating factors that connect the individual with the society. For this, interrogating and reflecting on the social bonding and the linkage and bridges that facilitate such bonds are important elements of comprehending social connection. At the level of operationalizing the concept of social connection, we looked at the participation and interaction of refugees in various social festivals, functions, celebrations, and any other social gatherings.

With social interaction in mind, we enquired about their course of interaction with the local population, and it was found that 85.5 percent of the respondents have close friends belonging outside their own community with whom they have regular social interaction, mostly this group belongs to the younger generation. However, the remaining 14.5 percent mentioned that they don't have any friends from the host society. This was particularly attributed toward those belonging to the older generation and among those who have not ventured outside the camp areas, arguing that the camp areas are secluded and are self-sufficient where they do not feel the need to make friends outside their community. However, if we look at Figure 5.1, it makes an interesting observation in relation to social interaction with the local population. As discussed in the first chapter, the settlement camps in the three regions—namely Darjeeling, Ravangla and Sonada—are relatively located in a socially and culturally homogeneous environment for the refugees. Hence, logically, the habitual environment for the refugee should be conducive in these three locations. However, Figure 5.1 suggests otherwise, with the lowest recorded non-interactive refugees located in Darjeeling (45 percent), Ravangla (22 percent), and Sonada (20 percent). Related to the above aspect, to comprehend their level of social interaction, we enquired whether they were invited by their Indian friends in their house, in which 69.5 percent of them responded positively, as reflected in Figure 5.2. The highest positive responses came from those refugees settled in the Dalhousie (cent percent) area, followed by those in Dharamsala (66 percent). In relation to Darjeeling, Ravangla, and Sonada, the level of social bonding with other communities are less as compared to Dalhousie and Dharamsala, with the lowest level in Darjeeling (40 percent). Therefore, it is interesting that despite the settlement camps in Darjeeling, Ravangla, and Sonada located in a socially and culturally homogenous environment, the level of interaction is lower as compared to Dalhousie and Dharamsala. This might be due to the competition for resources by virtue of being located in the same society. Also, Dharamsala and Dalhousie witness more flow of funds and resources from the Indian government and CTA, and thus the settlement camps in these areas face less competition for resources. Therefore, refugees residing in these camps witness more social interaction.

**Figure 5.1:** Respondents interacting with local population

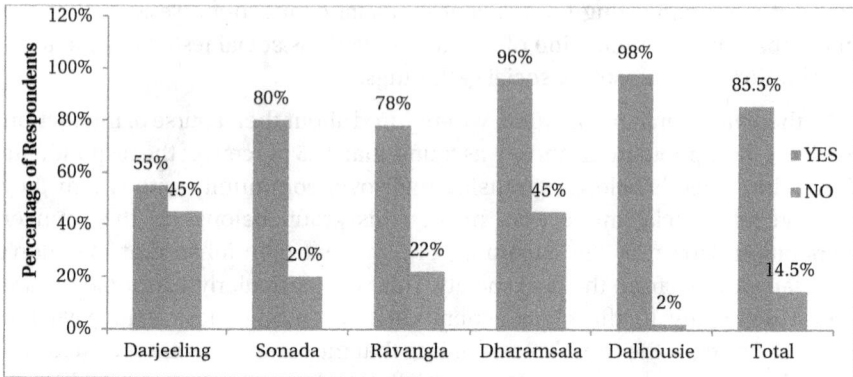

Source: Field Survey October 2016-August 2017

**Figure 5.2:** Respondents invited to friend's home

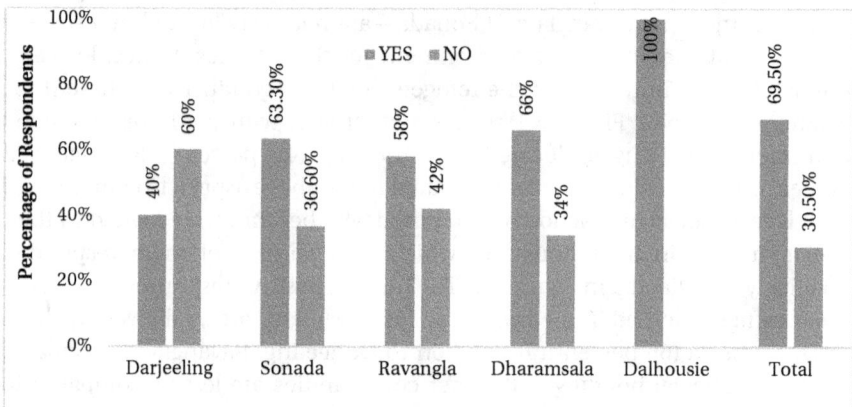

Source: Field Survey October 2016-August 2017

Further inquiry on the nature of occasion for such social bonding with host communities reflects that 70.5 percent are related to the festival, social interaction at the host home, and the second-highest being non-occasional visits (17.5 percent). However, the non-occasional visits were confined among the younger generations who were comfortable with their friends in the local communities. To a large extent, most of the younger generation were assimilated with the local populace due to such non-categorical boundless visits and interaction with their peer groups who are from the local communities. As highlighted in Figure 5.3, in Dharamsala, the visits to the host's home are only during festivals. Figure 5.4 suggests that the frequency of visits to the host's home in a year is higher in Dalhousie and Dharamsala compared to Darjeeling. Sonada and Ravangla. Again, this could be due to the occurrence of more social interaction at Dalhousie and Dharamsala. It is also interesting to note that despite existing in a socially and culturally homogenous environment, the social interaction related to work is also low in Darjeeling, Sonada and Ravangla. The most commonly answered response was related to whether their friend invites them over or not, following it the second-highest was those who were invited 2 to 3 times a week, if we correlate the two response with those aspects discussed earlier, then, to an extent we can argue that most of them visited frequently and were intimate. Extrapolating from the intensity of the friendships, the study further enquired whether they were also helped financially by their friends in local communities, to which 21 percent of them responded positively. The positive note was higher in Dharamsala (30 percent), followed by Darjeeling (25 percent) and Sonada (23.3 percent).

**Figure 5.3:** Purpose of their visits

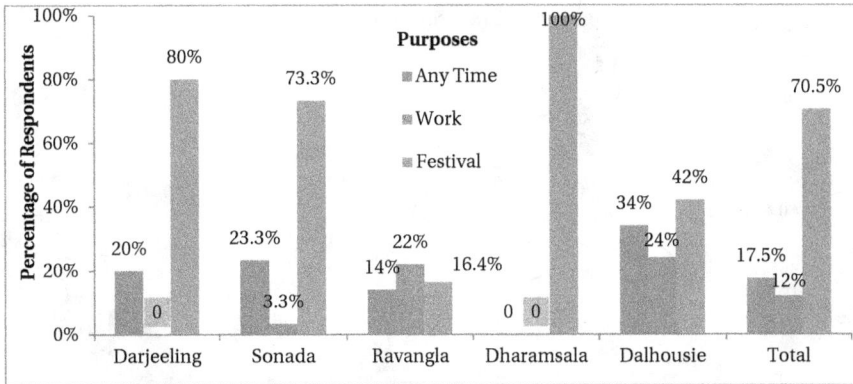

Source: Field Survey October 2016-August 2017

**Figure 5.4:** Frequency of the visits

| Frequency of Visit | Darjeeling | Sonada | Ravangla | Dharamsala | Dalhousie | Total |
|---|---|---|---|---|---|---|
| Everyday | NIL | 7% | 2% | 16% | NIL | 6% |
| Twice or Thrice a Week | NIL | 10% | 24% | 26% | 10% | 17% |
| Once in a Month | NIL | NIL | 10% | 20% | 34% | 16% |
| Once in a Year | NIL | NIL | 6% | 8% | 30% | 11% |
| Depends upon Friends | 100% | 83% | 58% | 30% | 26% | 51% |

Source: Field Survey October 2016-August 2017

**Figure 5.5:** Financial help received from friends belonging to different community

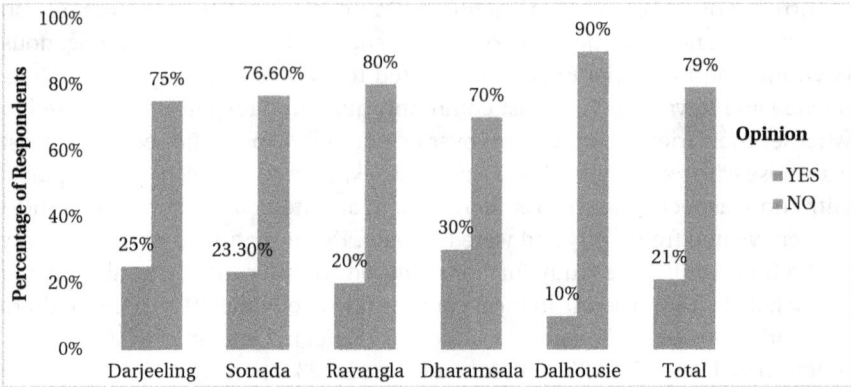

Source: Field Survey October 2016-August 2017

**Figure 5.6:** Inter-community marriage

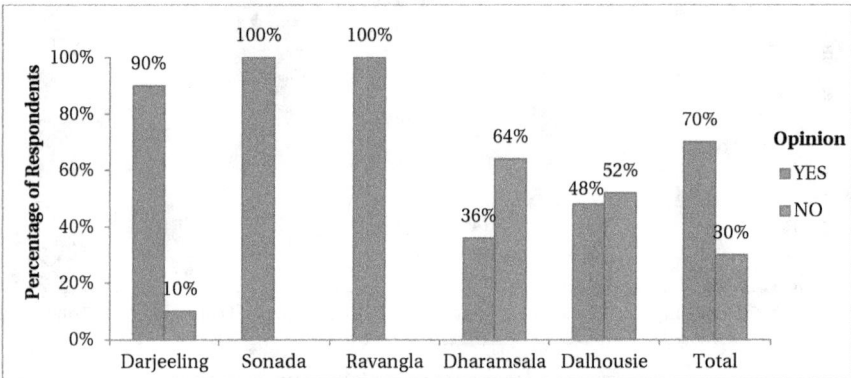

Source: Field Survey October 2016-August 2017

Further, extending the parameters for comprehending the level of social intercourse, we enquired about inter-community marriages. As reflected in Figure 5.6, 70 percent of the respondents have witnessed intercommunity marriages of the Tibetans with other communities of India. However, among the close-knit Tibetan settlements like Dalhousie and Dharamsala, inter-community marriages were not observed much and were reported by many respondents as non-preferable in their families. On the other hand, those settlements where the local population are relatively similar to their own in terms of race, culture, religion, and socioeconomic conditions, they did not opine to conservative and traditionalism in establishing conjugal relations with other community. These respondents were mostly concentrated in Ravangla and Sonada (cent percent), and Darjeeling with 90 percent. Mostly the respondents had also pointed out that among the younger generations, inter-community marriages are becoming more pronounced.

### *Facilitators*

#### *Language and Cultural Knowledge*

**Figure 5.7:** Significance of Hindi and local lingua franca

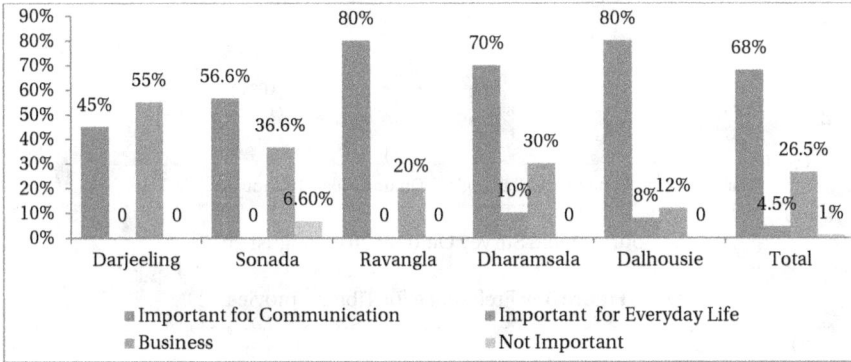

Source: Field Survey October 2016-August 2017

Language and knowledge of culture play a significant role in the process of integration of individuals into society. To assess their knowledge in the local lingua franca of the region, we requested the respondents to converse in the local dialect only. During the study, it was found that every single respondent was able to converse in the local language of the region with ease, Hindi and Nepali in the case of Darjeeling, Ravangla and Sonada, and only Hindi in the case of Dalhousie and Dharamsala. This aspect was not only confined to the younger generations, but it was equally found to be true with the older generations. In relation to 'Hindi' as one of the major languages of India for communication, 68 percent of them opined that since the Tibetan refugees travel to different places of India for pilgrimage and other purposes, they felt that knowing the language has helped them to communicate with other communities with ease. At the same time, many Tibetans are also engaged in business activities; 26.5 percent of them feel that having the knowledge of Hindi and the ability to communicate in it with the local population has broadened their scope of earning a livelihood and has boosted their economic transaction. Many of the younger generations also expressed that equipping themselves with the linguistic ability of local dialects made them easily accommodable to settle anywhere outside the settlement camps for various reasons, such as education and employment, including travels. In addition, 4.5 percent of the respondents believe that they should learn Hindi for their day to day interactions with the locals (Figure 5.7).

**Figure 5.8:** Preference of movies

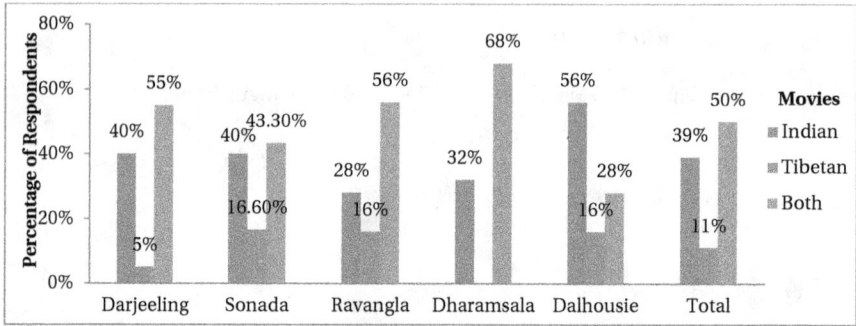

Source: Field Survey October 2016-August 2017

**Figure 5.9:** Preference for Tibetan movies

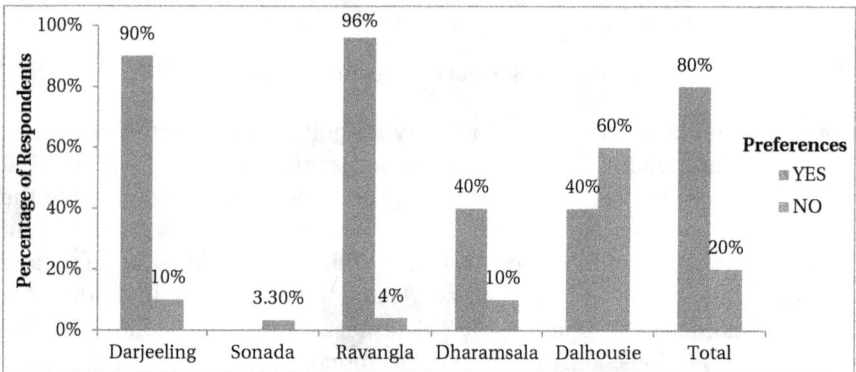

Source: Field Survey October 2016-August 2017

Movies are one of the important parameters that facilitate diffusion of culture, which in turn act as an assimilating tool to the cultural ethos of the larger society, to the extreme extent cultural homogenization and propagation of cultural hegemony. Hindi movies or Bollywood have always played a major role in the formation of the national identity of India (Miller, 2015). The movie as a form of entertainment attracted all the Tibetans interviewed regardless of age, sex, profession, and class. Therefore, it is important to observe and understand the preferences of Indian and Tibetan movies among the Tibetan refugees in India. In the option for choice as shown in Figure 5.8, 50 percent of the Tibetans preferred both Indian and Tibetan movies, whereas 39 percent of them only preferred Indian movies, particularly Hindi movies only, while 11 percent chose to stay with Tibetan movies, particularly among the older generation who are sentimentally attached to the ideology of Tibet. However, if the choices are conditioned to only one preference, then 20 percent of them prefer Tibetan movies, as given in Figure 5.9. In contrast, the remaining 80 percent of the respondents preferred to go for Indian movies only, with the reasons attributed to the wide range of selection of both movies and languages. The preference is also attributed due to technological sophistication in cinematography and subject matter of the movies, which they considered superior to most of the Tibetan movies. Few of the younger generation highlighted that they despise Tibetan movies.

**Figure 5.10:** Preference of different cuisines

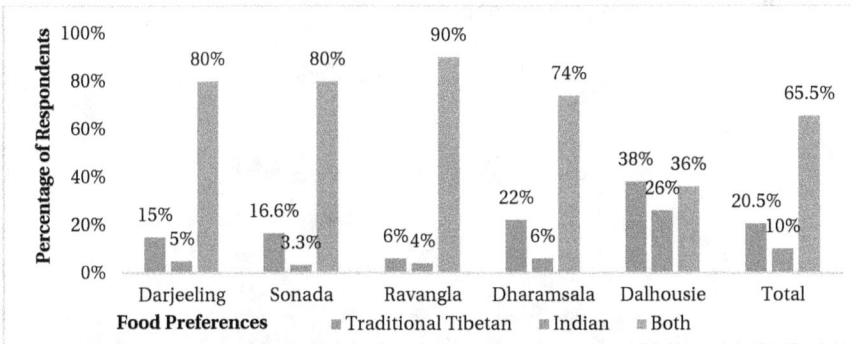

Source: Field Survey October 2016-August 2017

Food is not just about the dietary requirements of the body; it is also one of the most culturally significant aspects of our life. In a multi-cultural society, such as India, what kind of food one consumes defines what kind of social position/status one belongs to. For instance, the notion of *kaccha* and *pucca* food is associated with the caste system in Indian society. Or eating fermented food being a definition of primitiveness or of tribal practices. Statistically speaking, in a news article published by *Mirror UK*, on average, the British spend 34 minutes 51 seconds every day just on deciding what to eat (Mirror.co.uk, 2017).

Further, according to *Statista*, on average, an individual in India spends 87 minutes (men) or 80 minutes (women) every day eating and drinking (Statista, 2016). Therefore, understanding the preferences of food consumed by the Tibetans is a significant aspect to understand the level of their integration with Indian society. It is true that food is not just cultural, but what is cultural is also defined geographically vis-à-vis availability of certain food items. Nonetheless, changes in food habits and patterns can also be considered as a change in the cultural aspect of a community, thus suggesting cultural assimilation. It was found that 65.5 percent of the Tibetans consume both Indian and Tibetan cuisines, while 20.5 percent of the respondents only prefer Tibetan foods, and 10 percent showed a preference for Indian foods only. Most of the respondents pointed out that preference for Indian food is not out of compulsion due to the non-availability of Tibetan food items, but it is due to the taste of the foods which suits their taste buds. When posed with the question of whether they feel that they are assimilating with the Indian society and culture, and what are the various reasons for assimilation, 33.5 percent mentioned that it was because of business, 22.5 percent due to the educational institution, as highlighted in Figure 5.11. It was also found that respondents residing in Dalhousie and Dharamsala preferred more Tibetan food compared to Darjeeling, Sonada and Ravangla. Again, this could be due to these places located in a socially and culturally homogenous environment.

**Figure 5.11:** Domains of cultural assimilation

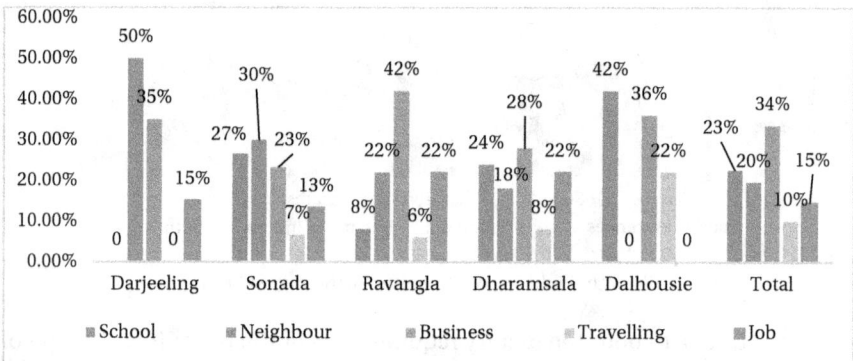

Source: Field Survey October 2016-August 2017

*Foundation*

*Citizenship and Rights*

Citizenship and rights are the foundation as well as the basis of entitlements that any nation is obliged to enshrine to its citizens. In relation to Tibetans, though, they have been staying in India for about six decades, yet they have not been accepted as citizens of India in accordance with their wishes. As discussed in the conceptual framework of the study, the question and issue of citizenship and rights are interdependent concepts as citizenship precedes rights. Citizenship comes with a sense of belonging and attachment to the nation. Nonetheless, issues pertaining to the question of whether Tibetans are entitled to be Indian citizens or not has been raised in the Lower House (Lok Shabha) of Indian

Parliament as early as 1951. The issue received enormous Parliamentary discussion after sheltering Dalai Lama from his flight from Tibet in 1959.

The Government of India took the standpoint that the Tibetans should be subjected to The Citizenship Act, 1955 and subsequent Amendments as foreign nationals like any other. But it has also been simultaneously pointed that the Government of India will consider their application if they voluntarily apply for Indian citizenship. Further, the reading of the Indian Citizenship Act, 2003 clearly documented that those Tibetans who are born in India before 1st July 1987 are entitled to become Indian citizen by birth, suggesting that most of the second-generation Tibetan refugees are eligible to obtain Indian citizenship. The citizenship issues of the Tibetan in India have been explored in great detail by Tarodi (2011). However, Falcone and Wangchuk (2008), based on their interviews with Tibetans, suggest that 'apart from bureaucratic impediments there seems to be a "bi-lateral though unofficial agreement among the CTA and Government of India officials" which denies Indian citizenship to the Tibetan applicants' (Falcone and Wangchuk, 2008 *as cited in* Tarodi, 2011, p. 8).

Based on the above notion, a question was asked about how the Tibetan refugees perceive themselves in India. From the figure below, we can state that apart from all the facilities to the citizenship issues as referred above, Tibetan refugees have assimilated well in India. When asked how they feel in India, 87 percent said they felt that they are at home and that they never get the feeling that they are away from home, whereas 13 percent of them said that they are refugees and still feel they are away from their homeland. The 13 percent—the older or the first generation born in Tibet—still feels a strong attachment towards the land, whereas most of the younger generation or the third generation feels that they are a part of India as they have been raised and brought up in India.

**Figure 5.12:** Refugees perception of being in India

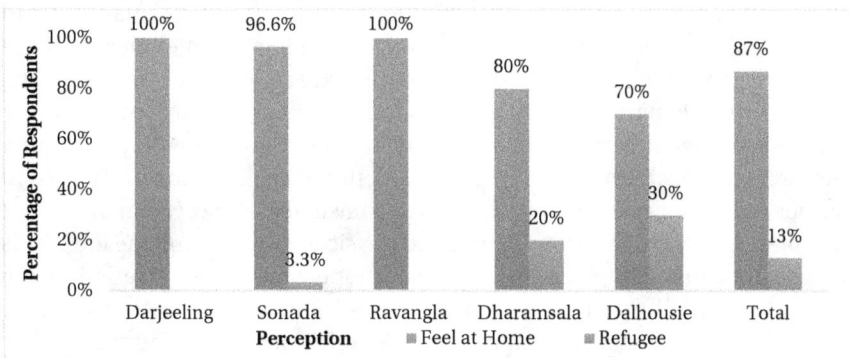

Source: Field Survey October 2016-August 2017

## Tibetan Identity

Identity, as Hogg and Abrams (1988) pointed out, is the concept of who we, as individuals, think we are. Studies on identity are broadly classified into two streams depending on what the study is examining, firstly those which examines 'the structure of identity and describe different facets (e.g., cultural, religious, gender identity), others concentrate on the question how individuals arrive at this structure, which underlies constant change' (Watzlawik, 2012, p. 253). For Bauman (1988), identity is forged and realized in the domain of what is social. However, those theorists who are inclined towards the interactionist perspective locate identity as constantly shaping and reshaping itself in close everyday social practices, which creates a sense of self among the individuals. However, these two theoretical paradigms are not mutually exclusive to each other; rather, it maintains an intimate dialectical relation despite its seemingly dichotomized projections. In a nutshell, identity is a subjective disposition of the ego in relation to her/his alter, yet such subjective disposition of the ego is the objective consequences emerging out of collectively shared values of the society. Therefore, despite identity being an individualized value-oriented subjective conception of the ego, it attains an intersubjective ontological status objectifying the nature of its existence. The subjective experiences are collectively shared by the members of the social entity, making the subjective identity possible for a collectively consensus-based formulation for an objective identity. The objective identity is constructed through numerous socio-cultural facts, such as nationality, place of birth, race and ethnic group, religion, language, food, attires, and the status acquired, etc. through which the objective criteria of identity is achieved. Turner and Oakes (1986) argued that psychologically, the social collectivity becomes self.

Basically, asking who I am has a lot to do with where one contextually locates oneself within the larger socio-cultural parameters of the society in which one belongs. The socio-cultural environment which conditions and defines an individual's identity is objectively achieved through the institutionalization of roles along with other primordial features outlining the membership. The process of institutionalization establishes role expectations from its members, helping consolidate the social identity of the individuals conforming to the cultural parameters of the society they inhabit. The consolidated social identity reinforces or transforms itself when these identities are lived and performed in various social contexts under numerous circumstances. However, in the face of uprootedness from the socio-cultural and physical environment, the identity is prone to becoming fragile under various extraneous pressures exerted by the external socio-cultural pressure from another group, leading to a crisis of identity of the individual, which can lead to a crisis of group identity also.

In relation to the Tibetan identity issue, Tibetans were displaced from their homeland and were struggling to re-root themselves in an alien terrain, which was physically and socio-culturally distinctively atypical from their own. This made it difficult for them to retain and maintain their unique socio-cultural and religious practices. Without which their identity of being Tibetan seems to be in flux when they are exposed to the cultural and religious dogmas of the host society. Such is more evident among the younger generation. In such a bleak situation, the idea and ideology of the Tibetan world seem on the verge of disappearance. Giles and Dorjee (2005, p. 147) pointed out that in the formative years of exile of the Tibetans in India, the Dalai Lama devoted himself to carrying out three important tasks relating to the situations of Tibetans in India and in other parts of the world relating to

> establishing the Tibetan government in exile, rehabilitating Tibetan refugees and providing Tibetan children with both Tibetan and modern education. Most notably, he drafted a Tibetan Democratic Constitution (Lama, 1963) and provided for his people the democratic Tibetan government in exile. Tibetan diasporas have modelled their political structures on India's parliamentary democracy. The Dalai Lama is the head of the government and supporting him is the *Kashag* – the Tibetan Cabinet – and below it are various departments including those of religion and culture, education, home affairs, security, information and international relations, and the general audit office. There is also the Supreme Commission of Justice that settles disputes among Tibetans in diaspora. Tibetans in diasporas elect their representatives to the Tibetan parliament in Dharamsala. In recent years, the Dalai Lama has initiated monumental changes in the Tibetan democratic set-up. For example, Tibetans directly elected their chairperson to the *Kashag*, thus creating a new chapter in Tibetan history. Under the *Kashag* fall offices of the representatives of the Dalai Lama in such cities as New Delhi, Geneva, New York, Tokyo, Moscow, Taipei and London. It is interesting to note how Tibetans have adopted democratic systems according to the changing needs of the time to maintain, preserve and promote (*Zin kyong pel sum*) their cultural identity.

The above steps taken up by Dalai Lama can be understood contextually looking in relation to preserving the sovereignty and socio-cultural integrity of the Tibetan identity. To further explore this subject matter, we need to consider the objective criteria and the worldview they have adopted.

### Language

The first aspect of the objective criteria is considering language. During the field interaction, 97.5 percent of the refugees feel that knowing the language and dialect is an important marker of identity, as shown in Figure 5.13. They express that being able to express themselves in the Tibetan language with their fellow Tibetans instills a sense of belonging with one another, language becomes a binding force for the whole Tibetan community. Regardless of generations, almost every respondent maintained the significate importance of language, and they pointed out that it is being taught to the kids at home; the rest of the respondents slightly disagreed and put forward the notion that the language is not important, but the teaching that distinguishes a Tibetan from the rest of the community is most vital, and this concept came from those Tibetan refugees who are born and brought up in India. Many from the older generation of the Tibetan feel that preserving language and religion is an important aspect of consistently maintain the Tibetan identity, also what defines Tibetanness, as mentioned in one of the narratives in the fourth chapter. This point was further extended in another narrative where it was pointed out that the '… language does not completely determine one's identity, language is secondary; it's the principles and ideas of spirituality that determine one's identity. He further added … because people are staying in different places in order to maintain their culture, they should know their language'. For him, being Tibetan is embodied in the spirituality of the religious practices which they are born into and following the dharma defines Tibetanness; language is a means to an end for transmission of the religious teachings to the coming generation. However, the view is contradicted in comparison with the younger generations. A young respondent pointed out that her parents insisted on her learning and speaking the Tibetan language at home as well as within the community; however, she rather feels comfortable with Hindi and argues that it doesn't matter which language she speaks to communicate; nonetheless, she remains a Tibetan. Therefore, language is a medium of communication and not a definite marker of identity.

**Figure 5.13:** Importance of language as a marker of Tibetan identity

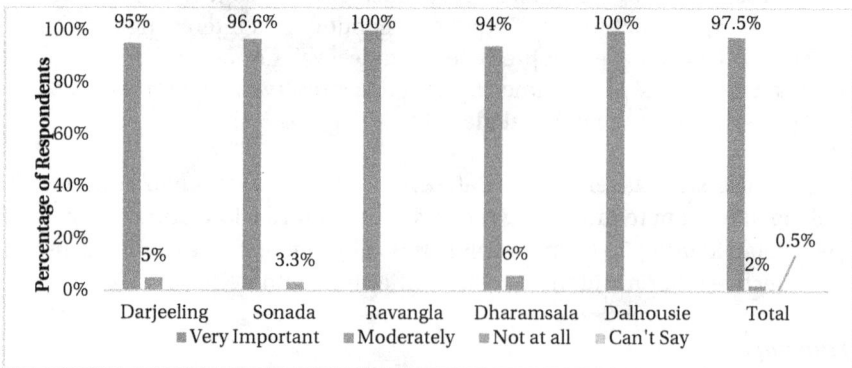

Source: Field Survey October 2016-August 2017

### Nationality/Birthplace as Marker of Identity

Citizenship in a nation-state has been argued to be the primary identity of an individual (Alonso, 1995). However, in relation to the Tibetan refugees in India, the question of citizenship is a problem of a contested issue; they are neither citizens of Tibet, strictly in the sense of being absent from the sovereign territory despite having the government in exile, and, on the other hand, they are not yet naturalized as citizens of India, which is as according to their wishes and the endeavors of returning, unlike other refugees in India. Therefore, for them, instead of citizenship, nationality seems to be rather a conducive conceptual frame to consider the conceptualization of Tibetan identity vis-à-vis corporeal territorial embodiment of Tibet into the Tibetan identity. As shown in Figure 5.14, 97 percent of respondents feel that it is an essential factor to be a Tibetan by birth, born within the territory of Tibet; whereas the remaining 3 percent of respondents slightly differed in the opinion and expressed that the criterion of birth within the territory is not as significant as maintaining and observing the moral ethos and philosophical principles of being a Tibetan. They all maintained a homogeneous response that being a part of the Tibetan generation is an important indicator of identity.

**Figure 5.14:** Significance of being born in Tibet for Tibetan identity

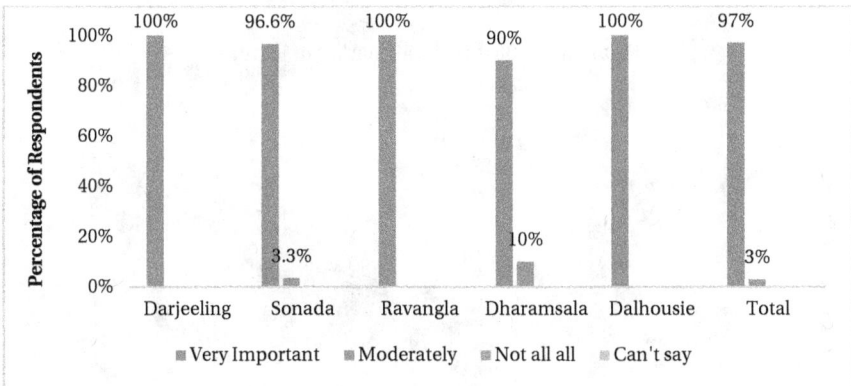

Source: Field Survey October 2016-August 2017

For many Tibetans, particularly among the first generations, the yearnings to return to Tibet is their solitary dream and goal, despite knowing that it will never be the same as before. A 75-year-old refugee narrated that Tibet was no longer the same, and all the religious structures and houses had been destroyed. However, despite the knowledge of all the predicaments of the situation and his age, he still yearns to go back some day and stay in his home and cherish the memories of all the struggles that the Tibetans have gone through. Another narrative also revealed a similar sentiment and expressed the view that it was an act of kindness. He narrated that '…Tibet is my first home and I always want to go and close the chapter of my life there at my homeland'.

However, a contradictory view is presented among the younger generations; for instance, as narrated, a respondent pointed out that he had heard a lot about Tibet and the struggles going on from his grandfather. However, since he was born in Sikkim, he prefers to stay in Sikkim as life for him is better when he compared it with the harshness of Tibet, which he heard from his grandfather. Therefore, even after Tibet is able to realize its freedom from China, he prefers to stay in India.

Further, if we look in Figure 5.15, it can be observed that the Tibetan refugees have a strong sense of belonging and attachment to the places that they were raised and brought up in, as we can see from the figure that 72.5 percent reported that the places where they were born and raised are integral and are very important to them. Most of the respondents, which constitute 72.5 percent, were born in India and belong to the second or third generation, followed by 22.5 percent who moderately think that the place of birth is an integral part of their identity. Only 0.5 percent had shown less interest as they are the new refugee group or the older generation who desires to return to their homeland.

**Figure 5.15:** Birthplace as marker of identity

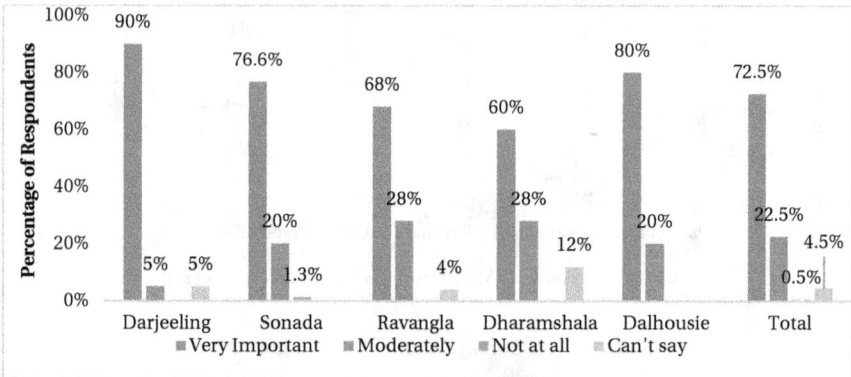

Source: Field Survey October 2016-August 2017

Therefore, the notion of Tibetan identity perceived to be realized through Tibetan nationality or attachment to imagined territorial belonging by those who imagine themselves to be part of the group, as championed by Anderson (2006), seems to be contradicting when contextualized with those Tibetan refugees born and brought up in India. For them, identity is bounded by and embodied in the corporeality of the physical boundaries of the land they inhabit. Tibetan identity, based on the observed phenomena and situated on the notion of affiliated national identity, rather presents itself as a more contested and contradicted perspective among the younger generation. However, if we look at Figure 5.16, 91 percent of the respondents, even if they were born in India, feel attached to the idea of Tibet as their homeland. The refugees reported that for them, Tibet is very important and it means a lot to them, it's their homeland and they wish to return someday, whereas for the rest of 8 percent they said its moderately important as they have never seen Tibet and have been living here in India since birth the only attachment they have is that it's a part of their identity and culture and their ancestors belonged from there.

**Figure 5.16:** Moral affiliation to Tibet

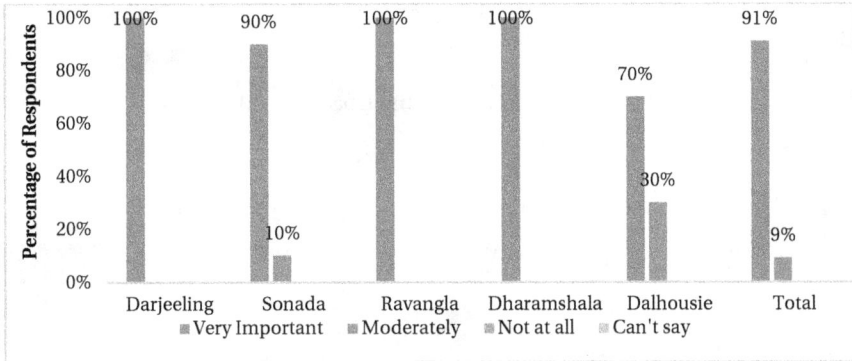

Source: Field Survey October 2016-August 2017

### Ethnicity and Religion

Another dimension of objective criteria of identity is ethnicity and religion. Ethnicity has been a much-discussed issue in contemporary third world societies. However, ethnicity and refugees have not been widely discussed in the academic world. Nonetheless, to understand the identity formation of the refugees, ethnicity becomes an important objective criterion, particularly when situating the refugees in a socio-culturally and racially alien world. The exposure to racial and ethnic differences plays a pivotal role in the identity formulation of the self in the multi-social context. Regmi (2003) pointed out that ethnic identity formation requires common descent, socio-culturally relevant physical attributes or characteristics and a set of attitudes and behaviors. Through these attributes, ethnic identities are replayed as ideologies of the ethnic groups. Often, these ethnic ideologies are in interplay with religious dogmas and practices. Further, there is a positive relationship between religion and identity, particularly among young adults (King, 2010). Oppong (2013) explored the close association between religion and identity, arguing that... (p. 10)

> Religion as an expression of deep sense of unity and its linkage with identity formation especially in the context of Durkheim's insights; the link between religion and ethnicity in terms of forging identity formation and the link between religion and identity formation especially with reference to youth's religiousness and search for identity.

He further expounded that the relationship between identity and religion is positively correlated with identity formation. It is argued that at the core of identity formation, religiosity plays a vital role in it as it acts as a forceful binding force. However, he further pointed, that the stated statement to be true in the olden days as compared to the modern era, it also varies both demographically and culturally.

**Figure 5.17:** Significance of race, ethnic background, and religion

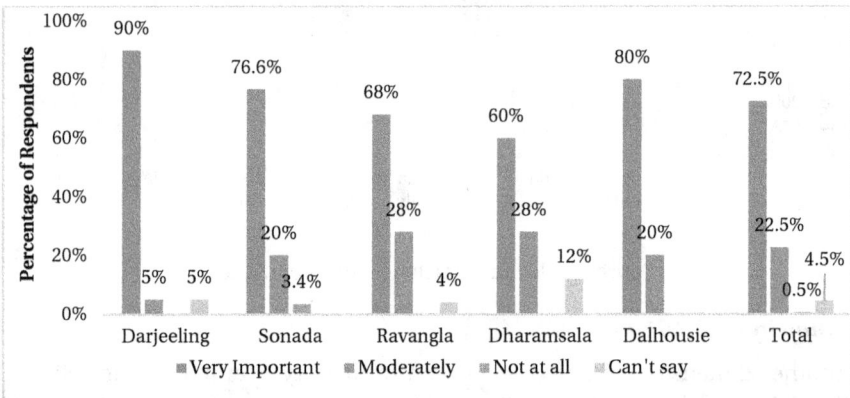

Source: Field Survey October 2016-August 2017

To address this dimension of identity, questions related to race, ethnicity or ethnic background and religion were put up to the refugees to assess their understanding and conceptualization of the Tibetan identity. However, during the process of interaction, the mentioned three categorical aspects of identity are not treated as mutually exclusive parameters; rather, they are expressed to them as interdependent and overlapping concepts. As highlighted in Figure 5.17, 72.5 percent of the respondents stated that race or ethnic background or religion is important to be a Tibetan, whereas 22.5 percent said its moderately important as we have seen cases of Tibetans who have converted to a different religion but still has a strong sense of Tibetan identity rest of the respondents were negative about the fact that religion or ethnicity has to do anything with identity, to be specific the older generation was more stringent about the religious and ethnic factor whereas the upcoming generations are more open towards the different religions and community. (Note: Though Figure 5.15 and 5.17 are observed to be similar, however, it must be noted that the similarities in the statistical data are due to the similarities in their response).

### *Values and Moral Standard*

Values and moral standard of Tibetan plays a pivotal role in the formation of both personal and social identity of being a Tibetan. Hitlin argued that 'Human beings anchor their sense of self across situations within feelings of right and wrong and the importance they place on various abstract, desirable goals' (2011, p. 515). The adherence to values and moral standards of the society established the sociological relationship between the individual and society. To assess the deeper insights of the refugees and to understand that the very conceptualization and determinant Tibetan identity is deeply rooted in their everyday life, questions related to their personal values and moral standard were administered. 93 percent of the respondents stated that the personal values and moral standard are important indicators of Tibetan identity; it is these qualities that make them unique, and wherever they reside in any corner of the world, the values and moral standards are going to remain the same, when questioned the younger generation about this view they had the exact same thing to say, they said that the values and the moral standards had been taught to them by their parents and grandparents since childhood and they had been with them since then. The rest of the 7 percent had differed on the terms of intensity; they believe it's an important factor but not so important as they are a part of the younger generation who are more modernized and have accepted change, as shown in Figure 5.18.

In relation to the above statement, another complimentary question was asked concerning the maintenance of core philosophical ideas of the Tibetans, and whether it has remained essentially intact or it had changed over the years through their practices involving external changes. As shown in Figure 5. 19, 51 percent of the respondent responded that it has remained intact since they were socialized and taught, and it has been engraved in them since then. They mentioned that they had followed the philosophy and teachings from one generation to another. The older generation said that the philosophy taught is based on logic, and logic remains the same and does not change. The teachings and philosophy have become a part of their identity, and it is associated with feeling, and feelings remain the same wherever we go. In comparison, 25.5 percent felt that it had changed moderately over the years. This is to point out that despite the cultural assimilation that has taken place through their gradual interaction with the host society, the Tibetan identity has basically remained intact. It was interesting to observe that at Ravangla majority of the respondents moderately or hardly believed in the maintenance of core philosophical ideas of Tibetan compared to other places like Darjeeling, Sonada, Dharmsala, and Dalhousie, where respondents very strongly believed in the maintenance of core philosophical ideas of Tibetan.

**Figure 5.18:** Importance of preserving moral standard as a Tibetan

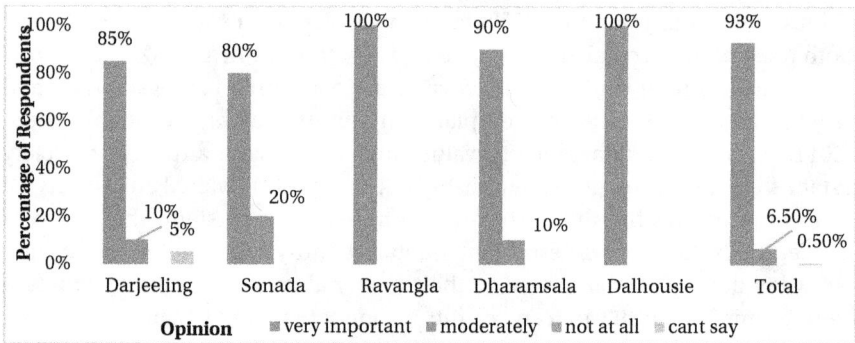

Source: Field Survey October 2016-August 2017

**Figure 5.19:** Views on maintenance of core philosophical principles of Tibetan ideologies in spite of external changes

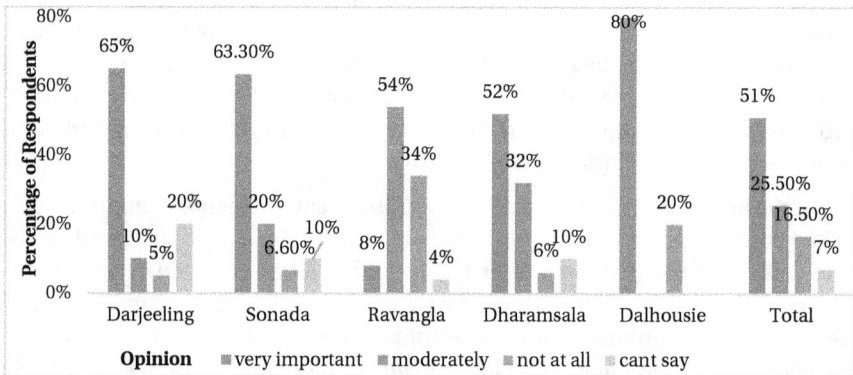

Source: Field Survey October 2016-August 2017

**Identity Crystallization**

The discussion on the objective criteria almost presented itself as a contradictory view between the younger generation and the older generations of Tibet, who have taken the toils in their body and embodied the identity of being born in Tibet in contrast to those who have not. This aspect presented itself as a major challenge on the very conceptualization of identity among the various generations of Tibetan refugees. For which, questioning the process of identity formulation and ossification or crystallization becomes an imperative aspect of the inquiry of the study, and also what various factors are involved in the process. Through our discussions with the refugees, particularly with the younger generation, it was found that the formulation and crystallization of the Tibetan identity is the product of unintended consequences through the gradual interaction within the community and outside the community. Traditionally, if we contextually locate the study from the interactionists' perspective, then the interaction is the constant supplier of images for imagination and conception of identity both on the part of the self as well as to the other. Therefore, being in a different land, alien from their own, often led to speculation and gossip both on the part of the Tibetan community and among the host community too. Keeping the aspect in mind, questions pertaining to their views on how they review themselves and the others and their reaction on it has been analyzed here.

The interactions played an important role in the formulation of their identity, which many of the respondents also agreed positively. They pointed out that what the host communities think and say matters a lot to them. In relation to their views within the community, it was usually seen that among the older generation, they were more concerned and worried about the social norms and values of being a Tibetan and had genuine sense and concerns about the social consequences in society. Whereas, among the younger generation they did not feel a need to feed to the needs and satisfy the society and believed it did not matter much what the society had to say. In the younger generation, cases were seen where a Tibetan refugee had married a girl from a different ethnic background, and it goes against their community sentiments, but the younger generation had an open outlook and had accepted changes.

The work by Penny-Dimri, in relation to host communities attitude towards the Tibetan refugees, brought out how Tibetans refugees being 'recipients of substantial financial assistance from the West they are today the focus of a good deal of envy from their less fortunate Indian neighbors' (1994, p. 280), as a result, a considerable event of conflict has occurred between the Tibetans and the local Indian population of Himachal Pradesh. Such conflicts also have, to a larger extent, brought internal solidarity among the refugees themselves, which can be theoretically linked with what Lewis Coser argued in his functional theorization of conflicts. Further, these conflicts have generated a sense of preserving and maintaining the Tibetan identity to keep intact and alive. The 'refugee tag' has also been acting as an identity marker for the Tibetans; in fact, this aspect has rather acted as a catalyst for the formulation and crystallization of identity among the Tibetans. As among the younger generation, they have narrated that many people from the host society have used the term 'refugee' as a gibe, which made them realize their social and political position of being a refugee. Contextually locating within the argued paradigm of thought, the respondents were enquired about their subjective feeling about being in India; 64.5 percent of the respondents said that being in India is very important to them as the older generation said that the feeling is as if they are living close to his holiness Dalai Lama and the place where lord Buddha preached. The younger generation believes it is important to them because they are getting opportunities that they could not have gotten if they were at their homeland; the rest of the respondents said it is not that important that they had to seek refuge and flee to India to save their lives. So, it is observed that most of the refugees in India are primarily due to the opportunity they get in terms of religious and spiritual proximity to the Dalai Lama.

**Figure 5.20:** Views on their stay in India

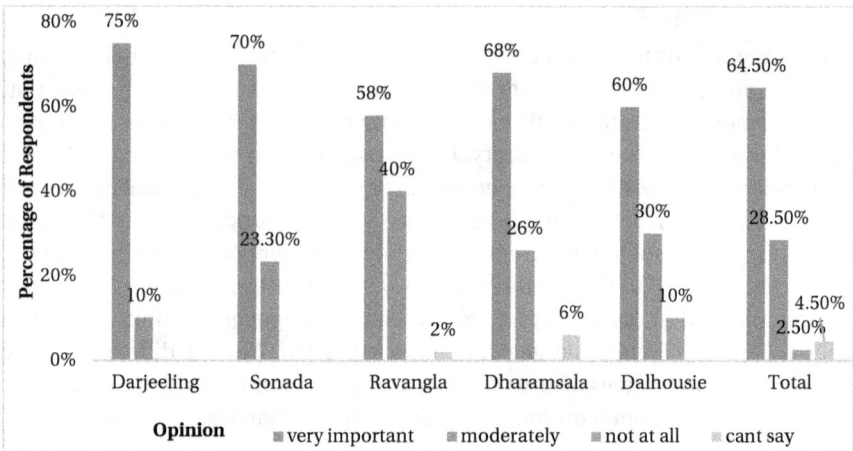

Source: Field Survey October 2016-August 2017

Further, as discussed in chapter four, particularly on the theme of the importance of preserving Tibetan identity, Tibetan culture and society are relatively better when compared with the social system of Indian society, as narrated by a respondent that '…In our society, everyone is treated equally, I heard of the caste system first time when I came to India, how does being born in a caste makes one lower and higher. In the Tibetan culture, everyone is respected, and we are all equal'. This aspect makes her re-evaluate her position of being a Tibetan and how the seemingly non-hierarchical structure of the Tibetan society gave her a pride in it and the morale boost to preserve and sustain the social structure. This aspect has been further accentuated by another argument as 'Nothing has changed for us, we are Tibetans, and we will remain Tibetans, whether we stay in Sikkim or any other part of India. We have a responsibility, and that is to preserve our culture, and we are doing that'.

Such aspects of Tibetan identity have been sustained for long during the lasting political struggle of the Tibetan refugees in India and around the world. During the interaction with the refugees in the Himalayan regions of India, 90 percent of the Tibetans stand for the cause and believe that the struggle should be kept alive until they achieve freedom of Tibet from communist China, as shown in Figure 5.21. They feel that it's very important for them and they should keep a track about the ongoing situation there as they are just refugees in India and they still have families living in Tibet; the rest said it's not that important and are not sure about how they feel about it, as they are more inclined towards their living situation in India as they have been residing here.

**Figure 5.21:** Support for political struggle in Tibet

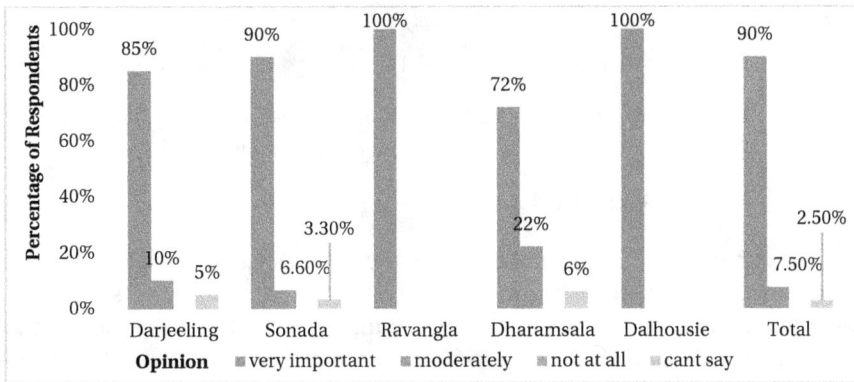

Source: Field Survey October 2016-August 2017

Relative to the above-stated inquiries, when asked about the importance of political activism in India in relation to the Tibetan issues, only 46 percent of the respondents said that the ongoing political issues and activities are very important to them as the second and the third generations are basically a part of India, being born and brought up there, and, as India is the host nation, being politically aware is always advantageous (Figure 5.22). However, 41.5 percent of the respondents feel that it is moderately important in India, but argued that it would have been more significant if they could take and carry out their struggle in Tibet itself under the most conducive democratic condition. In contrast, 5 percent of the respondents replied negatively, as they belonged to the older or the first generation, who have a different concept on the outlook of the world. In their view, the political matters of the host country matter less to them as they are satisfied with life and waiting to breathe their last, and the only thing that satisfies them is the fact that they are close to His Holiness. It was interesting to observe that at Ravangla majority of the respondents moderately or hardly believed in the maintenance of core philosophical ideas of Tibetan compared to other places like Darjeeling, Sonada, Dharmsala, and Dalhousie (fig. 5.19); however, in Ravangla, political activism in India vis-à-vis Tibetan issues is very important to them compared to other places.

**Figure 5.22:** Views on political activism in India vis-à-vis Tibetan issues

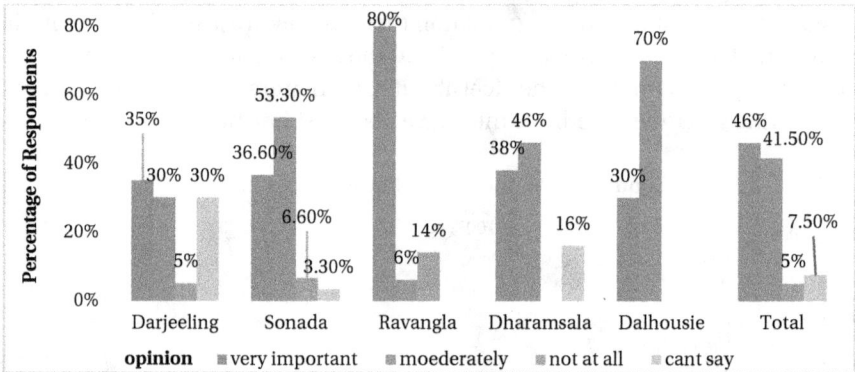

Source: Field Survey October 2016-August 2017

Their experiences in India in relation to the political support provided by the host country, 62.5 percent reported that the host country has been supportive and only 19.5 percent said that the host country has not been supportive. The same question in terms of the rehabilitation was asked, and 51 percent reported that the rehabilitation provided by the nation so far is good; 37.5 percent said that the rehabilitation is very good. 48 percent said that the funds allocated or received are okay, although they said it is not enough. Overall, it can be stated that the majority of the respondents were interacting well with the host community, and they were regularly invited and were helped by the host community. Their integration to host society is largely based on business and education. Most of their visit to the host's home is confined to only festivals. The majority of the respondents, especially those from the younger generations, were more open to inter-community marriages; however, generally, respondents from the older generations were not in favor of intercommunity marriages. The majority of the respondents agreed that knowing local languages like Hindi and Nepali is very important, which can help them integrate better in society. The majority of the respondents preferred to watch Indian movies only for reasons attributed to a wide range of selection. Tibetans consume both Indian and Tibetan cuisines, and they feel that Indian food is palatable and delicious. Even though the majority of respondents believed in better integration with the host society, the maintenance of Tibetan identity is very important for them; therefore, the majority of the respondents, even if they were born in India, feel attached to the idea of Tibet as their homeland. For them being a Tibetan, the race or ethnic background or religion of an individual is very important. Tibetan identity is deeply rooted in their everyday life, questions related to their personal values and moral standards were administered, and almost all of them believed in providing support to the political struggle in Tibet.

Chapter 6

# Gender and Identity Issues among the Tibetan Refugees

## Introduction

Western literature describes Tibetan women as independent and strong individuals, raised to play an active and responsible role in society. Men and women are not considered to be the same, but in organizing the community and its capacities in a geographically severe environment such as the Tibetan – it has proved more profitable to have a division between the sexes that is loose rather than strongly hierarchal. This way, women have gained equal responsibility that motivates them, and they play a significant role in society. However, in recent years this image has been questioned principally in Western gender literature (Goldstein-Kyaga, 1993). Modern scholars have argued that the political systems of the old Tibet were highly unequal. Campbell (1996) and Willis (1989) stress that Buddhism is categorized by rules and structures that continuously discriminate against women, and there is no gender equality. In exile, the democratic process initiated by the Dalai Lama has placed the old structures of Tibetan society in a modern context.

From their perilous flight into India, the Tibetan refugees are recognized as one of the most successful refugee communities today. Goldstein arrived at Bylakuppe, where a Tibetan settlement was established in 1962, and within five years the refugee settlement at Bylakuppe had 'become a tremendous economic success' (Goldstein, 1978, p. 399). He observed that there were little incidences of emotional or mental disorder. Girija Saklaini's (1984) research on Tibetan refugees living in Dharamsala mentioned work ethics, lack of sexual division of labor, and simple entrepreneurship as key to the success of the community. A lot of focus in research has been on studying their administrative setup, their attempt to continue their freedom struggle and in capturing their success stories in exile. However, very little attention has been given to the struggle the Tibetan women face in exile. The 1951 Refugee Conventions and international laws have been gender blind; refugee women continue to be discriminated in various spheres because of their gender, and emphasis continues to be on male-centric studies and policies.

The axial focus of this chapter is to address this lacuna in research, where there is scant information highlighting the struggle Tibetan women encounter. The aim is to study the status of the Tibetan women and the changes, if any, with regard to their autonomy, decision-making process, inheritance, marriage customs, and political participation. To understand the status of the women in the present Tibetan society, the structures of the pre-modern Tibet need to be explored.

## Status of Women in Pre-Modern Tibet

The relative isolation of Tibet with the rest of the world may be one of the reasons for the scant availability of literature and data on the status women had in Tibet prior to exile. Hence, there are conflicting views on the status of Tibetan women before their exile. Several studies claim that women enjoyed a remarkably high position in Tibetan society compared to their counterparts in other Asian societies (Chodon, 2007). Earlier, there were no distinctions in political, economic, or intellectual spheres; every task was attended and performed in accordance with one's aptitude and ability. Men and women in Tibet enjoyed equal rights and status in society (Chotsho, 1997). Bell (1991), who studied the social structure of Tibet, noted (pp. 155-156):

> When a traveler enters Tibet from neighboring China or India, few things impress him more vigorously or more deeply than the position of the Tibetan women. They are not kept in seclusion, as are Indian women. Accustomed to mix with the other sex throughout their lives, they are at ease with men, and can hold their own as well as any women in the world. There were regional differences, in the treatment of women. Also, being a deeply religious society and being relatively isolated from the world, modern education and democratic participation was unknown to them… The condition of Tibetan women with regard to men, especially in the provinces, may be considered as surpassing the ideal of western women, so far as the theory of equality of rights between the sexes is concerned.

He further mentioned that they did not rank a son higher than a daughter; therefore, female infanticide had never been found in Tibet. Women usually enjoyed much more freedom and prestige in old Tibet than in other Asian countries.

According to some scholars—Josh (1967), Sponberg (1992) and Harris (1999)—the high position Tibetan women occupy in society can be attributed to the influence of Tibetan Buddhism. Buddhism is promulgated as a gender-egalitarian religion; however, there is research that highlights the discrepancy between the ground reality and practice pertaining to the treatment and status of women. Chotsho, in her work *A Drop from an Ocean: The Status of Women in Tibetan Society*, has studied the status of women in society according to changes in lexical terms. She mentions that discrimination against women originated during King Srong btsan sgam po's era. Gradually terms were coined with a degree of comparisons based on gender. For instance, 'terms like *sky es bas rgyal* (victorious by birth), *sky es bas mtho* (higher by birth), *skyes bu rab* (superior person) and so forth are used to indicate men. Women were denoted by terms like *skyes dman* (lower by birth), *nag mo* (the black one), etc. Some common terms in the Tibetan language like *Kyemen* (inferior birth) and *tsamdenma* (she who has limitations) illustrate the low and denigrated perception of woman's position and her role in society' (Chotsho, 1997, p. 60). During King Srong btsan sgam po's rule, he initiated an open policy in the field of education and developed friendly relations with neighboring countries. Even in politically, economically, and intellectually developed countries like China and Nepal, the inegalitarian practice of discrimination against women was prevalent. In these countries, the dominion of men over women was strong, and the women had no rights; interracial marriages and cultural exchange with these countries may have instated the concept of male superiority in Tibet.

Historically, Tibetan families were patrilineal and extended. Within these clans, there were both polygamous and monogamous marriage systems. A wealthy and noble family would often marry one woman to two of her family's brothers, giving her 'special status' and wealth (Neumaier-Dargyay, 2002). She mentions that within monogamous marriages, divorce was not only common but initiated by both men and women.

According to Aziz (1987), the dominance and social status a woman had was in accordance with other rules of behavior. A woman had to be mindful of rules and protocol in public, which demanded passivity and compliance. Social situations demanded much more from a woman than a man could be forgiven (Aziz, 1987, p. 180). An aspect of the inequality of the position between men and women could be found observed in rituals. An important feature of the nomadic ritual was the yogurt vow. In this, the bride had to prepare the yogurt, which was considered an auspicious food, but there was no equivalent for the groom. Thus, whereas women might conduct trade as men did, men did not make yogurt (Klein, 1985 as cited in Rajput, 2012).

A Tibetan woman had very little choice when it came to the selection of her spouse. A son was consulted by the parents, but a daughter hardly ever was. It often happened that a girl was led away under the pretext of going on a pilgrimage and was introduced to her husband at the gate of his house where she was going to live (Aziz, 1987, p. 169). However, according to Bell, there was a growing practice where young men would choose their own brides. This was more common among the peasants and traders than among the gentry (Bell, 1991, p. 175). Marriage was arranged by parents and other relatives of the boy and the girl who was going to be married (Klein, 1985 as cited in Rajput, 2012). If there was a daughter in the family and no son, the daughter's husband lived in the house of her family. He adopted the family name and took a position subordinate to his wife in the management of the family estate (Bell, 1991, p. 157).

Unlike their other counterparts in Asia, Tibetan women were not limited or confined to their homes. There are written records that document the political participation of women, which increased dramatically when the Chinese Government instituted the first Tibetan women's patriotic organization in the early 1950s (Coelho, 2016).[5]

However, along with experiencing freedom in pre-modern Tibet, the women also faced restrictions related to their gender, which varied across regions, occupations, and class (Butler, 2007). These experiences influenced the Tibetan women refugees' response to their situation in exile. The issues and concerns of the women in exile are multidimensional. From our conversations and interaction with Tibetan women of different generations and in different field settings, we have attempted to understand Tibetan women's experience of their refugee status. Many Tibetan women are using their refugee status to empower themselves; although there is progress made on various fronts, some of the features of the traditional society have continued.

---

[5] On March 8, 1953 the Chinese Government formed the Lhasa Patriotic Women's Association. Various other women's organisation was established in Tibet during the next few years. The Chinese established these Women's organisations as a support group that would be pro Chinese and whom they could influence. But as Chinese atrocities in Tibet escalated, some Tibetans belonging to these Women's organisations, mobilised themselves to protest against Chinese aggression. The main concerns of the Tibetan women's organisations were the protection of the Dalai Lama, and the preservation of Tibetan culture. In the days leading up to the Tibetan Uprising of 10 March 1959, these women's' organisation got more proactive. In a celebration called by the Chinese to celebrate the anniversary of PWA on 8 March 1959, several Tibetan women shouted anti-Chinese slogans. On March 12 three thousand Tibetan women gathered outside the Potala Palace where they passed a resolution asking the Chinese to leave Tibet. They then marched on the streets of Lhasa raising anti-Chinese slogans and went to each of the Foreign missions in Lhasa, including the Indian mission, requesting their Government's support in expelling the Chinese. Chinese repercussions were quick, and many Tibetan women were subsequently publicly executed.

## Family

The designation 'head of the household', also termed 'head of the family', is applied to one who has the authority to exercise control on the family and to support the dependent members is founded upon a moral or legal obligation or duty. The head of the family is the one who caters to the need of the family and acts as the main backbone of the family. Taklha (2005), in her work *Women of Tibet*, affirms that

> [w]omen of Tibet did enjoy greater freedom than women of our neighboring countries... [b]ut Tibet's social structure was patriarchal. Although women had substantial power and freedom in the homes and in the community, the grandfather, father, or an elder brother took all the major decisions in the family. Women played a secondary and a submissive role in the community, but an important role.

According to a Tibetan saying, 'Father is the main person in the family, but the foundation of the home is the mother' (Taklha, 2005, p.4). This saying highlights the prevalence of patriarchy and its role in shaping the lives of Tibetan women and clearly demarcating the private space of the home for the woman.

### *Head of the Family*

**Figure 6.1:** Head of the family

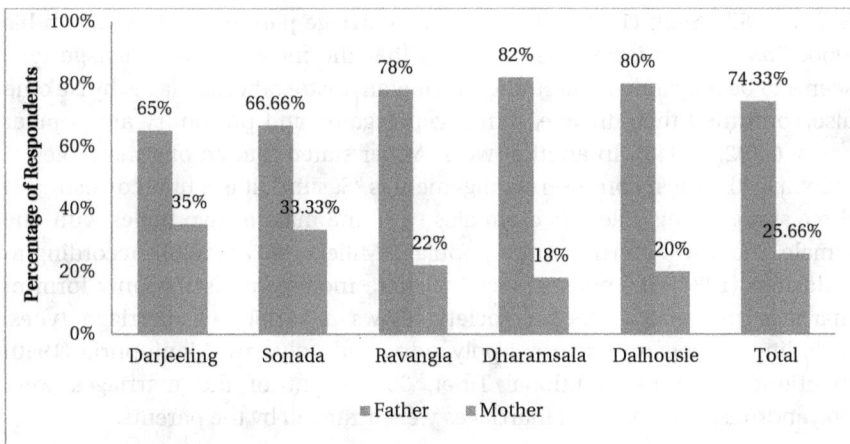

Source: Field Survey October 2016-August 2017

In order to find the prevalence of patriarchy and its role in shaping the lives of Tibetan women, first we checked on the Head of the family. It was found that

74 percent of the respondents in the study reported that the father is the head of the family, supporting the prevalent notion that the Tibetan community is patrilineal; 26 percent of respondents stated that their mother is the head of the family. Among the various field setting where the survey was conducted, Dharamsala recorded 82 percent of the respondents stated that the father is the head of the household. The joint family structure of Tibetan society is giving way to a nuclear type of family. The small areas allotted to the refugee families, lack of money, and no landholdings are some of the reasons for the disintegrating of the joint family. Majupuria (1990), in her work, mentioned that since Tibetans are leaving their country and settling in places where there is no land, the family structure is changing. The fact that most Tibetan refugees left Tibet not as families, but as individuals has affected the dynamics of kinship.

## Marriage

Works, like *Tibetans* by Liandi (1986) and *Tibetan Marriages and Families in Tibet before 'Democratic Reform'* by Chongzhong (1991) discussed the traditional form of marriage in Tibetan society and the social and economic reasons for the existence of these marriage practices. Jianhua, Rongqing, and Shuzhang's (1992) and Wenmei, Yi, and Rongjun's (1992) works have collected demographic data that focussed on marriage structure, the age difference between husband and wife, rates of unmarried, divorce, and widows in Tibetan society. In addition to this, there are works that describe the marriage patterns that are traditionally common in Tibetan culture (Stein, 1972; Nakane, 1992; Miller, 1987). Stein (1972) described the marriage patterns of Tibetans in his work *Tibetan Civilisation*. He believed that the most typical marriage type seems to be polyandry. The studies of Tibetan aristocracy marriages by Nakane also confirmed that 'divorce, remarry, polygamy and polyandry are popular cases' (1992, p. 343). In another work, Miller stated that among marriages of Tibetans, 'the most common arrangement is "Sasum", it is a unit consisting of three spouses, regardless two females with one male or two males with one female, the last pattern is more popular' (Miller, 1987, p. 338). According to Goldstein (1987), in modern society, where monogamy is the only form of marriage permitted, Tibetan society allows a variety of marriage types, including monogamy, fraternal polyandry, and polygyny. Manjupuria (1990) mentioned that in traditional Tibet, 30 percent of the marriages were polyandrous, and nearly all marriages were arranged by the parents.

## *Age of Marriage*

**Figure 6.2:** Age of marriage

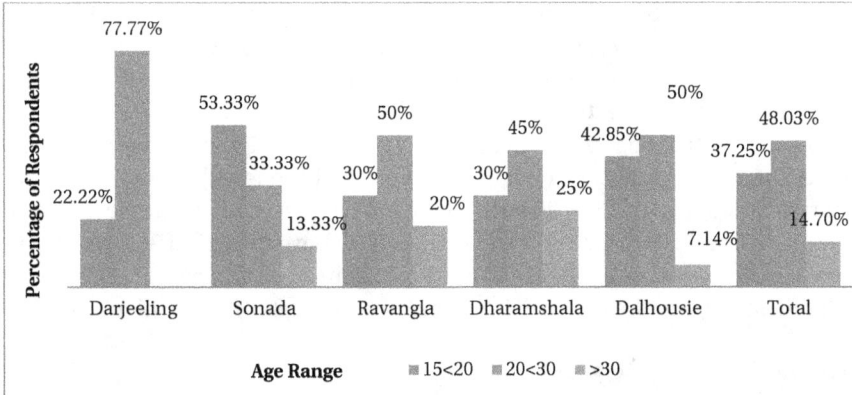

Source: Field Survey October 2016-August 2017

Marriageable age (or marriage age) is the minimum age at which a person is allowed by law to marry, either as a right or subject to parental or other forms of consent. Age and other prerequisites to marriage vary between jurisdictions, but marriage age for women is often 18. As seen from the above data, the age at which the female respondents got married varied. The age of marriage and the difference in the generation of Tibetan refugees are co-related. Likewise, the first generation of the Tibetan refugees were likely to marry at an early age looking at the customs and traditions of those times; with the time and in later generations, the age of marriage has increased. This may be due to the governing laws, education, and self-awareness that has increased over time. In Darjeeling, 77.77 percent of females married between the age of 20 to 30 years, while 22.22 percent of the respondents from Darjeeling got married between the ages of 15 to 20 years; it was seen that the first mostly belonged to the second and third generations of Tibetan refugees. Likewise, in Sonada, 55.33 percent of female respondents married at the ages of 15 to 20 years; the reason being the same as the above, the respondents are the first generation Tibetan refugees and in the time phase at which they got married, marrying at an early age was not an issue as it is now; 33.33 percent got married at the ages of 20 to 30 years which is an acceptable age, only 13.33 percent of the respondents had married at the age of above 30 years. In Ravangla, the age of marriage of 50 percent of the respondents was between 20 to 30 years; 30 percent married at the age of 15 to 20 years, and these early marriages were seen among the older generation; 20 percent married after 30 years, as the respondents did not find it necessary to marry early due to family obligation and situations, the age of marriage was delayed, and for the rest, it was about the compatibility. In Dharamsala, 30 percent of the female respondents married between the age of 15 to 20 years, 45 percent got married between the age of 20 to 30 years, and 25 percent married above the age of 30 years. Similarly, in Dalhousie, 42.85 percent of the female respondents got married at an early age (15-20 years), whereas 50 percent married at the age of 20 to 30 years, and only 7.14 percent of the female respondents married after attaining the age of 30 years; the early marriage is associated with the age group of the respondents: the higher the age group, the lower the marriage age. Overall, 37.25 percent of the female respondents got married at the age of 15 to 20 years, 48.03 percent got married at the age of 20 to 30 years, and only 14.70 percent got married above the age of 30 years. As we can see, the age composition of the respondents and the age of marriage is related: the higher the age of the respondents, the lower the age of marriage.

### Nature of Marriage Payments

Jack Goody (1974) has theorized that the nature of marriage payments depends on the extent of women's contributions to the domestic economy and that such contributions are more substantial under horticultural and pastoral regimes. Among Tibetans, the nature of marriage payment is the bridewealth; it is a gift of money or goods given to the bride's relatives by the groom or his kin. Marital payments usually included tools of production and other necessities such as tents, clothes, household goods, and so forth, but cash gifts are seldom given. Livestock is given priority as a marital payment since domestic animals are essential for work and life. Even for the Tibetans living in India, the nature of marriage payment has not changed, and the bridewealth has continued. However, the articles which were given earlier, such as livestock, are now being replaced by other goods and items of daily importance since many of the respondents were living in the settlement camps and did not have space to keep animals. 91 percent of the respondents in the study believed that there have been no changes in the marriage transaction; this was particularly felt by the respondents in Ravangla.

### Divorce

The voluntary separation of married couples might take four models: separation, divorce, forsaking, and marriage invalid, and there are different legal definitions in different countries for these models (Goode, 1982, p. 209). Divorce is defined as the legal termination of a marriage, but in its real sense, there is a lot more to it than just the end of a relationship. It has been argued that Tibetan society has no moral proscription against divorce; it usually occurred by mutual consent of the parties, because there had been no restrictive marriage registration systems for a very long time in Tibet, divorce was relatively a simple issue in most cases. 'There were no procedures required for divorce, and no need for witnesses or written documents. ...Women can remarry; remarriages of men and women were treated the same as the first marriage' (Liandi, 1986, p. 202). MA (2011) pointed out that there has been growth in the rate of divorce in urban areas of Lhasa. Tibetan refugee Settlements have Tibetan Settlement officers who, at times, adjudicate and decide disputes and decide on matrimonial offenses and divorce. So, Tibetan refugees living in India have followed and continued the custom of mutual divorce with the intervention of elders and village leaders (like Panchayat) and settlement officers. From Figure 6.3, it can be seen that in Darjeeling, Sonada, and Dharamsala, the women have full right to file for divorce; whereas in Ravangla and Dalhousie, 96 percent and 80 percent of women mentioned that they could file for divorce; overall, 94 percent of the women has a right to file for divorce.

**Figure 6.3:** Right to file divorce

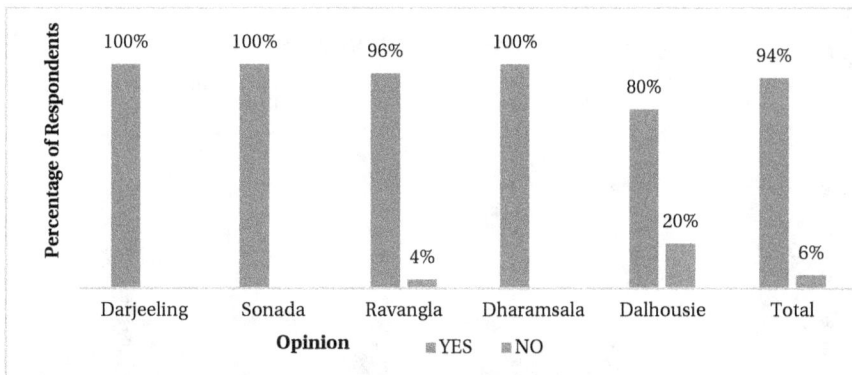

Source: Field Survey October 2016-August 2017

## *Family Planning*

Family planning is a program that allows individuals and couples to determine the number of children to have, when to have them, and at what intervals. This is achieved through the voluntary use of various devices, sexual practices, chemicals, drugs, or surgical procedures that interfere with the normal process of ovulation, fertilization, and implantation. In our study conducted in different states, we tried to determine if women had a choice in family planning practices. It has been found out that 92.5 percent of women had a choice in the family planning process, whereas only 7.5 percent of women mentioned that they did not have a choice. However, 7.5 percent reported that they could not voice their opinion regarding family planning; they belonged to the older generation of the Tibetan refugees who were conservative by nature. From the above graph, we can conclude that a Tibetan refugee woman in India has the freedom to practice family planning and control the family size.

**Figure 6.4:** Family Planning

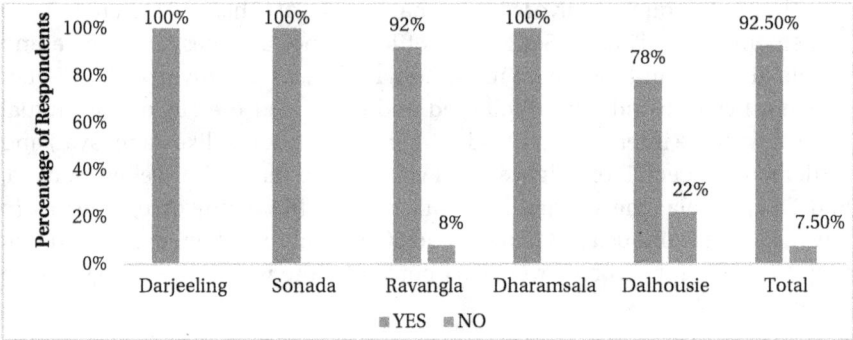

Source: Field Survey October 2016-August 2017

**Inheritance of Property**

**Figure 6.5:** Inheritance of Property

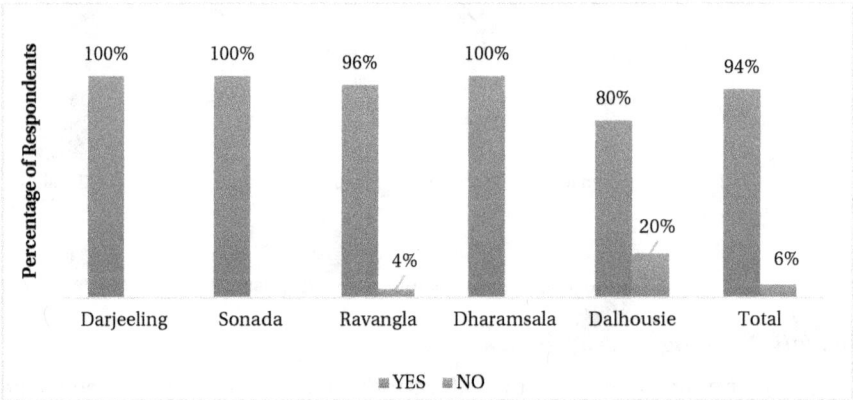

Source: Field Survey October 2016-August 2017

Lexically, in the legal sense, inheritance is defined as 'a perpetual or continuing right which a man and his heirs have to an estate; an estate which a man has by descent as heir to another, or which he may transmit to another as his heir; an estate derived from an ancestor to an heir' in the course of law' (Fine Dictionary, n.d.). The practice of Inheritance in all kinds of movable and immovable parental property is a global practice, but some of the traditional societies are characterized by gender discrimination in the form of either total deprivation or partial deprivation. The exploitation of women in the matter of inheritance is not an odd event of human history; rather, it is one of the disparities perpetuating women's suffocation in different compartments of life throughout the world. Inheritance is an integral part of family life, and depriving a child of each gender of entitlement in parental property is tantamount to diminish the conception of the family as a social unit (Leach, 1982). It is the cultural environment that degrades the status of women from all walks of life, including inheritance (Dascalopoulos, 1990). Marx considers women as a separate class of society and further makes the statement that they are vulnerable to various kinds of exploitation of men's dominance (Abraham, 1990). If a man fails to decide the distribution of his estate or leaves a will before he dies, the state stands responsible for doing it as per its framed law (Simon, 1978). Inheritance, in Tibetan society, was on a per capita basis: each son had a right to an equal share. In reality, people took efforts to prevent dividing their property. For example, they engaged in polyandrous marriages to concentrate male labor within the household and pass assets intact from one generation to the next.

Furthermore, the parents or eldest brother could refuse to bestow anything to a junior brother who wished to marry monogamously and establish a separate household (Goldstein, 1987). Parents could also eliminate sons from the inheritance equation by sending one to a monastery or to another household. In Tibetan society, the daughters of a family receive their bridewealth when they marry and leave their parents' family to join that of their husbands. There is one exception. If the family has no sons, they take the bridegrooms of its daughters into the family. In such a case the position of the daughter is stronger as she is the owner of the property, her family name is adopted by the bridegroom, and her sons have the same rights of inheritance.

**Figure 6.6:** Selection of Nominee

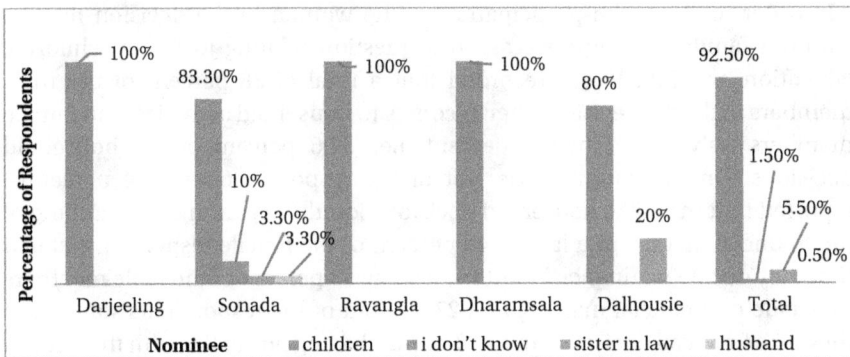

Source: Field Survey October 2016-August 2017

Not only the family structure, but marriage customs have also changed. In traditional Tibet, 30 percent of the marriages were polyandrous, and nearly all marriages were arranged by the parents. According to Majupuria (1990), although polyandry had died down, the paternal right on the property of the family still exists (Majupuria, 1990, p. 130). According to our study, in Darjeeling, Sonada, and Dharamsala, the women had the full inheritance right, whereas in Ravangla and Dalhousie it is 96 percent and 80 percent, respectively.

The nominee is the one that the individual nominates to give all the property after his or her death. According to the study, 92.5 percent of the women chose their children as their nominee to their property after death, this could be their sons or their daughters, whereas 1.5 percent was uncertain as to whom they would nominate; 5.5 percent mentioned that they nominate their sister-in-law and 0.5 percent mentioned that they would nominate their husbands.

## Decision Making

The decision-making authority in a family also helps us to analyze whether the authority rests with the male or the female members of the family.

Decision making is the ability to influence decisions that affect one's public and private life. Women's equal and meaningful participation and influence in decision-making at all levels, and in both formal and informal spaces, is fundamentally a question of social justice— women have the right to participate in decisions that affect their lives. Women's participation refers to women's ability to participate, at all levels, and in all aspects of household, public and political issues, including activism. The phrase 'participation and influence' refers to the equal and meaningful participation of women in decision-making. This means considering not only if women are represented but also the extent to which they are able to be actively involved and influence decision making processes through their participation.

In order to check the participation of the women in the decision making within a family, women were asked a question relating to family, children, education, religion. It was recorded that a total of 38 percent of the male members make the decision when it comes to household activities, and female members only lagged by 0.5 percent, i.e., 37.5 percent of the household decisions. On the contrary, the rest of the respondents—i.e. 24 percent— reported that they take household decisions jointly. Regarding the handling of the financial matters in a family, 40 percent of the female respondents stated that they decide on financial matters, leaving 33 percent of the male members to decide on financial matters, and 27 percent of the respondents stated that they take financial decisions jointly. The purchasing power lies with the female, i.e., 41 percent of the female members make the decision on what should be purchased; likewise, 40 percent of female members decide on the education,

37 percent female of members make the decision on travel, and 39 percent of the male members decide on religious activities. Although the father or the man is the head of the household, women in the family decide either jointly or separately.

**Figure 6.7:** Spheres of decision making by Tibetan men and women

| Domains of Decision | Sex | Darjeeling | Sonada | Ravangla | Dharamsala | Dalhousie | Total |
|---|---|---|---|---|---|---|---|
| Household Matters | Male | 35% | 26.6% | 48% | 32% | 42% | 38% |
| | Female | 55% | 50% | 28% | 30% | 40% | 37.5% |
| | Total | 10% | 23.3% | 24% | 38% | 18% | 24.5% |
| Financial Matters | Male | 15% | 20% | 28% | 54% | 32% | 33% |
| | Female | 75% | 53.3% | 42% | 26% | 30% | 40% |
| | Total | 10% | 26.6% | 30% | 20% | 38% | 27% |
| Purchase of Goods | Male | 30% | 30% | 40% | 32% | 28% | 32.5% |
| | Female | 60% | 43.3% | 42% | 32% | 42% | 41.5% |
| | Total | 10% | 26.6% | 18% | 36% | 30% | 26% |
| Education | Male | 20% | 16.6% | 44% | 36% | 48% | 36.5% |
| | Female | 70% | 50% | 36% | 38% | 28% | 40% |
| | Total | 10% | 33.3% | 20% | 26% | 24% | 23.5% |
| Travel | Male | 40% | 20% | 30% | 38% | 30% | 31.5% |
| | Female | 45% | 53.3% | 38% | 32% | 28% | 37% |
| | Total | 15% | 26.6% | 32% | 30% | 42% | 31.5% |
| Religious Ceremonies | Male | 45% | 30% | 42% | 40% | 20% | 39.5% |
| | Female | 40% | 40% | 40% | 30% | 40% | 37.5% |
| | Total | 15% | 30% | 18% | 30% | 20% | 23% |

Source: Field Survey October 2016-August 2017

### Bank Account or Savings for Women

Banking and savings are a small gesture in the path of empowerment of women. Having a bank account or savings account makes them independent and strong. Amongst all the survey areas, only in Dalhousie 0.2 percent had no savings or bank account, whereas all the field setting female members had a savings or bank account. The reason to validate the case of 0.2 percent having no bank or savings account could be that they belonged to the older generations of Tibetan refugees, and did not understand the banking mechanism.

*Spending Power*

Figure 6.8 shows that 98 percent of the respondents can spend their money and save as per their desire, and only 2 percent of the respondents were seen not having a say in terms of spending their money as desired.

**Figure 6.8:** Spending power

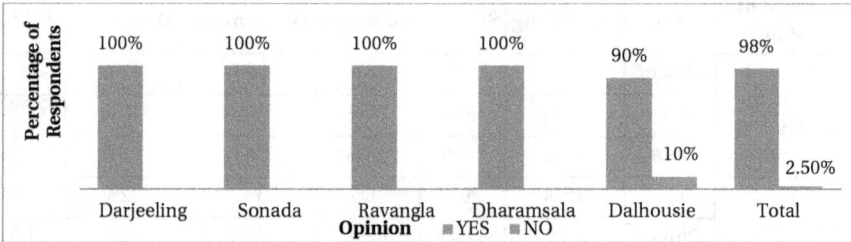

Source: Field Survey October 2016-August 2017

*Recreational Activities for Women*

The purpose of recreation is to give mental relaxation to the women after all the household chores. In the case of Tibetan women, recreational activities are different since religion is an integral part of their lives. The data shows that 44.5 percent of the respondents were involved with religious work as their recreational activities, for 26.4 percent of the respondents' recreation takes the form of community work, and 24 percent of the respondents enjoy going out with friends, which is predominant in Darjeeling. Similarly, more female respondents from Darjeeling and Sonada watch television for their recreational activity.

**Figure 6.9:** Activities of refugee women during their recreational time

| Recreational Activities | Darjeeling | Sonada | Ravangla | Dharamsala | Dalhousie | Total |
|---|---|---|---|---|---|---|
| Community work | 20% | 16.6% | 24% | 56% | 8% | 26.5% |
| Watching Television | 30% | 33.3% | 4% | 4% | 4% | 11% |
| Shopping | 10% | 16.6% | 6% | 2% | 2% | 6% |
| Religious work | 35% | 20% | 56% | 34% | 62% | 44.5% |
| Outing with friends | 55% | 13.3% | 10% | 4% | 24% | 24% |

Source: Field Survey October 2016-August 2017

## Domestic Violence

**Figure 6.10:** Domestic violence

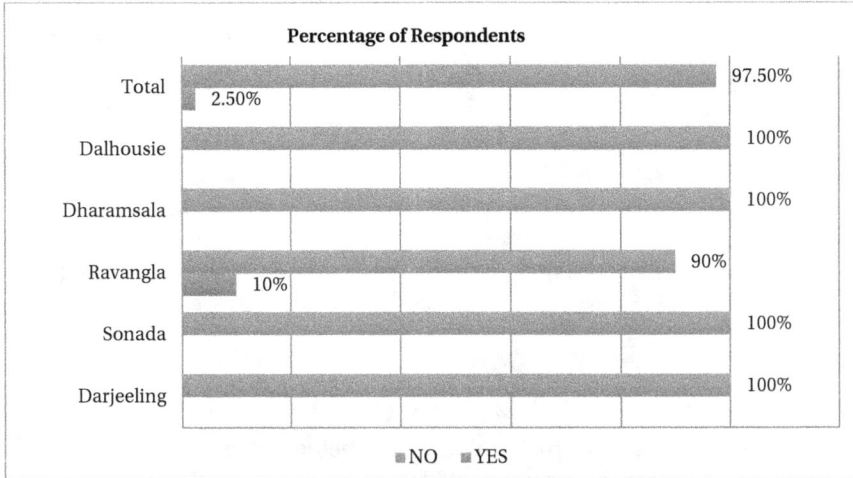

Source: Field Survey October 2016-August 2017

While a large number of Tibetans have suffered from some form of abuse or the other in exile, women are victims of additional abuse where gender, religion, patriarchy and refugee status - all combined to form a concoction which becomes very oppressive and abusive towards women. Domestic violence means any violent or aggressive behavior of any person within the home. Violence may take the form of physical aggression, sexual abuse, and emotional abuse etc. During the interview, many of the community members opined beating is acceptable if a wife does not behave herself or if she crosses her boundary. However, it was considered unacceptable to beat a woman if she performed her duties diligently and with sincerity. The notion that beating is acceptable if a wife commits a mistake or does not properly perform her duties and tasks has also been recorded in the study *When Wife-Beating is not necessarily Abuse* by Rajan (2018). She mentions that women are being taught to adhere to abuse and accept community norms that help them socialize. In our study, only 2.5 percent of the respondents had reported domestic violence. Ravangla had reported 10 percent of domestic violence cases against women. However, the figure does not mean that violence against women is almost non-existing as it seems when looking at it. The sample is not representative in comparison with the number of Tibetan women living in the areas where the survey took place. According to our understanding, violence against women exists among the Tibetans, but it is not something they want to talk about; it is often hidden in Tibetan society.

## Women's Political Participation

**Figure 6.11:** Political participation of women

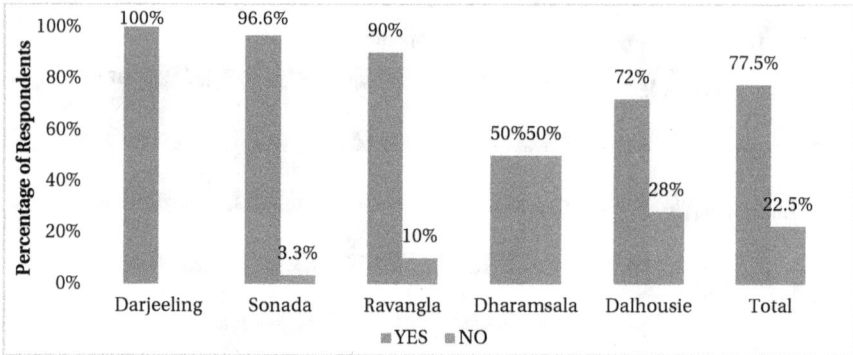

Source: Field Survey October 2016-August 2017

Political participation is broadly defined as being a process through which individual plays a role in the political life of his society, has the opportunity to take part in deciding what the common goals of that society are and the best way of achieving these goals. Political participation refers to actual participation in these voluntary activities by which members of the society share in the selection of rules and directly or indirectly in the formulation of public policy Singh (2000). Tibetan women were politically active even prior to their exile. But this assertiveness and articulation in the political sphere have only grown in exile. The present study shows that 78 percent of women support and take part in political activities.

### *Women's Participation in the Tibet Freedom Movement*

The Tibetan Women's Association is the second largest Tibetan NGO in exile, established in 1959, and again re-established in exile in 1984. Currently, the TWA has fifty-six regional chapters all over the world and seventeen thousand members. Being a women's organization, it is politically involved on various levels and addresses many issues relating to women. According to our study, women participate in the freedom movement of Tibet; in places like Darjeeling, Sonada, and Ravangla, there is 100 percent participation of the women, whereas in Dharamsala and Dalhousie it is 64 percent and 90 percent participation of the respectively.

**Figure 6.12:** Women's participation in Tibet freedom movement

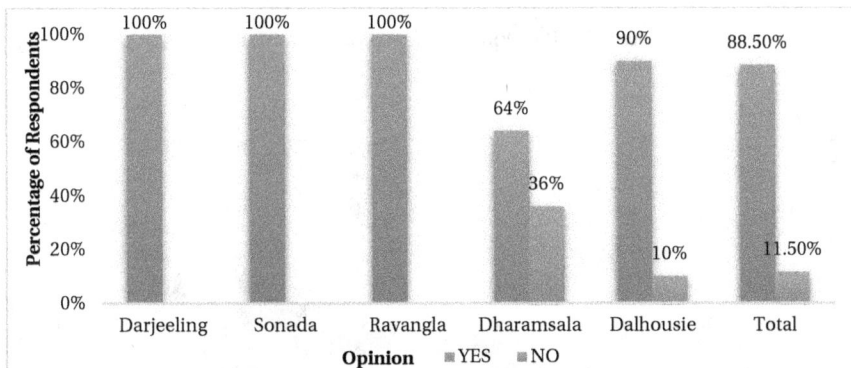

Source: Field Survey October 2016-August 2017

## Priority in Life

**Figure 6.13:** Priority in life

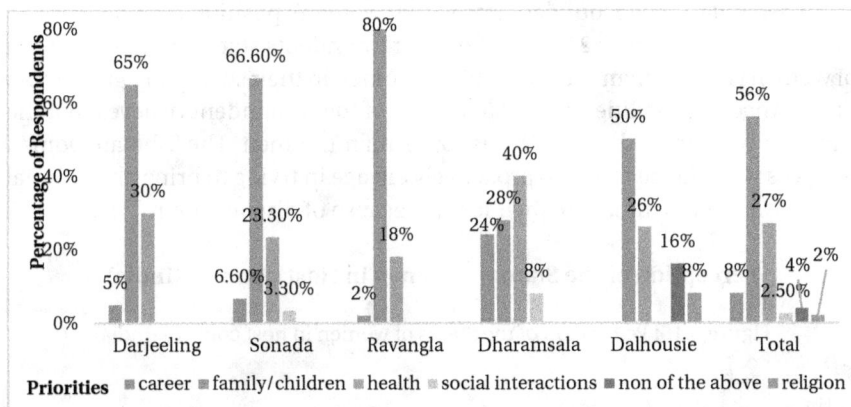

Source: Field Survey October 2016-August 2017

Financial security is the top phrase that comes to mind when thinking of success, but women prioritize their children. From Figure 6.13, we can see that the most important thing in the lives of the respondents was their children, i.e., 56 percent. 27 percent mentioned that health should also be a priority, 8 percent mentioned career, 2.5 percent felt that social interactions should be important as it helps in integration, for 2 percent religion and participation in religious activities was important, and 0.4 percent mentioned that none of the above was important for them.

## Position of Women Comparative to Men

**Figure 6.14:** Position of women comparative to men

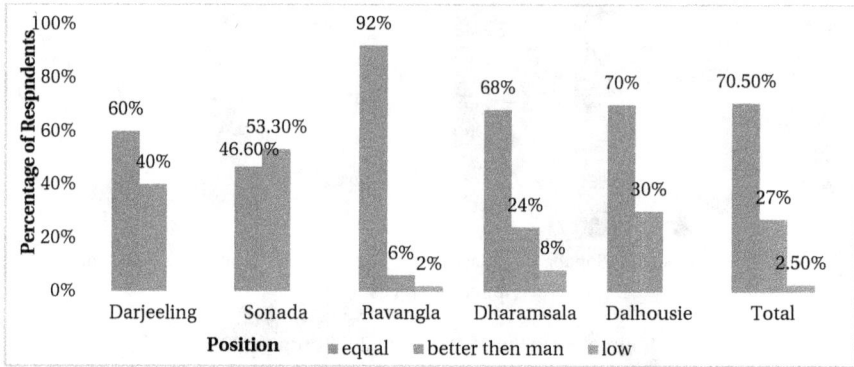

Source: Field Survey October 2016-August 2017

Tibetan refugee believes that the status of the women in their society is good, 70.50 percent of the respondent stated that women's position is equal to men's in their society, another 27 percent of the respondents stated that the position of women is better than the men and the women in their society are given more importance and facilities. Only 2.5 percent of the respondent believes that the status of women in their society is lower than the men. The Tibetan women refugees in India are trying to proactively engage in trying to bring about social transformation to minimize their losses because of displacement.

## Perception of the Status of Women in Host Country (India)

**Figure 6.15:** Perception of the Status of women in host country (India)

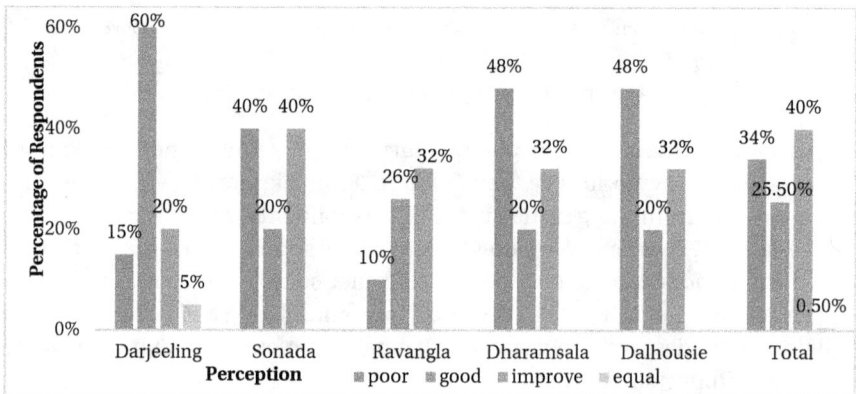

Source: Field Survey October 2016-August 2017

Studying the position of the Indian women, 40 percent of the respondents believe that the position of the Indian women is better from earlier times, 34 percent of the respondent believes that the position of the women in India is still in poor condition and needs to be improved and 25.5 percent believes that the position of women is good in India.

Many felt that the low position and status that the Indian women experience is to go with the prevalence of the caste system. According to their understanding, the interplay of caste, gender, and patriarchy is responsible for the subordinate position of Indian women.

## Observation and Discussion

The concerns and issues that the Tibetan women refugees experience in exile are multidimensional and manifold; they have tried to counter their experiences of loss and displacement by improving their conditions of life. The refugee status is seen as a tool of empowerment by many of the women.

Generally, women experience higher rates of unemployment than men due to cultural and educational handicaps arising out of illiteracy and lack of occupational experience. In our study, Figure 3.5 shows that 14.2 percent of female family members have education below matriculation, 8.8 percent are illiterate, 6.5 percent are graduate, 3.5 percent are postgraduate, and 1.7 percent have a diploma. Unlike the female family members, male members of the family are more educated, but female members are enrolled in postgraduate and diploma courses more than the men (2.5 percent of the male members are postgraduate which is lesser than the females; 1.5 percent of the male members are diploma holders, again lesser than females).

However, among the Tibetans in India, it is observed that occupational disparity between the sexes is minimal. Tibetan women in all the study areas were seen to be engaged in seasonal occupations like sweaters and jewelry selling. In fact, the seasonal business of sweaters and jewelry selling is one of the major occupations of Tibetans in exile. A 45-year-old respondent from Dharamsala narrated that 'when we came to India, we were given jobs as road construction workers ... this was very difficult for many of us as we had never done it, many of us were not well and then working on high altitudes made us further sick. When we were relocated to different settlements, we started selling sweaters to earn extra income, and we realized that this was a very profitable business'. It was an interesting observation that when women took to sweater selling, the men stayed back to look after the family. This seasonal occupation of the Tibetan women has changed the family dynamics in their exile homes.

Another respondent sharing her experience mentioned, '... most of the women in our society work, Tibetan women are tough ... (laughed) and added we can take care of our men. She further mentioned that earning gives confidence and self-esteem'. As apparent from the data, women had a choice in decision making, in important matters relating to children, health, saving and this is attributed to their economic empowerment. They took decisions either independently or along with their husbands. It was interesting that children took priority over health or career for most of them. They were also seen having their own shops and selling goods of religious significance or seen running small tea stalls and supporting their family. According to another respondent, '... I feel confident with the money I earn; I can spend the money I have; I have a saving bank account, and being economically independent gives me more space to share my thoughts'. The household continues to be headed by a male member, as evident from the data, but many of the households are now headed by women; this can be a socio-cultural consequence of the economic empowerment of women. In the words of a respondent, '... father being the head of the family is just in conversation, in most of the houses now women have taken center stage and do all the work ... they are the breadwinners'. Further, with facilities and support from the Government of India, many Tibetan women are getting scholarships and are receiving modern education, and hence are on the lookout for diverse occupations.

Earlier, polygamous marriages—particularly polyandric form and 'marriage by capture'—were traditionally prevalent among the Tibetans. Haddix (1999) pointed out that polyandry was a widespread practice among the Tibetans, which, to an extent, had become the cultural ideal of Tibetans prior to Chinese occupation. Studies have shown that the probabilistic rationale and advantages behind polyandric practices were for population regulation as well as for broadening the support base for countenance in overcoming the harsh and difficult environment. However, the study has not encountered any prevalence of such institutional practices, which could be because of different environmental locales both in terms of social and natural. Socially, the spirit of the host society discourages polygamy of all forms. Presently, monogamy has become the most acceptable form among Tibetans in India. However, there are no visible changes in the system of marriage payment, and the bridewealth continues as the acceptable form of payment.

Further, the story voices the dilemma of the woman as socially constructed norms of the society are changing, bigamy is quite prevalent in the Nepali society, but it creates a problem for the Tibetan women '... My husband brought another woman; she was a Nepali lady and was beautiful ... I looked quite old in front of her. I accepted her'. She recounted, '... this woman would drink with my husband and enjoy. I learnt that she had left her husband and small children to stay with my husband. One day while they were drinking, her first husband came and started fighting with my husband ... in that altercation, my husband hit her husband, and he started bleeding. The police took my husband, and I had to part with my gold ring to save him ... that woman never came back again'. She mentioned that her ordeal did not stop here; her husband continued to visit other women, and one fine day he brought a Tibetan woman who was at least ten years older than him, following which she left him and took her children away.

In the process of integration and assimilation, some of the women have married local men and were happy in their lives. However, some of them were often ridiculed and mocked at by their own family members as their children could not converse in Tibetan, and being a mother/woman, it is their duty to preserve the Tibetan language. According to a respondent, ' ... I went against the wishes of my parents and married a Bhutia man from Sikkim. Although I was welcomed in my husband's house, I was criticized for my Tibetan identity. When my children were born, my in-laws said that they would not speak in any other language except Sikkimese, and on the other hand, my parents and relatives would insist that they speak the Tibetan language ... I did not know where I belonged, who I was'. This ontological narrative reflects the pain and confusion the women face about their identity; they are constantly struggling and trying to draw a balance between their Tibetan identity and gender identity. According to many respondents, as a woman, there is more pressure to maintain Tibetan identity. They constantly get questioned about their identity and must modify their clothing, and when they try to mingle with the local population, it is viewed as a step towards abandoning one's culture. The young generation of Tibetan women try to integrate all that they learn from an Indian university and non-Tibetan friends, and they have a more nuanced definition of Tibetanness.

The Tibetan women in exile are financially empowered; thus, the age of marriage has considerably gone up, as evident from the data. Many of the women are marrying much later than their mothers and fathers did. They also exercise choice in the selection of their spouse. Divorce was a mutual consent basis. Property, which was initially only inherited by men, can now be inherited by women as well. Domestic violence was not experienced by the women in the study sample; however, time and again, they have been subjected to ridicules for different reasons. The narrative of a 62-year-old woman highlights one such incident '... in Tibet because of the cold we do not take a bath for many days, but my mother-in-law always commented on my hygiene. I was not allowed to enter the kitchen till I took a bath'. Some women mentioned that they were also chastised for their appearance, eating raw meat, and even marrying so many men.

We know from the literature that Tibetan women were politically active even prior to their exile. Since the Constitution, which was framed in exile, proclaimed equality between the sexes, it was observed that the women have become more articulate, assertive, and forthcoming in the political sphere. Tibetan women were seen politically engaged in governance in the settlement camps. Whenever there are protest movements, women are seen mobilizing and participating. The younger generation takes to social media to voice their opinion, as evident in many of the narratives Tibetan women refugees are making progress, and their success is the success of the entire community.

Chapter 7

# Conclusion

## Introduction

As introduced, the present book focuses on the socioeconomic profile and the question of Tibetan identity among the diasporic Tibetan communities, particularly those settled in the Indian Himalayan belt. Identity broadly defined is 'people's concepts of who they are, of what sort of people they are, and how they relate to others' (Hogg and Abrams, 1988, p. 2). The fundamentals of human interaction or with other social objects are contingent on the identification of the objects involved. In other words, before we can act toward or interact with some object, it must be situated in time and place. To do so is to give the object a name in the sense of classifying it as a member of a category; such a categorization process helps in the identification and formulation of the nature of interaction and orient accordingly. The way identity is conceptualized and analyzed is largely based on orienting perspectives of essentialist, dispositional, and constructionist, which has been discussed in the previous chapter.

The question of identity among the Tibetans has been thoroughly discussed at first by trying to incorporate the notion of integration, which is essential in the formation/formulation of the identity of individuals in terms of whether they feel integrated and shared a consensus among themselves and with others or they experience a sense of dislocation. The book explores the question of the identity of the Tibetan refugees in India by questioning and investigating whether the notion of identity among the Tibetan refugees is constant regardless of spatial organizational settlement and historical position in time or is differential and in flux. Exploring the question on identity of the Tibetan refugees, particularly among the youth, is pertinent, as, on the one hand, the CTA and the Tibetan Parliament in Exile (TPiE) are in the hope of returning to Tibet, which, to an extent, imposes restrictions on the practice and maintenance of their distinctive cultural and traditional identity; and on the other hand, due to their social linkages and bridges in their social interactions for various purposes they are more attuned towards the host society. Aspects of cultural assimilation in their outlooks are observed among the Tibetan youth, thus leading to the question of how the youth negotiate between the identity they are ascribed with and the identity they accultured to. Here, the question of identity crisis among Tibetan youths is one of the important dimensions that the study seeks to comprehend. In relation to the crisis of identity, the conflicting gender role identities of the Tibetan women refugees is yet another significant element that the study endeavors to comprehend along. Therefore, the main motif of the book was to delineate how the construction of Tibetan identity differs among those who came to India seeking refugee asylum status from Tibet and those generations who are born to refugee parents in India since they have not struggled and lived through the same experiences as their parents, who directly descended from Tibet during the crisis period. Secondly, among those refugees who are confined in cluster settlements in large Tibetan refugee communities, such as those which are in McLeod Ganj and Dalhousie. Their settlements are located and surrounded by communities that are distinctively different from their own, in terms of culture, religion, and race. These factors posed a severe challenge in the process of their integration with the host society, making them maintain their distinctive identity. Fourthly, those refugees who are settled in parts of India where the mentioned distinctive differences are less, such as those refugee settlements in Ravangla, Darjeeling and Sonada. Therefore, the level of differential integration among these settlements with the communities of the areas also determines the formation and crystallization of their identity. Finally, in relation to the importance of the gender dimension in the formulation and assertion of Tibetan identity. To do so, the objectives of the study were outlined by questioning the socioeconomic status and the question of the identity of the Tibetans Refugees in general, and the youths and women in particular. This was done by undertaking a comparative analysis of the refugees at various camps accessing the level of integration and assimilation and their variations regionally.

The identity question was addressed on two levels; first, on the question of what constitutes the idea of Tibetanness. Secondly, to see how that has changed over the years vis-à-vis variation in terms of generational difference, for which understanding the level of integration and assimilation of the refugees to the society and culture of the host society is important. This was carried out by using the conceptual model developed by Ager and Strang (2008) in their work. *Understanding integration: A conceptual framework*, where the level of integration of the refugees at four domains of integration was assessed. Firstly, at the level of major public arenas, which tries to analyze their access to employment, housing, education and health care system, which Ager and Strang refer to as 'Markers and Means' to reflect the achievement of integration and the potential means in attaining integration.

### Integration of Refugees

In terms of employment, it was found that 48 percent of the respondents were employed in various occupations such as teachers, army, nurses, officials, etc., whereas 26 percent were involved in various kinds of business activities, and 7.5 percent were engaged as drivers. In a nutshell, 81.5 percent of the Tibetan refugees are economically integrated into Indian society. The remaining 18.5 percent constitute homemakers; however, these groups of women are not to be seen as economically unproductive; they engage in various kinds of seasonal micro-economical activities such as making candles, jewelry, incense sticks, weaving and selling seasonal clothes, etc. In relation to housing facilities, in all the Tibetan settlement areas, the GOI has provided agricultural lands for their livelihood and resettlement in lease. They also have been availing basic facilities of households like cooking gas connections, water supply, even some of them have been availing the subsidized groceries, and other household requirements as some of they are in possession of BPL card for subsidies in PDS items. Education and health are also one of the important indicators for the integration of the refugees; it was found that 76.5 percent of the respondents were found to be literate and educated as per the Indian education system. For health, more than 50 percent rely on the modern medical facilities available in India; however, the remaining were found to be more inclined towards traditional Tibetan medicine – Amji.

Secondly, considering the questions on how well they are socially connected and bonded with people and families of their own community as 'proximity to family …enabled them to share cultural practices and maintain familiar patterns of relationships. Such connection played a large part in them feeling 'settled'. It was found that 85.5 percent of the respondents have close friends belonging outside their own community with whom they have regular social interaction with the local populace; the remaining 14.5 percent, however, have not interacted with the local population as most of them belong to the older generation, and also it became difficult for them to venture outside the camp areas as most of the housing areas are fairly secluded and almost self-sufficient, making them feel the non-necessity of doing so. The social bridges between the refugees and the host communities were related to occasional visits on festivals at the premise of the host's home, dictating a majority of 70.5 percent of such social connections. The social ties between the two were also found to be intimate to an extent as 21 percent of the respondents positively responded in relation to financial helps extended towards them in the time of need by the host communities; further, 70 percent of the respondents have also highlighted that they have witnessed inter-community marriages between the Tibetans and the other communities of the host society, such was found to be highest (90 percent) among the refugees in Darjeeling.

Thirdly, as 'language and cultural knowledge' and 'safety and stability' are the specialized facilitators for integration, linguistic and cultural competence of the larger society is an important aspect consideration for effective integration.

Language, when sociologically investigated, is an important medium for cultural transmission. Accessing the cultural and linguistic information about the refugees who are born in India is an important parameter of the study. The study found that every single respondent could converse in the local language of the region with ease, Hindi, and Nepali in the case of Darjeeling, Ravangla and Sonada, and only Hindi in the case of Dalhousie and Dharamsala. They expressed that having the knowledge of Hindi and the ability to communicate in it with the local population has broadened their scope of earning a livelihood and has boosted their economic transaction with the others. Among the younger generations, they expressed about accommodability with the local population when they leave the camps for education, employment, and travel. Movies play a significant role in the process of cultural transmission and integration; the study found that 50 percent of the Tibetans prefer both Indian and Tibetan movies. This helped them learn the culture and language of the place and assisted in the process of cultural assimilation. In relation to food, it was found that 65.5 percent of the Tibetans consumes both Indian as well as Tibetan cuisines. When posed with the question of what the areas are, they feel they are assimilating with the Indian society and culture, 33.5 percent mentioned that it was because of business, 22.5 percent due to the educational institution. Within this parameter, as highlighted above, both safety and stability are another aspect of integration as the refugees themselves felt 'at home' if the community or their place of settlement gives them a sense of stability and security. The facilitators are an important dimension of understanding the level of integration and assimilation of the refugees.

Finally, in relation to 'citizenship and rights', the concept is intertwined together as the sense of right comes along with citizenship equipped by the sense of identity emerging from the fact of belonging to a nation. In the case of Tibetan refugees in India, the question of citizenship and right is thus misleading to an extent. The issue of citizenship of Tibetans came up repeatedly in the Lok Sabha after 1959 due to the huge influx of refugees following the flight of the Dalai Lama to India. From 1959 to 1976, questions were repeatedly raised in Parliament about whether Tibetans had applied for citizenship, whether their children could acquire citizenship, and whether the Tibetans would be treated as Indians or foreigners. The Government's stand, as per the Citizenship Act of 1955, as well as subsequent Amendments, has been that Tibetans will be treated as foreigners, it is up to them to apply voluntarily for Indian citizenship if they so desire, and the Government would consider their application as per the rules and the Act. So, the issue of citizenship is not obligatory to the refugees, and they are left with choices whether to remain as Tibetan citizens in exile as refugees or to adopt and naturalize as Indian citizens.

## Question of Tibetan Identity

We know that identity is people's concept of who they think they are, and using that conceptualized frame of self-reference, they come into social ties and relations with others, where their concept of self is further reinforced in such social interactions. Asking who I am, has to do with where one contextually locates oneself within the larger socio-cultural parameters of the society in which one belongs. The socio-cultural environment which conditions and defines an individual's identity is objectively achieved through the institutionalization of roles along with other primordial features outlining the membership. The process of institutionalization establishes role expectations from its members, helping consolidate the social identity of the individuals conforming to the cultural parameters of the society they inhabit. The consolidated social identity reinforces or transforms itself when these identities are lived and performed in various social contexts under numerous circumstances. However, in the face of uprooting from the socio-cultural and physical environment, the identity becomes fragile under various extraneous pressures exerted by the external socio-cultural pressure from another group, leading to a crisis of identity of the individual, which also can lead to a crisis of group identity. In relation to the Tibetan identity issue, Tibetans were displaced from their homeland and were struggling to re-root themselves in an alien terrain, which was physically and socio-culturally distinctively atypical from their own. This made it difficult for them to retain and maintain their unique socio-cultural and religious practices, without which their identity of being Tibetan seems to be in flux when they are exposed to the cultural and religious dogmas of the host society. Such become more evident among the younger generation, particularly those who are born in India. Nonetheless, steps were taken up at the initiative of the Dalai Lama in preserving the sovereignty and socio-cultural integrity of the Tibetan identity.

For preserving the socio-cultural and religious identity of the Tibetan refugees, language becomes an important marker for the cultural identity; 97.5 percent of the respondents pointed out that preserving the Tibetan language is an essential step that needs to be taken to maintain the integrity of Tibetan identity. However, many instances of challenges were encountered during the study as many of the Tibetans expressed their concerns stating that staying in a heterogeneous alien environment as a minority makes it difficult for them to maintain the cultural integrity. There is a constant infringement of cultural elements of the dominant society, which homogenizes the distinctive Tibetan culture in the line of the host society. At the same time, the children, through their social interaction with the 'other' community, find it more convenient to converse and adopt the dominant culture. Another dimension of the identity issue of the Tibetan is in concern with ethnicity and religion, as ethnicity and religion become an important objective criterion, particularly when situating the refugees in a socio-culturally and racially alien world. The exposure to the racial and ethnic differences plays a pivotal role in the identity formulation of the self as ethnic identities are replayed as ideologies of the ethnic groups. Often, these ethnic ideologies are in interplay with religious dogmas and practices. 72.5 percent of the respondent stated that race or ethnic background or religion is important to be a Tibetan, whereas 22.5 percent said it is moderately important as we have seen cases of Tibetans who have converted to a different religion but still have a strong sense of Tibetan identity. To be specific, the older generation was more stringent about the religious and ethnic factors whereas the upcoming generations are more open towards the different religions and communities. Respondents stated that personal values and moral standards are important indicators of Tibetan identity. It is these qualities that make them unique, and wherever they reside in any corner of the world, the values and moral standards are going to remain the same. When inquired from the younger generation about this view, they reiterated that these values and moral standards had been taught to them by their parents and grandparents since childhood, and it has since been with them.

Additionally, drawing on the richness of the 'lived through' experiences of the interviewees, the significance of subjective interpretation or subjects as active meaning-making beings situated in the backdrop of the peculiarities of one's socio-historical and temporal settings surfaces as an important theme. Particularly, in the case of identity as a phenomenon, the narratives of the refugees problematize the simplistic narrative of characterizing 'Tibetan identity' as a monolith and immutable category common for all generations of Tibetans living in exile. The lived experiences of the interviewees, therefore, question and disrupt the assumption that all Tibetans in exile harbor dreams of returning to their homeland whilst conjuring images of utopia and an idyllic/peaceful existence. Tibetans in exile and their collective experiences of nationhood, identity, and culture, therefore cannot be expressed in watertight congealed classifications insulated from external factors but instead should be viewed as an embodied and engaged exercise wherein subjects actively partake in the meaning process whilst simultaneously being impacted with the extant meanings produced via intersubjectivity and other dominant social, cultural and political discourses. Such narratives of lived experiences also appeal to the body of work categorized under the rubric of symbolic interactionism wherein Cooley rightly articulates the mutual processes shared by the subject and the society in which he/she is embedded in. This mutually symbiotic relationship is evident when examining the experiences of Tibetan refugees pertaining to identity, culture, and nationality. The upshot, therefore, remains that the experiences of individuals emanate from a complex stream of embodied activity fused seamlessly with one's consciousness and corporeality. The subject in his/her seamless engagement with the world, therefore, is continuously acted upon and actively acts upon (or reacts) to any given phenomenon. Identity in itself is a broad rubric, and the Tibetan refugees, in their everyday experiences and coping with the world, contest the postulation that Tibetan identity is indubitably tethered with the idea of a fundamental unchanging 'Tibetanness' anchored by one's language, culture, a hope of a return to one's land, and religion. However, the very indicators that sustain or supposedly preserve the authenticity of a Tibetan identity are perpetually counter-challenged or become eroded (in some regard) when Tibetan refugees embody practices that are not in complete alignment with the ideals prescribed by their larger community/society. In a similar vein, Sen speaks of multitudinous identities embodied and expressed by individuals in their everyday lives. They may profess several affiliations or express loyalties for more than one community or organization. Sen therefore critiques the existing belief that subjects must compulsorily associate themselves with a dominant/singular determiner of identity viz. religious, ethnic, racial, or political categories whilst relegating other identities as trivial or inconsequential. In this regard, Bauman's premise of uncertainty bequeathed by the modern globalized world holds true as it is immediately experienced by the Tibetan refugees who have lost their homes and hearth owing to socio-political instability and the continuation of such 'palpable fear of uncertainty' in their present experiences as refugees in India or other host countries wherein they question the possibilities of maintaining the sanctity of their native identity whilst simultaneously engaging with one's socio-political and cultural realities. The Tibetan refugees thus become sites of 'uncertainty' themselves, embodying what Bauman calls as 'liquid fear', fear of losing their dominant identity or fear of surrendering their aspirations of 'returning' to the solidity of their homes and fusing freely with one's local/regional spaces thereby negotiating with the contours of their identity in the process.

### Among the Generations

Tibetans who came to India seeking refugee asylum status from Tibet and those generations who were born in India have marked differences in their conceptualization of Tibetan identity, as interactionists argue our experience defines who and what we are. Since the older refugees struggled and lived through their experiences, their attachment to the land, people, and the struggle will be different as compared to younger generations.

### Older Generation

Older generation refugees are happy and contented to be in India. They justify the notion by saying they are close to His Holiness Dalai Lama. The other reason was the relatives they had there are long gone, and they do not have a reason to go back as they are now settled in India with their family and children. They say the only way to keep the identity intact is through the teaching, beliefs, customs, and language that they have been following. They mentioned that these are cultural components and are going to stay with them and will continue to help them in building their identity. Another factor was in terms of marriage; they believed that marrying within one's own community will help them strengthen their bond with their community and will later help them fight back the oppression. The narratives reveal that the journey of escape for most of the refugees escaping from Tibet was frightening and difficult. Many reported that they suffered from psychological trauma, but it was not documented in this research. Many refugees suffered both serious psychological hardships and serious physical injuries because of their journey. We documented that many of them had faced beatings, torture, and sexual assaults, robbed, and had to part away with their personal items and belongings. Some were caught by the Chinese and given the choice to return, but they insisted on following His Holiness. Nevertheless, there are narrations of strength, struggle and survival and the desire to be with his Holiness and follow him to the unknown land. Those refugees who crossed the Nepal border to reach Himachal Pradesh reported more atrocities and hardships; however, those coming to Sikkim felt that the people were more hospitable and cooperative.

When questioned about what it means for them to be a Tibetan, how they perceive their own identity and what it means to them, the general response was that Tibetans need to be compassionate, peace-loving, hardworking, and honest. Buddhism has been a way of life for them, and the philosophy of Buddhism is compassion, love and surrender. They believed that it is this Dharma that differentiates them from others. Some described their culture as unique because it has the blessing of His Holiness, the Dalai Lama. They were proud of being born in a Tibetan family and being part of the Tibetan culture. A few also mentioned that although they liked the Indian culture, this is not their nation; their nationality is Tibetan because that is their country of birth.

The older generations of Tibetans have a sense of nostalgia about their homeland. They are consistently engaged with present-day Tibet even if it is from a distance, they are aware of the changes taking place in Tibet, and it has changed the perception for some of them, but still, they dream of going back. For many, Tibet remains their first home and India their second home. The nostalgia is often replaced by a pragmatic understanding that the past is no longer there when interacting with other refugees who have recently come from Tibet. The middle and the younger generations know Tibet has undergone irreversible changes, but it still finds a place in the imagination of the exiled community.

*Younger Generation*

They follow the teachings of their parents but are more receptive to change. They have accepted the host nation and are comfortable living here. They state that they have a responsibility towards the host nation and want to serve here. They have assimilated with the host nation more than their older generation. They say they don't perceive themselves as refugees till later in their lives. They are open towards inter-community marriages and are seen comfortable wearing western apparel. They want to go back to their country, but the desire is not that strong, especially for those who have comfortably adjusted here.

The younger generation of Tibetans is connected to Tibet through the internet. It gives them an opportunity to exchange views, share information and discuss the changes in the exiled community as well as in Tibet. There are very active on Tibet networks, forums on the internet, Tibet.Net, Free Tibet, etc. For many of the younger generation of Tibetans born in India mentioned that India is home for them. They also added that they 'eat, dress and live' the Indian way. The younger generation enjoys Indian cuisine, and Indian snacks are as popular as *thupka* and *momos*. The youth are familiar with Hindi and Bollywood songs, and most of them wear western clothes or the comfortable Indian Kurta. There are multiple narratives on whether India is a home or a potential home, and for many of the respondents, since Tibet is the homeland of their parents, Tibet is their 'homeland', but since they were born and brought up in India, they enjoy the comfort of the home there also. Many of the respondents felt that since there was no freedom in Tibet, the longing to go back is absent. Nonetheless, they desire Tibet to be a free country. Some mentioned that their generation was not really interested in the issue of identity, and they were often used by the politicians for their ulterior motives. The young respondents felt that they enjoyed cultural freedom and felt that India could be used as a launchpad and was a gateway for many of them to go to foreign countries, which otherwise would not be possible being in Tibet. This can primarily be contributed to their age, as establishing social ties at a later age becomes difficult for the people. Social uprooting is rather exaggerated at an older age.

**Regional Variance**

The conceptualization of the identity among the Tibetan population is being problematized in terms of regional variation. On the one hand, are those refugees who are confined in cluster settlements in large Tibetan refugee communities, such as those in McLeod Ganj and Dalhousie. These settlements are located and surrounded by communities that are distinctively different from their own, in terms of cultural, religious, and racially. These factors posed a severe challenge in the process of their integration with the host society, making them maintain their distinctive identity. On the other hand, those refugees who are settled in Ravangla, Darjeeling and Sonada are settled in a homogeneous socio-cultural environment, which makes it accommodative for them in terms of similar food habits like the locals, there is a notable number of Buddhist followers in these states. Therefore, the level of differential integration among these settlements with the communities of the areas also determines the formation and crystallization of their identity.

*Darjeeling, Ravangla and Sonada*

The Tibetans in Sikkim almost gave identical answers regarding their cultural closeness with the Nepali and Bhutia communities. They mentioned that the population in the Himalayan region was like them culturally and ethnically. The Bhutia's belonging to the Namgyal dynasty in Sikkim shared the same religion and is believed to have migrated from Tibet in the 17th Century. They, however, do not feel the same closeness with the Nepali Community because apart from the difference in religion, most of their traditions, culture and customs are different. They felt the Nepali caste system was very discriminating, unlike Tibetan society, which is more egalitarian in nature. Some of the respondents also mentioned that they did not appreciate the treatment meted out to the women in the Nepali community; they felt that in the Tibetan community, there is no gender bias, and women are treated at power with men; they were given the same place in society as men, sometimes they are even more authoritarian then men. In Ravangla (Sikkim), there was a lot of intermarriage between the Tibetan and Nepali communities and most of these marriages were successful. In fact, according to one male respondent, '… I am very happy marrying my Nepali wife, she really cares for me, and she is very nice'. A similar positive sentiment was shared by a Nepali woman, '…. My husband is a very nice human being, he is very religious and cares a lot for me, we work together, and I have so much more freedom than many of my friends, who have Nepali husbands'. In Ravangla, cultural assimilation to the host society was more visible. Few who married Nepali women have now started sharing their religious spaces and even visiting temples and performing puja's. Even in West Bengal (Darjeeling and Sonada), the respondents expressed similar closeness with the local population. There was intermarriage with the local population, and respondents who married Nepali women felt they made better wives than Tibetan girls. They believed that the Nepali's being Hindus strongly profess patriarchy, and this teaches the women to be subservient towards men.

Many women respondents were seen adorning the marriage symbols of both the Tibetan and Nepali community, highlights the efforts the Tibetans have made to integrate themselves with the local population. There were cases of marriage with westerners also. Surprisingly, Tibetans feel much more closeness to the westerners because they are open-minded and take a lot of interest in learning different aspects of a new culture. They also appreciated the interest westerners take in Buddhism and Buddhist philosophy, they, however, did not like the way they treat the Buddhist text, '.... for them it is just books, and they eat food while reading them, but for us it is our life, our Dharma'. However, surprising it may seem, almost all respondents stated that they experience full emotional comfort and support with the local population.

### Dalhousie and Dharamsala (McLeod Ganj)

In terms of the Darjeeling, Sonada, and Ravangla communities and their assimilation with the local population, it has been greater in comparison to Dharamsala and Dalhousie. The former centers are in an area where adaptation with the local population has been easy due to the similarities mentioned above. Also, the facial structure of locals of these host states is similar, giving the refugees a sense of oneness.

Relating to the above aspect, in order to comprehend their level of social interaction, we enquired whether they were invited by their Indian friends in their house, in which 69.5 percent responded positively, as reflected in Figure 5.2. The highest positive responses came from those refugees settled in the Dalhousie (cent percent) area, followed by those in Dharamsala (66 percent). In relation to Darjeeling, Ravangla, and Sonada, the level of social bonding with other communities are less as compared to Dalhousie and Dharamsala, with the lowest level in Darjeeling (40 percent).

On the other hand, in our study at Himachal Pradesh, we did not come across any cases of intermarriage between the Tibetan and the local community. A plausible reason could be that Dharamsala is the headquarter of the Government in Exile with the presence of His Holiness, and a lot of emphasis is placed on the preservation of culture, and hence marriage with community members is encouraged. However, there have been instances where the respondents have faced hostility and suspicion from the members of the host community since they felt that their resources were being shared and have been referred by deprecatory terms like *Chin-bhote* (Chinese Bhutia) as mentioned by one of our respondents.

Tibetan culture has been preserved untouched until the middle twentieth century. It is a rich cultural heritage incorporating Indian spiritual practices, Chinese culinary traditions, amalgamated with the tradition of Buddhist philosophy, traditional medicine, and astrology. The Tibetan language, probably being unique linguistically, belongs to the Sino-Tibetan family; the writing is based on Sanskrit, and it doesn't have a hieroglyphic structure, and it is used in several Mahayana Buddhist texts. The current scenario in Tibet puts a threat to language preservation, and it is on the verge of extinction. However, it seems that the Tibetan language is flourishing in exile, particularly in India and Nepal, because many westerners are studying it and investing in educational institutions. According to Mountcastle (1997), Tibetan spoken inside Tibet is becoming very sinicized; the writing and reading competence and purity of the language have become weak, and lay Tibetans feel that the English language is easier to comprehend and understand. The Tibetan tradition of Buddhism is practiced in many other countries all over the world, including the Western world (Powers, 2007). People are attracted to the ideas of compassion and wisdom, and it inspires them to make pilgrimages to Tibet, India, Nepal, etc., but Tibetan Buddhism is in danger because a lot of organizations recognize and promote the Tibetan issue, but China's power and significance in the world are unshakeable. Therefore, the three most important aspects that need to be preserved are language, religion, and the desire to return to Tibet. Language is not only a medium of communication among them, but it is also a feature of cultural identity, a medium for preserving their religious tradition, Buddhist philosophy and values, which also incites a yearning to go back to roots.

Nevertheless, some of the traditions and rituals which were there earlier—for example, polyandry—have been reconsidered since it generated a negative reaction from members of the Indian community. The older generation felt factors like materialism and western influence are hindering the culture, and human values are slowly eroding. Therefore, the younger generations need to be guided more. Multiple narratives mention the need to preserve the Tibetan culture, but sometimes integration is also essential; otherwise, it creates antagonism among the inhabitants of the host community—since it was a question of survival, they have learnt the local language. This also reflects on the effort made by the member in exile to avoid the mistrust of the host community. It was interesting that in our study, even the younger respondents could converse in their native language. However, they were more comfortable in English while interacting with their friends.

Other respondents also pointed out that there must be mutual learning and sharing; the exchange is important because it enriches an individual. The respondents at Dharamsala gave more emphasis to human values because that is the teaching of Dharma. Many respondents mention that people deserve to be respected regardless of their culture. They claim there is no contradiction between cultures because it depends on geographical and historical factors; every culture is unique and caters to the needs of its people.

A teacher of Tibetan Philosophy at Dharamsala, in his discussion mentioned that there is nothing called cultural difference; it is something used by politicians to gain political gains. He mentioned that they all worshiped nature before organized religion came, some worshiped some animals, and others killed them for sacrifice. For him to think that culture is different is wrong; what is important is to understand the cultural difference. He added that he is Tibetan and Buddhist in his heart, but open to learning and understanding all cultures. However, he did agree that if the Tibetan religion could be preserved, humanity could be preserved, because Buddhism is a religion based on compassion and love. There were others also who demonstrated a universal outlook and spoke of pan-human values. The Project officer at Ravangla also spoke in the same strain and mentioned that there is no difference between Buddhist or Non-Buddhist However, from these responses it is clear that 'same culture' does not mean uniform; it means equal. Therefore, the universalism does not eliminate cultural differences or merge people into a culturally homogeneous mass, but rather it celebrates the cultural variety, exchange, and learning, creating space for different cultures to co-exist being different in form and essence, but equal in rights and importance. A universal attitude does not necessarily lead to a gradual loss of one's culture. On the contrary, if one keeps to one's culture and enriches it with intercultural encounters, it is more likely to increase cultural identity

When asked how religious beliefs help them in coping with difficult situations with non-Tibetans, most respondents mentioned that it has really helped them in their life; it has helped them overcome negative emotions and tolerate difficult conditions. The majority of respondents mentioned their belief in the law of karma, and this helps them to deal with a difficult situation.

On a personal level, some respondents also saw intermarriage as a threat to the preservation of Tibetan culture. They expressed their fears that the pure Tibetan race is at risk when they marry people from a different community because the culture is compromised, and they will lose their identity. Respondents at Dharamsala were appreciative of the role of the Central Tibetan Administration (CTA) established by the Dalai Lama, which monitors and helps to preserve Tibetan culture.

The question of how Tibetans negotiate their identity was analyzed; the trend among the answers is that there are dissimilarities with the local Hindu population, but they were not criticized. Regardless of the differences with the local population, most of the respondents were comfortable with the local inhabitants. Nevertheless, individuals are judged primarily in terms of their personal qualities and actions rather than the cultural background. People who share the same beliefs and values are seen close; the local Buddhists—for example, in Ravangla and Darjeeling—who are close to Tibetans culturally, religiously, and ethnically, share relative closeness with them. Most respondents manage to keep the balance between rootedness and openness by linking their traditional values with the universal human ones, thus making a step from individuation to universalization (Kim, 1988, 2001, 2005).

When asked about the transformation and identity changes Tibetans are undergoing in India, the respondents give varying answers. About half of them said, with different levels of certainty, that their cultural identity remains consistent. A respondent at Dharamsala opined that '… had we been in Tibet, maybe we would not have been so conscious, but now we are in a different part of the world and 'our world' needs to be protected and preserved'. Further, the respondents at Dharamsala shared that the presence of His Holiness here in Dharamsala was a constant reminder that whatever their suffering might be, they must preserve the culture.

It was a consensus among respondents of the three-study area that education is the reason for the transformation taking place in the mindset of Tibetan society. The educated younger generation of Tibetans felt that knowing and understanding the situation in Tibet, it is impossible for them to go back there, and they should instead use India as a gateway and passport to other countries so that they can have a better life. After living in India for so long, some of them even born here, they felt that life here is good, they have access to most of the things, the only thing they do not have is an Indian Citizenship, but they do have the yellow card which allows them to travel anywhere in India and a green card by which they can travel overseas. They were particularly happy after the Aadhaar card because at least it was proof of Identification in India. The younger generation was not concerned with the question of 'Tibetan Identity'; they felt holding on to one's identity closes all doors for progress, growth, and advancement; identity takes them away from being global. However, there were respondents who felt that the Government creates conditions for discrimination, and there is a defiance to cooperate because they see them as immigrants. This was seen while interviewing some of the respondents in Sikkim, who shared that the Nepali inhabitants of the state feel that if the Tibetans were not here in Sikkim, they would have captured the entire economic sphere. In the words of a respondent from Sikkim '…. Tibetans are all over Sikkim, they are very good at business, and they take away all the customers, all the big shops in Sikkim are owned by Tibetan … we only gave them refugee, not our resources'. However, this was not a general sentiment, and it was observed that the Tibetans shared very cordial relations with the local population.

The size of the Tibetan community, the settlement structure, the vicinity of cultural and religious objects all have a positive effect on the preservation of culture and assimilation. Almost all our respondents were fluent in their language; even the younger generation could converse in their native language. Some of the respondents at Dharamsala mentioned that the proximity is a blessing in India to preserve their culture and their identity; for Tibetans who have gone to foreign countries, the situation may be different. One respondent at Dharamsala shared the story of his son, who is now living in America. His son shared with him that in the West, people are not hospitable and friendly to them; it is a very competitive and isolated society. Living in America is very expensive, and to maintain a standard of living, everyone must work very hard. There is no time for evaluating one's identity. He also shared that his grandchildren do not know the language, and his son has no time to teach them. The narrative of a young boy from Darjeeling also highlighted how being in Darjeeling, he never understood the meaning of identity and how he was (re)introduced to Tibetan identity for the first time when he went to Dharamsala and started attending Tibetan prayer sessions, participating in cultural shows and was surrounded by Tibetan classmates and teachers. He narrated that language helps in building a bond with one's community. During the two years he spent in Dharamsala, speaking, and writing in Tibetan, truly gave him a sense of his Tibetan identity. In India, despite the struggle, there is a good environment for identity rootedness; on the contrary, moving towards the West might become a threat to the preservation of culture and assimilation.

### *Gender Difference*

There is less gender difference, and importance is given to both the genders; women are seen a bit stronger in their position, they are active and hardworking, there is no notion regarding the difference of work—it's done equally and without any prejudice. During informal conversations, many men said the women are in a stronger position in their society, and if they are willing, they can marry for the second time.

The focus of the chapter on Gender and Identity Issues among the Tibetan Refugees highlighted that the issues and concerns of the women in exile are multidimensional. The aim was to learn about the status of the Tibetan women and the changes, if any, regarding their autonomy, decision-making process, inheritance, marriage customs, and political participation. Generally, women experience higher rates of unemployment than men due to cultural and educational handicaps arising out of illiteracy and lack of occupational experience; however, in the study, female members are enrolled in post-graduation and diploma courses more than the men (2.5 percent of the male members are postgraduate which is lesser than the females, 1.5 percent of the male members are diploma holders, again lesser than females). Even occupational disparity was minimal, and women were seen engaged in seasonal occupations like sweaters and jewelry. Support from the Indian

Government and from CTA in the form of scholarships, and other facilities, now more Tibetan women are getting educated, and this education has transformed the nomadic herding Tibetan society and has opened new opportunities for Tibetan women (Rajput, 2012).

The Tibetan families were Patrilineal, and this is further corroborated in the findings of the book. Monogamy was the most preferred form of marriage, and traditional cultural marriage practices like polyandry were non-existent in the study. There are examples of bigamy which reflects the helplessness of the women in not being able to accept their husband's second wife. Brideprice as the form of marriage payment still existed, although there were some changes, the gifts, livestock has been replaced with other items of daily use. Since many women are getting educated and are financially empowered, the age of marriage has gone up. The Tibetan refugees living in India have followed and continued the custom of mutual divorce with the intervention of elders and village leaders and settlement officers. Most of the women reported that they could control the size of the family by using several birth control methods and experience freedom. Inheritance in Tibetan society was on a per capita basis, and each son had a right to an equal share in the property. But it was seen in the study that women also inherited property and gave property to their daughters. Despite the patrilineal nature of Tibetan society, there was no discrimination meted to the girl child; on the contrary, there were instances from the field where old Tibetan women lived in the old age home because they had been deserted by their son.

In the decision-making process regarding family, children, education, religion, women took decisions either singly or jointly with their husbands. Almost all the women had bank accounts and could spend all their money as per their desire. Recreational activities for women were mostly related to religious work. In the study sample, Tibetan women did not face much violence in their homes. But this does not mean that they did not experience violence, but they refrained from talking about it.

Tibetan women were politically active even prior to their exile. But this assertiveness and articulation in the political sphere have only grown in exile. According to the study, 78 percent of women support and take part in political activities. According to the study, women participate in the freedom movement of Tibet; in places like Darjeeling, Sonada and Ravangla, there is 100 percent participation of the women. Whereas in Dharamsala and Dalhousie, there is 64 percent and 90 percent participation, respectively. Tibetan women have on their shoulders the onus of preserving the Tibetan identity, whether it is language, religion, or purity of the race. Almost all the respondents mentioned that they had to learn the Tibetan language and participate in prayer and rituals. The elders in the family constantly emphasized the importance of learning the language, and this task was taken up by the mother. Tibetan women born in India were more closely monitored as they had to pass it on to their children.

However, many Tibetan women faced a dilemma regarding their identity. As part of the process of assimilation with the local populace, many of the women married non-Tibetan men. In one of the narratives, a woman shared that she married a Sikkimese man. Although ethnically and religiously both the communities are very similar, they have a different language. After her children were born, her in-laws did not permit her children to converse in Tibetan and asked her to ensure that they only spoke in Sikkimese. According to many respondents, the onus of maintaining the Tibetan identity lies more with the women. If they are married, they should ensure that their children learn the language and the Tibetan way of life. On the contrary, when they are not seen wearing their traditional clothes, it is again seen as forsaking one's culture. In this regard, a young respondent posed a relevant question '… why are men not asked to wear the traditional clothes? Their identity is not questioned; it looks like identity also has a gender connotation'.

## Concluding Remarks

The question on the identity of the Tibetan refugees in India is in delirious condition due to factors such as the compartmentalized settlement of the refugees non-homogeneously across various locations in India—39 major and minor settlement to be precise. As discussed, the settlement in these various locations created the difference in the opinion formation and conceptualization of the identity itself. On the other hand, the differences are also observed while comparing the older and the younger generation. The difference is problematized not based on age, rather on the basis of their struggles as a first-hand encounter and those who have experienced about the struggle from the tales of their parents; and finally, the difference based on gender, as in all patriarchal societies, women have always been sidelined in the social discourses, and Tibetan society is no different. These three domains presented a sharp difference in the conceptualization of the Tibetan identity formation.

Further, it also has been discussed how the differences could, to an extent, overcome when it encounters other communities and contrast their culture with them. This was observed when in relation to the conflict between host communities, as Penny-Dimri discussed in her work; further, the refugee tag among the younger generation as discussed in the narration were taken by the Tibetan youths who are born in India as a humiliation and taunt, which made them realize and visualize their social and political position of being a refugee. These factors have instilled a sense of belonging to the Tibetan objective identity bringing a sense of shared consensus among them despite all the differences.

# References

Abraham, M.F. (1990) *A modern sociological theory: An introduction*. New York: Oxford University Press.

Adams, W.F. (2005) 'Tibetan refugees in India: Integration opportunities through development of social, cultural and spiritual traditions', *Community Development Journal*, 40(2), pp. 216–219.

Ager, A. and Strang, A. (2008) 'Understanding integration: A conceptual framework'. *Journal of Refugee Studies*, 21(2), pp. 166-191.

Alonso, W. (1995) 'Citizenship, nationality and other identities', *Journal of International Affairs*, 48(2), pp. 585-599.

Anand, D. (2000) '(Re)imagining nationalism: Identity and representation in the Tibetan diaspora of South Asia', *Contemporary South Asia*, 9(3), pp. 271-287.

Appiah, K.A. and Gates, H.L.Jr. (1995) 'Introduction, multiplying identities', in Appiah, K.A. and Gates, H.L. (eds.) *Identities*. Chicago: Chicago Press, pp. 1-6.

Ardley, J. (2003) 'Learning the art of democracy? Continuity and change in the Tibetan government-in-exile', *Contemporary South Asia*, 12(3), pp. 349-363.

Avedon, J. (1984) *In exile from the land of snows: The Dalai Lama and Tibet since the Chinese conquest*. New York: Harper Perennial.

Aziz, B. (1987) 'Moving towards a sociology of Tibet', *The Tibet Journal: A Special Issue on Women and Tibet*, 12(4), pp. 72-86.

Banjan, V. (2009) 'Illegal Bangladeshi migrants in Mumbai', *The Indian Journal of Political Science*, 70(4), pp. 1007-1020.

Basu, S. (2008) 'Interpreting the Tibetan diaspora: Cultural preservation and the pragmatics of identity', *CEU Political Science Journal*, 4, pp. 419-445.

Basu, S. (2018) *In diasporic lands: Tibetan refugees and their transformation since the exodus*. Hyderabad: Orient Blackswan Private Ltd.

Basu, S. (n.d.) Organizing for exile! "Self-Help" among Tibetan refugees in an Indian town. [Online]. Available at:
http://www.mcrg.ac.in/rw%20files/RW35/1.Sudeep%20Basu.pdf (Accessed: 14 February 2018).

Bauman, Z. (1988) *Freedom*. Milton Keynes: Open University Press.

Bell, C. (1991) *People of Tibet*. London: Oxford University Press.

Bentz, A.S. (2012) 'Being a Tibetan refugee in India', *Refugee Survey Quarterly*, 31(1), pp. 80-107.

Berger, P.L. and Luckmann, T. (1966) *Social construction of reality*. New York: Doubleday.

Bernstorff, D. and Welck, H. (eds.) (2004) *Exile as challenge: The Tibetan diaspora*. New Delhi: Orient Longman.

Bhat, Md.Y. and Ali, K. (1994). 'Tourism and socioeconomic profile: A case study of Sindh valley (Kashmir)', *Pakistan Economic and Social Review*, 32(2), pp. 117-133.

Bhattacharjea, A. (1994) *Tibetans in exile: The democratic vision.* New Delhi: Tibetan Parliamentary and Policy Research Centre.

Bloch, A. and Hirsch, S. (2016) '"Second generation" refugees and multilingualism: Identity, race and language transmission', *Ethnic and Racial Studies.* [Online] DOI: 10.1080/01419870.2016.1252461 (Accessed: 19 June 2017).

Bogdandy, A.V., Häussler, S., Hanschmann, F. and Utz, R. (2005) 'State-building, nation-building, and constitutional politics in post-conflict situations: Conceptual clarifications and an appraisal of different approaches' in Bogdandy, A.V., Wolfrum, R. and Philipp, C.E. (eds.) *Max Planck Yearbook of United Nations Law* (9 vols). Leiden: Martinus Nijhoff Publishers, pp. 579–613.

Bose, A. (2004) 'Afghan Refugees in India', *Economic and Political Weekly,* 39(43), pp. 4698-4701.

Boswell, C. (2002) 'New issues in refugee research Addressing the causes of migratory and refugee movements: The role of the European Union', *Working Paper No. 73.* [Online]. Available at: https://www.unhcr.org/3e03005fa.pdf (Accessed: 15 June 2017).

Boyd, H.R. (2004) *The future of Tibet: The government-in-exile meets the challenge of democratization.* New York: Peter Lang.

Braun, V. and Clarke, V. (2006). 'Using thematic analysis in psychology', *Qualitative Research in Psychology,* 3(2), pp. 77–101.

Bureau Reporter (2003) 'Interview with Mr. Thubten Samphel', *Central Tibetan Administration.* [Online]. Available at: https://tibet.net/interview-with-mr-thubten-samphel/ (Accessed: 25 March 2018).

Burke, P.J. (1980) 'The self: Measurement implications from a symbolic interactionist perspective', *Social Psychology Quarterly,* 43, pp. 18-29.

Burke, P.J. and Reitzes, D.C. (1981) 'The link between identity and role performance', *Social Psychology Quarterly,* 44, pp. 83-92.

Butler, A. (2007) *Feminism, nationalism and exiled Tibetan women.* New Delhi: Zubaan.

Campbell, J. (1996) *Traveller in space: Gender, identity, and Tibetan Buddhism.* Revised edition. London and New York: Continuum.

Cassinelli, C.W. and Ekvall, R.B. (1969) *A Tibetan principality: The political system of SasKya.* Ithaca, N.Y: Cornell University Press.

Castles, S., Korac, M., Vasta, E., and Vertovec, S. (2001) 'Integration: Mapping the field', *Report of a project carried out by the centre for migration and policy research and refugee studies centre,* University of Oxford.

Central Tibetan Administration http://tibet.net/, (May 2, 2014).

Cerulo, K.A. (1997) 'Identity constructions: New issues, new dimensions', *Annual Review of Sociology,* 23, pp. 385-409.

Chambers, R. (1994). 'Participatory rural appraisal (PRA): Analysis of experience', *World Development,* 22(9), pp. 1253-1268. [Online]. Available at: https://entwicklungspolitik.unihohenheim.de/uploads/media/Day_4_-_Reading_text_6.pdf (Accessed: 16 November 2017).

Chapman, T. and Hockey, J. (eds.) (1999) *Ideal homes? Social change and domestic life.* London: Routledge.

Chaudhuri, B., and König, L. (2017) 'The Aadhaar scheme: A cornerstone of a new citizenship regime in India?', *Contemporary South Asia*, 26(2), pp. 127–142.

Chimienti, M., Bloch, A., Ossipow, L. and Wihtol de Wenden, C. (2019) 'Second generation from refugee backgrounds in Europe', *Comparative Migration Studies*, 7. [Online]. DOI: https://doi.org/10.1186/s40878-019-0138-2

Chimni, B.S. (2000) 'Globalization, humanitarianism and the erosion of refugee protection', *Journal of Refugee Studies*, 13(3), pp. 243–263.

Chodon, Y. (2007) T*ibetan women and higher educational experience: An exploratory study.* Unpublished Dissertation (PhD.), University of Massachusetts, Amherst.

Choedup, N. (2015) *From Tibetan refugees to transmigrants: Negotiating cultural continuity and economic mobility through migration.* Unpublished Dissertation. [Online]. Available at: https://doi.org/10.7936/K75D8Q30 (Accessed 25 April 2019).

Chotsho. T. (1997) 'A drop from an ocean: The status of women in Tibetan society', *The Tibet Journal*, 22(2), pp. 59-68.

Clarck, B. (1995) *The quintessence tantras of Tibetan medicine.* Massachusetts: Snow Lion.

Coelho, P.J. (2016) 'Empowerment and marginalisation of Tibetan women in India', *Social Research Foundation*, 4(1), pp. 1-10.

Coleman, G. (1993) *A handbook of Tibetan culture: A guide to Tibetan centres and resources throughout the world.* London: Rider.

Collyer, M. (2007) 'In-between places: Trans-Saharan transit migrants in Morocco and the fragmented journey to Europe', *Antipode*, 39(4), pp. 668-690.

Congzhong, W, (ed.) (1991) *Collected papers of studies of feudal serfdom system in Tibet.* Beijing: Chinese Press of Tibetan Studies.

Cooley, C.H. (1902) *Human Nature and Social Order.* New York: Scribners.

Cooper, C. (1976) 'The house as symbol of the self', in Proshansky, H.M., Ittelson, W.H. and Rivlin, L.G. (eds.) *Environmental Psychology: People and Their Physical Settings.* 2nd edn. New York: Holt, Rinehart, and Winston.

Cornell, S. and Hartmann, D. (1998) *Ethnicity and race: Making identities in a changing world.* London: Pine Forge Thousand Oaks.

Crescenzi, A., Ketzer, E., Van Ommeren, M., Phuntsok, K., Komproe, I., and de Jong, J.T.V.M. (2002) 'Effect of political imprisonment and trauma history on recent Tibetan refugees in India', *Journal of Traumatic Stress*, 15, pp. 369–375.

CTA (n.d.) 'Background of CTA', *Central Tibetan Administration.* [Online]. Available at: https://web.archive.org/web/20100803041342/http://www.tibet.net/en/index.php?id=14 (Accessed: 15 February 2018)

CTA (n.d.) 'The Office of the Auditor General', *Central Tibetan Administration.* [Online]. Available at: http://tibet.net/about-cta/office-of-the-auditor-general/ (Accessed: 21 February 2018)

Dargay, L. (1988) 'Tibetans in Alberta and their cultural identity', *Ethnic Studies*, 20(2), pp. 14-123.

Dascalopoulos, C.S. (1990) 'The notion of female property: A comparative study of property', *J. Legal Plural and Unofficial Law*, 2(4), pp. 330-352.

Dasgupta, A. (2003) 'Repatriation of Sri Lankan refugees: Unfinished tasks', *Economic and Political Weekly*, 38(24), pp. 2365-2367.

Datta, K. (2002) 'Transformation of the Tibetan women in exile', *Proceedings of the first Biennial Conference*. Indian Association for Asian and Pacific Studies.

Datta, K. and Chakaravorty, R. (2001) 'Freedom in exile: The Tibetan refugees in India in pursuit of rights and identity', in Roy, S.K. (ed.) *Refugees and Human rights*. Jaipur and New Delhi: Rawat Publications.

Deng, F.M. (1995) *War of visions: Conflict of identities in the Sudan*. Washington, DC: Brookings.

Diehl, K. (2002) *Echoes from Dharamsala: Music in the life of a Tibetan refugee community*. California: University of California Press.

Dodin, T. and Räther, H. (2001) *Imagining Tibet: Perceptions, projections and fantasies*. Boston: Wisdom Publication.

Dolma, D. (2016). *Survival and revival of Tibetan ethnic identity in India*. Unpublished Master's Dissertation, Central European University, Hungry.

Dolma, S., Singh, S., Lohfeld, L., Orbinski, J.J. and Mills, E.L. (2006) 'Dangerous journey: Documenting the experience of Tibetan refugees', *American Journal of Public Health*, 96(11), pp. 2061-2064.

Donden, Y. and Hopkins, J. (1997) *Health through balance: An introduction to Tibetan medicine*. Delhi: Motilal Banarsidass.

Douglas, M. (1991) 'The idea of a home: A kind of space', *Social Research*, 58(1), pp. 287-307.

Dreyer, J.T. and Van Walt Van Praag, M.C. (1988) 'The status of Tibet: History, rights, and prospects in international law', *Pacific Affairs*, 61(2), p. 340. [Online]. DOI: 10.2307/2759325

Dreyfus, H.L. (2014) *Skillful coping: Essays on the phenomenology of everyday perception and action*. New York: Oxford University Press.

Elsass, P. and Phuntsok, K. (2009) "Tibetans' coping mechanisms following torture: An interview study of Tibetan torture survivors' use of coping mechanisms and how these were supported by western counselling', *Traumatology*, 15, pp. 3-10.

Erffa, V.W. (1996) *Uncompromising Tibet: Culture, religion, politics*. New Delhi: Paljor Publications.

Erikson, E.H. (1968) *Identity, youth and crisis*. New York: W.W. Norton Company.

Falcone, J. and Wangchuk, T. (2008) 'We're not home: Tibetan refugees in India in the twenty-first century', *India Review*, 7(3), pp. 164-199.

Fearon, J.D. (1999) *What is Identity (as we now use the word)?* [Online]. Available at: https://web.stanford.edu/group/fearon-research/cgi-bin/wordpress/wp-content/uploads/2013/10/What-is-Identity-as-we-now-use-the-word-.pdf (Accessed: 25 August 2018).

Fine Dictionary (n.d.) 'Inheritance', *Fine Dictionary*. [Online]. Available at: http://www.finedictionary.com/inheritance.html (Accessed: 19 June 2020).

Forrest, J. and Kusek, W. (2016) 'Human capital and the structural integration of Polish immigrants in Australia in the first, second and third generations', *Australian Geographer*, 47(2), pp. 233–248.

Fox, J. (2013) *An introduction to religion and politics: Theory and practice.* London and New York: Routledge.

Francke, A.H. (1994) *History, folklore and culture of Tibet.* New Delhi: Sumit Publication.

Frechette, A. (2007) 'Democracy and democratization among Tibetans in exile', *The Journal of Asian Studies,* 66(1), pp. 97-127.

French, R.R. (1995) *The golden yoke: The legal cosmology of Buddhist Tibet.* Boston: Snow Lion Publications.

Frilund, R. (2019) 'Tibetan refugee journeys: Representations of escape and transit', *Refugee Survey Quarterly,* 38(3), pp. 290-313.

Frilund, R. (2020) 'Exploring (transit) migration through a postcolonial lens: Tibetans migrating to India and beyond', *Journal of Ethnic and Migration Studies,* 46(7), pp. 1425-1441.

Giddens, A. (1991) *Modernity and self-identity: Self and society in the late modern age.* Stanford: Stanford University Press.

Giles, H. (1978) 'Linguistic differentiation between ethnic groups' in Tajfel, H. (ed.) *Differentiation between social groups.* London: Academic Press, pp. 361-393.

Giles, H. and Dorjee, T. (2005) 'Cultural identity in Tibetan diasporas', *Journal of Multilingual and Multicultural Development,* 26(2), pp. 138-157.

Gleason, P. (1983) 'Identifying identity: A semantic history', *A Journal of American history,* 69(4), pp. 910-931.

Goffman, E. (1959) *The presentation of self in everyday life.* New York: Anchor Books.

Goffman, E. (1963) *Stigma. Notes on the management of spoiled identity.* New York: Simon and Shuster.

Goldstein, M.C. (1978) 'Ethnogenesis and resource competition among Tibetan refugees in South India: A new face to the Indo-Tibetan Interface', in Fisher, J. (ed.) *Himalayan Anthropology: The Indo-Tibetan interface.* The Hague: Mouton Publishers.

Goldstein, M.C. (1987) 'When brothers share a wife: Among Tibetans, the good life relegates many women to spinsterhood', *Natural History,* March, pp. 39-48.

Goldstein, M.C. (1989) *A history of modern Tibet, 1913-1951: The demise of the lamaist state.* New York: University of California Press.

Goldstein-Kyaga, K. (1993) *The Tibetans: Schools for survival or submission. An investigation of ethnicity and education.* Stockholm. HLS.

Goode, W.J. (1982) *The Family.* 2nd edn. New Jersey: Prentice-Hall Inc.

Goody, J. (1974) *Production and reproduction. A comparative study of the domestic domain.* Cambridge: Cambridge University Press.

Government of India (GOI) (1984) *Report of the Finance Commission, 1984.* New Delhi: Ministry of Finance.

Grenard, F. (1974) *Tibet: The country and its inhabitants.* Translated by A. Tiexeira De Nathat. New Delhi: Cosmo Publications.

Grunfeld, T.A. (1987) *The making of modern Tibet.* New Delhi: Oxford University Press.

Gyatso, P., Shakya, T. and Palden, G. (1997) *The autobiography of a Tibetan monk.* New York: Grove Press.

Haddix, K.A. (1999) '"Excess women": Non-marriage and reproduction in two ethnic Tibetan communities of Humal, Nepal', *Himalayan*, 9(1). [Online]. Available at: https://digitalcommons.macalester.edu/himalaya/vol19/iss1/9 (Accessed: 19 June 2017).

Hale, S. (2000) 'The reception and resettlement of Vietnamese refugees in Britain', in Robinson, V. (ed.) *The international refugee crisis.* Basingstoke: Macmillan, pp. 280-290.

Haneda, M. (1997) 'Emigration of Iranian elites to India during the 16-18th centuries', *Cahiers d'Asiecentrale.* [Online]. Available at: http://asiecentrale.revues.org/480 (Accessed: 3 January 2018).

Harris, E.J. (1999) 'The female in Buddhism' in Tsomo, K.L. (ed) *Buddhist women across cultures: Realizations.* New York: State University of New York Press, pp. 49-65.

Hess, M. (2009) *Immigrant ambassadors: Citizenship and belonging in the Tibetan diaspora.* Stanford: Stanford University Press.

Hindustan Times (2010). '127935 Tibetans living outside Tibet: Tibetan survey', *Hindustan Times*, 4 December. [Online]. Available at: https://www.hindustantimes.com/india/127935-tibetans-living-outside-tibet-tibetan-survey/story-ELAHRcCZQ8NFNxTdCbWoMM.html (Accessed: 13 February 2018).

Hitlin, S. (2011) 'Values, personal identity, and the moral self' in Schwartz, S.J., Luyckx, K. and Vignoles, V.L. (eds.) *Handbook of identity theory and research.* New York: Springer, pp. 515-529.

Hogg, M.A. and Abrams, D. (1988) *Social identifications: A social psychology of intergroup relations and group processes.* London: Routledge.

Holtz, T. (1998) 'Refugee trauma versus torture trauma: A retrospective controlled cohort study of Tibetan refugees', *Journal of Nervous and Mental Disease*, 186, pp. 24-34.

Houston, S. and Wright, R. (2003) 'Making and remaking of Tibetan diasporic identities', *Social and Cultural Geography*, 4(2), pp. 217–232.

Human Rights Law Network (HRLN) (2007) *Report of Refugee Populations in India.* [Online]. Available at: http://www.hrln.org/admin/issue/subpdf/Refugee_populations_in_India.pdf (Accessed: 13 February 2018).

International Campaign for Tibet (2005) *Dangerous crossing: Conditions impacting the flight of Tibetan refugees*, 2004 update. Washington, DC: Author.

Jacobs, D. and Maier, R. (1998) 'European identity, construct, fact and fiction', in Gastelaars, M. and de Ruijter, A. (eds.) A *united Europe: The quest for a multi-faceted identity.* Maastricht: Shaker Publishing, pp. 13-34.

James, W. (1890) *The principles of psychology* (2 vols.). New York: Holt.

Janes, C.R. (2002) 'Buddhism, science, and market: The globalisation of Tibetan medicine', *Anthropology and Medicine*, 9(3), pp. 267-289.

Jha, H.B. (1992) *Tibetans in Nepal.* Delhi: Book Faith, India.

Jianhua, W., Rongqing, D. and Shuzhang, Y. (1992) 'Analysis of population in the Tibet autonomous region', in Jingxin, S. (ed.) *Tibetan Population in Contemporary China.* Beijing: China Tibetology Press.

Josh, L.M. (1967) *Studies in Buddhist culture of India.* Delhi: Motilal Banarsidass.

Kabuya, K. (2008) Social integration of Congolese refugees in a town in Southern Norway. Unpublished Master's thesis, Faculty of Social Sciences, University of Tromsø.

Kapstein, M. (2006) *The Tibetans.* (12 vols. Peoples of Asia Series). New Jersey: Wiley Blackwell.

Karthak, P.J. (1991) 'A Personal look at the Tibetan exiles', *Tibetan Review*, 16(8), pp. 15-18.

Kasur, T.N.T. (2005) *The Art and politics of Tibet.* Lecture at the Asian Art Museum. June 2005 in WTN, June 20.

Keller, A., Lhewa, D., Rosenfeld, B., Sachs, E., Asher, A., Cohen, I., Smith, H and Porterfield, K. (2006) 'Traumatic experiences and psychological distress in an urban refugee population', *Journal of Nervous and Mental Disease*, 194, pp. 188-194.

Kim, Y.Y. (1988) *Communication and cross-cultural adaptation: An integrative theory.* Clevedon, UK: Multilingual Matters.

Kim, Y.Y. (2001) *Becoming intercultural: An integrative theory of communication and cross-cultural adaptation.* Thousand Oaks, CA: Sage Publications.

Kim, Y.Y. (2005) 'Adapting to a new culture: An integrative communication theory', in Gudykunst, W. (ed.) *Theorizing about intercultural communication.* Thousand Oaks, CA: Sage Publications, pp. 375–400.

King, P.E. (2010) 'Religion and identity: The role of ideological, social, and spiritual contexts', *Applied Developmental Science*, 7(3), pp. 197-204.

Klieger, C. (1989) *Accomplishing Tibetan identity: The constitution of a national consciousness.* Unpublished thesis (PhD.), University of Hawaii.

Kolstø, P. (2000) *Political construction sites: Nation-building in Russia and the post-Soviet States.* Boulder, Colorado: Westview Press.

Korom, F.J. (ed.) (1997) 'Tibetan culture in the diaspora', Papers presented at a Panel of the 7th *Seminar of the International Association of Tibetan Studies*, Graz 1995. Vienna: Verlag der Osterreichischen Akademie der Wissenschaften.

Lama, D. (1962) *My land and my people.* New York: McGraw Hill.

Lama, D. (1990) *Freedom in exile.* New Delhi: Rupa & Co.

Lama, Y. (2001) *The essence of Tibetan Buddhism: The three principal aspects of the path and the introduction to tantra.* Boston: Lama Yeshe Wisdom Archive.

Leach, E. (1982) *Social Anthropology.* New York: Oxford University Press.

Liandi, Lu. (1986) 'Tibetans', in Ruxian, Y. (ed.) *Marriages and Families of Ethnic Minorities in China.* Beijing: Chinese Women Press.

Lindesmith, A.R. and Strauss, A.L. (1956) *Social Psychology.* New York: Holt, Rinehart and Winston.

Lopez, D. (1998) *Prisoners of ShangriLa: Tibetan Buddhism and the West.* Chicago: Chicago University Press.

MA, R. (2011) *Population and society in contemporary Tibet.* Hong Kong: Hong Kong University Press.

Macdonald, D. (1978) *Cultural heritage of Tibet: A description of a country of contrasts and of its cheerful happy-go-lucky people of hardy nature and curious customs, their religion, ways of living, trade, and social life*. New Delhi: Light and Life publishers.

Majupuria, I. (1990) *Tibetan women: Then and now*. Madhya Pradesh: M. Devi.

Mallett, S. (2004). 'Understanding home: A critical review of the literature', *The Sociological Review*, 52(1), pp. 62–89.

McCall, G.J. and Simmons, J.L. (1978) *Identities and interactions*. New York: Free Press.

McConnell, F. (2009). 'Democracy-in-exile: The 'uniqueness' and limitations of exile Tibetan democracy', *Sociological Bulletin*, 58(1), pp. 115-144.

McLagan, M.J. (1996) *Mobilising for Tibet: Transnational politics and the diaspora culture*. Unpublished thesis (PhD.), New York University.

McLellan, J. (1986) 'Religion and ethnicity: The role of Buddhism in maintaining ethnic identity among Tibetans in Lindsay, Ontario', *Canadian Ethnic Studies*, 19(l), pp. 63-76.

Mead, G.H. (1934) *Mind, Self, and Society*. Chicago: University of Chicago Press.

Menon, R. and Bhasin, K. (1993). 'Recovery, rupture, resistance: Indian state and abduction of women during partition', *Economic and Political Weekly*, 28(17), pp. WS2-WS11.

Mercer, S.W., Ager, A. and Ruwanpura, E. (2005) 'Psychosocial distress of Tibetans in exile: Integrating western interventions with traditional beliefs and practice', *SocSciMed*, 60, pp. 179-189.

Methfessel, T. (1995) *Music in the life of a Tibetan refugee community*. Berkeley, New York: Berghahn.

Michael, F. (1982) *Rule by incarnation: Tibetan Buddhism and its role in society and state*. New York: Routledge.

Michael, F. (1985). 'Survival of a culture: Tibetan refugees in India', *Asian Survey*, 25(7).

Miller, B.D. (1987) 'Status of women in Tibet', Translations of *Tibetan Studies in the West*, 3. Lhasa: Academy of Social Sciences of Tibet, pp. 328-344.

Miller, J.R. (2015). 'The world and Bollywood: An examination of the globalization paradigm', *Anthós*, 7(1), Article 5.

Mills, E.J., Singh, S., Holtz, T. H., Chase, R. M., Dolma, S., Santa-Barbara, J., and Orbinski, J. J. (2005) 'Prevalence of mental disorders and torture among Tibetan refugees: A systematic review', *BMC International Health and Human Rights*, 5(1).

Mirror.co.uk (2017) 'Brits will spend 18 MONTHS of their lives deciding just what to eat – that's 35 minutes every day', *Mirror UK* [Online]. Available at: https://www.mirror.co.uk/news/uk-news/brits-spend-18-months-lives-10697904 (Accessed: 28 April 2018).

Mishra, M. (2014) *Education of Tibetan refugees in India: Issues of culture, ethnic identity and opportunity*, Unpublished thesis (PhD.), Jawaharlal Nehru University.

Moore, J. (2007) 'Polarity or integration? Towards a fuller understanding of home and homelessness', *Journal of Architectural and Planning Research*, 24(2), pp. 143-59.

Moraes, F. (1960). *The revolt in Tibet*. New York: The Macmillan Co.

Moran, D. and Cohen, J. (2012) *The Husserl dictionary.* London: Continuum Philosophy Dictionaries.

Morse, M. and Field, A. (1995) *Qualitative research methods for health professionals.* London: Sage Publications.

Nachmias, C., and Nachmias, D. (1992) *Research methods in the social sciences.* 4th edn. New York: St. Martin's Press.

Nakane, C. (1992) 'Nobles in Tibet', Translated Papers of *Tibetan studies abroad,* 9. Lhasa: People's Press, pp. 336-388.

Neumaier-Dargyay, E. (2002). 'Tibetan women', in Tierney, H. (ed.) *Women's Studies Encyclopedia.* Revised and Expanded Edition. Westport, Connecticut: Greenwood Press, pp. 1409-1412.

Nezer, M. (2013) 'Resettlement at risk: Meeting emerging challenges to refugee resettlement in local communities', Research report prepared for the J.M. Kaplan Fund, HIAS.

Norbu, D. (1979) 'The 1959 Tibetan rebellion: An interpretation', *The China Quarterly,* 77, pp. 74-93.

Norbu, D. (1987) *Red star over Tibet.* New Delhi: Sterling Publication.

Norbu, D. (1997) *Tibet: The road ahead.* London: Harper Collins.

Norbu, D. (2001) 'Refugees from Tibet: Structural causes of successful settlements', *The Tibet Journal,* 26, pp. 3-25.

Nowak, M. (1984) *Tibetan refugee youths and the new generation of meaning.* New Brunswick: Rutgers University Press.

Oppong, S.H. (2013) 'Religion and identity', *American International Journal of Contemporary Research,* 3(6), pp. 10-16.

Palakshappa, T.C. (1978) *Tibetans in India: A case study of Mundgod Tibetans.* New Delhi: Sterling Publishers Pvt Ltd.

Patel, S. (1980) *Tibetan refugees in Orissa: An Anthropogenetic study.* Kolkata: Punthi Pustyak.

Patterson, G.N. (1960) *Tibet in revolt.* London: Faber and Faber.

Pennix, R. (2009) 'Decentralizing integration policies managing migration in cities, regions and localities', *Research program "managing migration in times of economic turbulence".* Barrow Cadbury Trust.

Penny-Dimri, S. (1994) 'Conflict amongst the Tibetans and Indians of north India: Communal violence and welfare dollars', *The Australian Journal of Anthropology,* 5(1-2), pp. 280-293.

Polletta, F. and Jasper, J.M. (2001) 'Collective identity and social movement', *Annual Review of Sociology,* 27, pp. 283-305.

Rajan, H. (2018) 'When wife-beating is not necessarily abuse: A feminist and cross-cultural analysis of the concept of abuse as expressed by Tibetan survivors of domestic violence', *Violence against Women,* 24(1), pp. 3-27.

Rajput, M. (2012) 'Tibetan women: Past and present', *Dialogue,* 14(2). [Online]. Available at: https://www.asthabharati.org/Dia_Oct%20012/madh.htm (Accessed: 23 March 2018)

Rapport, N. and Dawson, A. (1998) *Migrants of identity: perceptions of home in a world of movement.* Oxford: Berg.

Ray, R. (2001) *Secret of the vajra world: The tantric Buddhism of Tibet.* Boston: Shambhala Publications.

Regmi, R. (2003) 'Ethnicity and identity', *Occasional Papers in Sociology and Anthropology*, 8, pp. 1-11.

Richardson, H.E. (1962) *Tibet and its history.* London: Oxford University Press.

Robinson, V. (1998) 'Defining and measuring successful refugee integration', *ECRE International Conference on Integration of Refugees in Europe*, Antwerp, November 1998, Brussels, ECRE.

Roemer, S. (2008) *The Tibetan government-in-exile: Politics at large.* New York: Routledge.

Routray, B.P. (2007) 'Tibetan refugees in India: Religious identity and the forces of modernity', *Refugee Survey Quarterly*, 26(2), pp. 79–90.

Sachs, E., Rosenfeld, B., Lhewa, D., Rasmussen, A. and Keller, A. (2008) 'Entering exile: Trauma, mental health, and coping among Tibetan refugees arriving in Dharamsala, India', *Journal of Traumatic Stress*, 21(2), pp. 199-208.

Saklani, G. (1978) 'Tibetan Refugees in India: A sociological study of an uprooted community', *The Tibet Journal*, 3(1).

Saklani, G. (1984) *The uprooted Tibetans in India: A sociological study of continuity and change.* New Delhi: Cosmo Publication.

Sarkar, T. (2010). 'Infiltration from Bangladesh: A sub-continental dimension', *The Indian Journal of Political Science*, 71(2), pp. 683-686.

Sarup, M. (1995) 'Home and identity', in Robertson, G. (ed.) *Travellers' tales: Narratives of home and displacement.* London: Routledge, pp. 93-104.

Saunders, P. and Williams, P. (1988) 'The constitution of the home: Towards a research agenda', *Housing Studies*, 3(2), pp. 81–93.

Schell, O. (2007) *Virtual Tibet: Searching for Shangri-La from the Himalayas to Hollywood.* New York: Henry Holt and Company.

Schopflin, G. (2001) *The construction of identity.* [Online]. Available at: http:documents.mx/documents/schopflin-the-construction–of-Identity.html (Accessed: 4 February 2017).

Servan-Schreiber, D., Lin, B. L., and Birmaher, B. (1998) 'Prevalence of posttraumatic stress disorder and major depressive disorder in Tibetan refugee children', *Journal of the American Academy of Child and Adolescent Psychiatry*, 37(8), pp. 874–879.

Seventeen-Point Plan for the Peaceful Liberation of Tibet (SPPPLT) (1951) The Agreement of the Central People's Government and the local Government of Tibet on measures for the peaceful liberation of Tibet, p.182. [Online] Available at: http://www.tibetjustice.org/materials/china/china3.html (Accessed: 17 February 2018).

Shakabpa, W.D. (1973) *Tibet a political history.* Yale: Yale University Press.

Shakya, T. (1999) *The dragon in the land of snows: A history of modern Tibet.* New York: Penguin Compass.

Sharma, S., and Sharma, U. (1997) *Religious heritage of Tibet.* New Delhi: Anmol Publisher.

Simon, R.J. (1978). 'Preferences and opinions concerning the distribution of property at death', *Int'l Sociol. Assoc.*, 2(6), pp. 125-127.

Singh J.P. (2000) 'Indian democracy and empowerment of women', *The Indian Journal of Public Administration*, 46(4), pp. 617-630.

Smith, B. and Smith, D. (2005) *The Cambridge Companion to Husserl.* New York: Cambridge University Press.

Smith, W. (1975) *Tibetan refugees: A second life in a new land.* Ottawa: Canada Research Project Group, Department of Manpower and Immigration.

Snellgrove, D. (2002) *Indo-Tibetan Buddhism, Indian Buddhists and their Tibetan Successors.* Boston: Shambhala Publications.

Snellgrove, D. and Richardson, H. (1986) *A Cultural History of Tibet.* Boston: Shambala Publications.

Snow, D.A., Oselin, S.S. and Corrigall-Brown, C. (2004) 'Identity', in Ritzer, G. (ed.) *Encyclopedia of Social Theory* (1 vols). California: Sage Publications, pp. 390-393.

Somerville, P. (1992) 'Homelessness and the meaning of home: Rooflessness and rootlessness?', *International Journal of Urban and Regional Research*, 16(4), pp. 529-539.

Sponberg, A. (1992) 'Attitudes toward women and the feminine in early Buddhism', in Jose, I.C. (ed.) *Buddhism, sexuality, and gender.* New York: University of New York Press, pp. 3-36.

Statista (2016) 'Average minutes per day spent eating and drinking in OECD countries plus China, India and South Africa by gender, as of 2016', *Statista.* [Online]. Available at: https://www.statista.com/statistics/521972/time-spent-eating-drinking-countries/ (Accessed: 28 April 2018).

Stein, R. A. (1982) *La Civilisation Tibetaine.* Lhasa: Academy of Social Sciences of Tibet.

Stein, R.A. (1972) *Tibetan Civilization.* London: Faber & Faber.

Stone, G.P. (1962) 'Appearance and the self', in Rose, A.M. (ed.) *Human behavior and the social processes: An Interactionist approac*h. New York: Houghton Mifflin, pp. 86-118.

Subba, T.B. (1990) *Flight and adaption: Tibetan refugees in the Darjeeling-Sikkim Himalaya.* Dharamsala: LTWA.

Tajfel, H. (1972) 'Social categorization. English manuscript of "La categorisation sociale"', in Moscovici, S. (ed.) *Introduction a`la psychologie sociale* (1 vols). Paris: Larousse, pp. 272–302.

Taklha, N. L. (2005) *Women of Tibet.* Dehradun, India: Songtsen Library, Center for Tibetan and Himalayan Studies.

Tarodi, T. (2011) 'Revisiting home: Tibetan refugees, perceptions of home (land) and politics of return', *Working paper 266.* Institute for Social and Economic Change, Bangalore.

Terheggen, M., Stroebe, M., and Kleber, R. (2001) 'Western conceptualizations and eastern experience: A cross-cultural study of traumatic stress reactions among Tibetan refugees in India', *Journal of Traumatic Stress*, 14, pp. 391-403.

Thondup, T. (2000) 'Indian cinema and Tibetan refugees', *Tibetan Review*, November.

Thondup, T., and Sinclair, R.L. (1999) 'Improving Tibetan education in exile', *Tibetan Review*, 34(5), pp. 16-19.

Tucci, G. (1967). *Tibet: Land of snows.* Translated by J.E. Stapleton Driver. London: Elek Book.

Turner, J. (1999) 'Some current issues in research on social identity and self-categorization theories', in Ellemers, N., Spears, R. and Doosje, B. (eds.) *Social identity: Context, commitment, content.* Oxford: Blackwell Publishers, pp. 6–34.

Turner, J. C. and Oakes, P.J. (1986). 'The significance of the social identity concept for social psychology with reference to individualism, interactionism and social influence', *British Journal of Social Psychology,* 25, pp. 237-252. (Special issue on the Individual/Society Interface).

United National High Commissioner for Refugees (UNHCR) (2011) *The 1951 Convention relating to the Status of Refugees and its 1967 Protocol, Geneva.* [Online]. Available at: http://www.unhcr.org/about-us/background/4ec262df9/1951-convention-relating-status-refugees-its-1967-protocol.html (Accessed: 24 October 2017).

United National High Commissioner for Refugees (UNHCR) (n.d.) *Convention and protocol relating to the status of refugees: 1951 Convention 1967 Protocol.* [Online]. Available at: https://www.unhcr.org/4ae57b489.pdf (Accessed: 27 May 2018).

United States Bureau of Citizenship and Immigration Services (USBCIS) (2003) *India: Information on Tibetan refugees and settlements.* [Online]. Available at: http://www.refworld.org/docid/3f51f90821.html (Accessed: 15 February 2018).

United States Department of State (USDS) (2002) *Country Reports on Human Rights Practices: India 2001.* Washington, D.C.: Bureau of Democracy, Human Rights, and Labor. [Online]. Available at: https://2009-2017.state.gov/j/drl/rls/hrrpt/2001/sa/8230.htm (Accessed: 13 February 2018).

Vahali, H.O. (2009). *Lives in exile: Exploring the inner world of Tibetan refugees.* New Delhi: Routledge India.

Van Walt Van Praag, C.M. (1987) 'The Status of Tibet: History, rights and prospects', *American Journal of International Law,* 84(4), pp. 996-999.

Venturino, S. (1997) 'Reading negotiations in the Tibetan diaspora', in Korom, F.J. (ed.) *Constructing Tibetan culture: Contemporary perspectives.* Quebec: World Heritage Press, pp. 98–121.

Vijaykumar, V. (1998) 'Institutional response to refugee problem in India', *Conference of Scholars and other professionals working on refugees and displaced persons in South Asia.* Held in Rajendrapur, Bangladesh, organised by Regional Centre for Strategic Studies, Colombo, in collaboration with the Refugees Studies Programme of Oxford University.

Warner, S. (1998) 'Immigration and religious communities in the United States', in Warner, R. and Wittner, J. (eds.) *Gatherings in diaspora: Religious communities and the new immigration.* Philadelphia, PA: Temple University Press, pp. 3-34.

Watzlawik, M. (2012) 'Cultural identity markers and identity as a whole: Some alternative solutions', *Culture and Psychology,* 18(2), pp. 253-260.

Wenmei, C., Yi, L. and Rongjun, S. (1992) 'Characters of marriages and families in Tibetan population', in Jingxin, S. (ed.) *Tibetan Population in Current China.* Beijing: Chinese Press of Tibetan Studies, pp. 167-179.

Willis, J.D. (ed.) (1989) *Feminine ground: Essays on women and Tibet.* Ithaca, New York: Snow Lion Publications.

Wright, G. (1991) 'Prescribing the model of home', *Social Research*, 58(1), pp. 213-225.

Yeh, E.T. (2007) 'Exile meets homeland: Politics, performance, and authenticity in the Tibetan diaspora', *Environment and Planning D: Society and Space*, 25(4), pp. 648-667.

# Index